Dagmar Pruin, Rolf Schieder, Johannes Zachhuber (Eds./Hg.)

# Religion and Politics in the United States and Germany
# Religion und Politik in Deutschland und den USA

# Religion – Staat – Kultur

## Interdisziplinäre Studien aus der Humboldt-Universität zu Berlin

herausgegeben von

Christina von Braun
Volker Gerhardt
Wilhelm Gräb
Herfried Münkler
Richard Schröder

Band 4

LIT

# Religion and Politics in the United States and Germany

## Old Divisions and New Frontiers

# Religion und Politik in Deutschland und den USA

## Traditionelle Differenzen und neue Herausforderungen

edited by
herausgegeben von

Dagmar Pruin
Rolf Schieder
Johannes Zachhuber

LIT

Umschlagbild: 1. Freiheitsglocke im Rathaus Schöneberg,
© Pressestelle Bezirksamt Tempelhof-Schöneberg, Berlin
2. Bell of Liberty in Philadelphia,
© http://flickr.com/photos/zesmeralda/136685870

Gedruckt mit Mitteln aus dem deutschen Programm für Transatlantische Begegnung aus dem ERP-Sondervermögen

**Bibliographic information published by the Deutsche Nationalbibliothek**
The Deutsche Nationalbibliothek lists this publication in the Deutsche Nationalbibliografie; detailed bibliographic data are available in the Internet at http://dnb.d-nb.de.

ISBN 978-3-8258-9622-5

**A catalogue record for this book is available from the British Library**



Auslieferung/Verlagskontakt:
Fresnostr. 2 48159 Münster
Tel. +49 (0)251–62 03 20 Fax +49 (0)251–23 19 72
e-Mail: lit@lit-verlag.de http://www.lit-verlag.de

Distributed in the UK by: Global Book Marketing, 99B Wallis Rd, London, E9 5LN
Phone: +44 (0) 20 8533 5800 – Fax: +44 (0) 1600 775 663
http://www.centralbooks.co.uk/acatalog/search.html

Distributed in North America by:

Transaction Publishers
New Brunswick (U.S.A.) and London (U.K.)

Transaction Publishers
Rutgers University
35 Berrue Circle
Piscataway, NJ 08854

Phone: +1 (732) 445 - 2280
Fax: + 1 (732) 445 - 3138
for orders (U. S. only):
toll free (888) 999 - 6778
e-mail:
orders@transactionspub.com

# Contents

# Introduction: Religion and Politics in the United States and Germany

## Old Divisions and New Frontiers

JOHANNES ZACHHUBER/DAGMAR PRUIN/ROLF SCHIEDER

To all appearance, recent political developments have strained transatlantic relations in a way that goes far beyond occasional disagreements about policy issues, however weighty these might be. A deeply felt awareness exists in Western democracies on both sides of the Atlantic of some fundamentally divergent perceptions of, and approaches to, political and social realities. Particularly prone to the kind of mutual misunderstandings and suspicions inevitably ensuing from those differences are questions about the role of religion in public life and the relation of politics and religion. Western Europe and North America, two parts of the world that have much in common, seem to be worlds apart with regard to this particular issue.

For Germany, the problem is exacerbated as it comes as part of a broader challenge. Here, the relation of politics and religion had long been considered a topic of marginal relevance. Modernisation, it seemed, inevitably brought about a decline in religious affiliation, which would continue to exist, if at all, in domesticated forms of which one could think as one chose, but which certainly were without real importance for political decision making. Consequently, academics, politicians, and other public leaders turned a blind eye to questions of that kind and, with their return to the fore of public awareness, find they lack the intellectual resources needed for addressing them.

In this situation, the current volume is intended to attain a twofold objective. On the one hand, and primarily, it will explore configurations of public religion and their relation to the political realm in Germany and the US thus offering its own contribution to transatlantic communication in general. On the other hand, it is meant to further, more generally, an understanding of the role religion can and does play in contemporary political developments. The individual chapters, therefore, address various aspects of religion and politics in either or both of the two countries (VOIGT, FISHER, PALLY), but by doing this, they also elucidate more general aspects of the interplay between religion and politics, from the role of elites (OERMANN, FISCHER) to the construction of identities (PECK, ZACHHUBER), to issues like pluralism (DENEEN), civil religion (SCHIEDER), religious education (GRELLE, SCHIEDER), and inter-faith dialogue (PRUIN).

The following is meant as an introduction to both these larger aims of the book. Through a largely historical contextualisation of the religious divide between Germany (and Western Europe more generally) and the US it is intended to present one important background to current perceptions, approaches, and conceptualisations of religion and politics on both sides of the Atlantic, but also a template for actual or potential interactions between the two areas.

Initially, however, some clarification may be needed about the character of those differences. From the German perspective an intuitive first answer might be this. Politics and religion should ideally be separated from each other. Religion is at its best where it is as little political as possible; politics in turn ought to be as far as possible free from religious influence. For religious groups not accepting this division we quickly and easily employ the word ›fundamentalists‹. Politicians, who use religious symbolism in their rhetoric or who back up their argument by reference to religious beliefs, would seem suspicious. The US, by this standard, appears as a country to which these insights have not yet transpired. Not only are large parts of its population more intensely religious than the vast majority of Western Europeans, they often belong to religious communities which Germans routinely call ›fundamentalist‹ as they draw immediate public and political consequences from their religious beliefs: from the rejection of the theory of evolution to the hope of a restoration of Greater Israel and, in any case, the justification of a special role of their own country on the world stage. Political rhetoric in the US is religiously charged in a way which, to Europeans, sounds only either ridiculous or menacing.

And yet, as KARSTEN VOIGT will show in detail, this is only one part of the picture. The separation of the two domains in Germany (as in many other European countries) is by no means as unequivocal as public perception would have it. On the contrary, the state is accorded traditionally the right to support religious communities and to co-operate with them—a right which it may (and does) exert discriminately based on political considerations. This principle has led to remarkable forms of co-operation between state and church in social and health services, in areas such as Religious Education at schools, theological faculties at universities and the collection of financial contributions to religious communities through the state tax system. At the same time, as the religious landscape has grown ever more diverse in recent decades, the difficulties of the political discernment implied in this system have repeatedly been challenged. Only recently Jehovah's Witnesses have won a Constitutional Court case granting them the privileges mentioned above, which the government had previously refused to do.

In comparison, the legal separation of church and state in the US is much stricter. There the forms of co-operation current in Germany are either altogether impossible or, at least, highly controversial—as is illustrated, in this volume, through the matching chapters by BRUCE GRELLE and ROLF SCHIEDER on Religious Education. Direct political involvement of churches or of Christian interest groups, such as the so-called Religious Right, is a relatively new development of the last three decades and still widely observed with suspicion.

The two systems are thus not as easily contrasted as might have seemed at first sight. In order to understand their differences a historical detour may be useful. Crucial decisions in both Europe and the US were made in the 18th century. In Germany this was the time of enlightened absolutism. Characteristic is the Prussian King Frederick II (›the Great‹: 1712-1786). Being a cynical and successful war strategist, he was also a great personal friend of Voltaire and thus imbued by the ideas of the French enlightenment. In his so-called *Political Testament* of 1752 he describes his religious policies as follows:

> Lutherans, Catholics, Reformed, Jews and many other Christian sects live in Prussia, and they coexist peacefully. If the ruler had the idea, out of misplaced zeal, to favour one of them, at once there would be parties, and rows would erupt ...
>
> For politics it is altogether unimportant whether the ruler is religious or not. If one gets to the bottom of any religion, they are all founded on a more or less irrational system of fables ... However, one must be careful not to hurt the religious feelings of the big masses whatever their religion.
>
> I am, so to speak, the pope of the Lutherans and the ecclesiastical head of the reformed. All the other Christian sects are tolerated in Prussia. The first one trying to unleash a civil war must at once be silenced, and the teachings of the would-be reformer will be exposed to ridicule.[1]

In the 18th century, this view was probably extreme in its professed religious scepticism, yet it rests on a fairly representative principle. This starts from the observation that, in dealing with religion, the state confronts a plurality of groups, which are potentially hostile towards each other, and, as such, a threat to order and peace. In the 18th century, such an assessment gained its force on the backdrop of the religious wars of the previous two centuries, which seemed to have demonstrated both the inability of competing religious groups to settle their differences peacefully and the disastrous consequences of too much interference of religion in political matters. A state with a religiously diverse populace (on religious pluralism see the chapter in this book by PATRICK DENEEN) would therefore need an active policy to pacify those groups and contain their aggressive potential.

This principle, it should be noted, was common to conservative and liberal approaches. They differed, of course, in the role they assigned to the state. Frederick represents the liberal strand by advocating a neutral position: the state ought to be the impartial umpire between rival denominations; to be

[1] Friedrich der Große, Testament politique (1752). German edition: Das Politische Testament von 1752, Stuttgart (Reclam) 1974, 44f.

accepted by all of them, it must not favour any. In opposition to this, the more conservative position would advocate, in the name of tradition, aligning the state specifically with the one church or religious community that used to dominate public life in the respective territory. Its ideal is not so much the state as neutral arbiter between religious groups but rather, the state as guardian of traditional religious values.

Both these positions have their own problems. As for the liberal one, Frederick's text distinctly shows that his claim to ›neutrality‹ rests on a critical distance from any religion. Ultimately then, the agnostic who feels the same indifference or even hostility towards any religion might appear as the most competent arbiter—though the ›impartiality‹ of his judgment could be questioned. The liberal position thus has the tendency to be opposed to religion. The conservative position, on the other hand, tends to be opposed to plurality thus running counter to the very reason that necessitated its adoption in the first place.

In the present place, however, the principal agreement between the two positions may be more important than their differences, for it allows perceiving some underlying commonalities and continuities that have worked on the European mind the more strongly as they were not subject to controversy. For Europe, the fundamental paradigm has been secularisation, the process, in which a form of organising communal life on the basis of pragmatic (›secular‹) considerations emerged from the shadows of domination by (frequently competing) theological and ecclesiastical interests. This process has never been uncontroversial, but its underlying perception of reality has deeply informed the European world view. Therefore, in whatever way the separation between the two realms has been executed, the overriding concern has always been to protect the secular, political sphere from religious dominance. The separation of church and state was therefore aimed—explicitly or implicitly—against the real or imagined threat to that sphere from the side of organised religion.

In the US precisely this consideration has played no or—at least—a much less significant role than it has in Europe. For this reason their constitutional separation between state and religion is in principle different from the various forms of such separation that exist in Europe as it reflects primarily respect for religion and the concern that government could impinge on the religious rights of its citizens. A famous witness for the classical form in which this separation was introduced is Alexis de Tocqueville who, as a European, travelled through the United States in 1830 and 1831. In the resulting classic, *Democracy in America*, one reads as follows:

> Religion, which, among Americans, never mixes directly in the government of society, should [...] be considered as the first of their political institutions; for if it does not give them the taste for freedom, it singu-

> larly facilitates their use of it. It is also from this point of view that the inhabitants of the United States themselves consider religious beliefs. I do not know whether all Americans have faith in their religion—for who can read to the bottom of hearts?—but I am sure that they believe it necessary to the maintenance of republican institutions. This opinion does not belong only to one class of citizens or to one party, but to the entire nation; one finds it in all ranks.[2]

Elsewhere in that book one reads:

> There is an innumerable multitude of sects in the United States. All differ in the worship one must render to the Creator, but all agree on the duties of men toward one another.[3]

On this premise rests the indirect influence which those sects have on the political life:

> Therefore one cannot say that in the United States religion exerts an influence on the laws or on the details of political opinions, but it directs mores, and it is in regulating the family that it works to regulate the state.[4]

Underlying this system is a number of principles quite different from those of the Prussian Frederick. Religions, first and foremost, are assumed to live and coexist peacefully. There is no hint that they, left to themselves, might do any harm to each other or to the larger community. Without the historical background of the European religious wars the moral and social relevance of religion is seen here as almost entirely positive. And it is not only *this* background that is lacking. Equally missing is the experience of one mighty church dominating communal life and threatening to exert undue influence on the state, without which the strict separation of religion and state rests on the firm conviction that religious communities, by doing their proper work, can make their own unique and most important contribution to a free and democratic (or, in Tocqueville's phrase, ›republican‹) society. For this reason the government's policies towards organised religion will largely be passive interfering as little as possible with the internal matters of religious communities.

This separation of the two realms, then, is intended chiefly to protect religious freedom from the kind of state intervention many American immigrants had known in their European home countries; indeed, these ›interventions‹ had often been the very reason for their immigration. This principle of a separation for the sake of religion is acknowledged today as much as it has been at any

[2] A. de Tocqueville, Democracy in America, transl. H.C. Mansfield/D. Winthrop, Chicago 2000, 280.

[3] Op. cit., 278.

[4] Loc. cit.

time. Senator Joe Lieberman of the Democratic Party enjoys widespread support for saying that ›our constitution promises freedom of religion, not freedom from religion‹.

Given all this, it still needs explaining why American political rhetoric contains such an abundance of religious language. Why do American politicians find it appropriate frequently to mention God or the Bible? Why do they speak so openly about their own religious life? Why can they argue for central decisions by alluding to biblical or theological themes? Any of this would be unthinkable for mainstream politicians in practically all European countries. Is this not, then, an indication that the ›wall of separation‹ between church and state is not as strong as Thomas Jefferson (and many after him) claimed it is?[5] In the past few years, Europeans have been quick to establish a connection between the personal religious faith of the present American president, his self-definition as a born-again Christian, and his use of what one might call messianic rhetoric in his political speeches. Statements like the following are typical and famous: ›The liberty we prize is not America's gift to the world, it is God's gift to humanity‹.[6] Are they not incontestable proof of the hijacking of American politics by a religious fundamentalist?

The question of the actual influence of groups from the Religious Right on the policies of the present American administration, specifically its foreign policy is complex; it cannot and will not be discussed in this place.[7] What seems to be clear, however, is that equating George W. Bush's membership in a particular kind of religious community (whatever its character) and his use of phrases like the aforementioned one, is a typically European misunderstanding. For, while we may talk, in Europe today, habitually about the relation between politics and religion, what we really mean is still the relation between (normally one, dominant) *church* and the state. In the US, however, the differentiation between religion, sometimes called ›civil religion‹ and churches has been for a long time crucial in defining that relation.

The direct link which many Europeans perceive between Bush's religiously charged rhetoric and his own religious affiliation is, then, a *misunderstanding* because it ignores that for most Americans there exists a clear-cut distinction between the beliefs and creeds of singular religious communities, which must be absent from the political sphere, and a supposedly universal or, at least, consen-

[5] Cf. Jefferson's famous letter to the Danbury Baptist association of 1 January 1802; online at: `http://www.usconstitution.net/jeffwall.html`.

[6] George W. Bush, Presidential Message, in: USA TODAY, 24 December 2003.

[7] Cf. J.C. Green/M.J. Rozell/C. Wilcox, The Values Campaign? The Christian Right and the 2004 Elections, Washington DC 2006; C. Wilcox/C. Larsen, Onwards Christian Soldiers. The Religious Right in American Politics, Boulder CO, 2006; J. Braml, Die religiöse Rechte in den USA. Basis des Bush-Administration? SWP-Studie S35, September 2004; online at: `http://www.swp-berlin.org/de/produkte/swp_studie.php?id=3794`.

sual religion of the citizens, a civil religion. It is for this reason that essentially the same type of rhetoric was used in an amazing continuity throughout much of US history and in spite of varying religious affiliations and personal religious commitments of the incumbent presidents, as MARCIA PALLY demonstrates at length in her contribution to this volume.

Such a misunderstanding, further, is *typically European* because, to Europeans, the presence of religious phrases and symbols in the public realm appears almost inevitably as a remnant of the old system of a state church, the traditional, and to many now notorious, alliance of throne and altar. At the very least, such presence would be taken in the European context as an indication of the long standing intertwining between Western culture and the Christian religion. The fundamental notion underlying the ›civil religion‹ in the US is radically different from this line of reasoning. The American appreciation of religion does not derive from the specific contribution of one religion or of one denomination to the formation of American society or culture (even though, arguably, the actual shape of that ›civil religion‹ does mirror the specific religious inheritance of American society).

The fundamental tenet of American civil religion has been described, once again, with admirable clarity in Tocqueville's classical work. He observed that the appreciation of religion in the US was not directed towards any particular denomination, but to religion in a more general sense:

> In the United States, when a political man attacks a sect, it is not a reason for the partisans even of that sect not to support him; but if he attacks all sects together, each flees him, and he remains alone.[8]

The practically undisputed place of religion in US public life and, particularly, its strong presence in political rhetoric, which for Europeans is a perennial source of amazement, concern, or ridicule, is based on this distinction between ›religion‹ as such and any particular system of religious beliefs or any specific form of organised religion. One must take this deep-seated distinction into account to understand why, according to a recent survey, only a small majority of Americans think that churches ought to speak up on political issues (52% vs. 44%), whereas a vast majority finds that politicians speak of their own faith either ›the right amount‹ or ›too little‹ (70%) against only 21% who find they do it ›too much‹Americans, these figures would suggest, wish to see religious faith, religious commitment in their national leaders, as they see religion as an important and fundamental source of human life and of human society. Incidentally, this general assessment is explicitly applied to the incumbent president. Only 10% of those surveyed said his personal faith was influencing his political

[8] Tocqueville, op. cit. (n. 3), 280.

decisions ›too much‹. Even among those Americans who call themselves ›secular‹ (they make up approximately 16% of the population) this figure rises to only 30% against 60% (of that particular group) who answer that his faith has ›right‹ or ›too little‹ influence on his political decisions.[9]

Thus, while Europeans normally identify ›religion‹ with (often one) church and nurture a scepticism, which is deeply ingrained in their history, towards its political influence, the American position, as CATHLEEN FISHER will demonstrate in her chapter, is characterised by a distinction between religion in general and particular religious communities in combination with a strong appreciation of ›religion‹ (precisely thus understood) in its influence on politics and society.

We started by pointing out that current developments on both sides of the Atlantic are regularly perceived as a process of increasing estrangement. Yet, whatever truth there may be in such a blanket claim, it may be worthwhile concluding this introductory overview by adducing some observations which may open up new opportunities for mutual understanding.

The first one is this. Europeans may today be in a better position than at any point in the more recent past to re-evaluate the American appreciation for religion and religious faith within and for a democratic society. This is the case even though (perhaps precisely because) the developments of religious practice and religious affiliation in Europe and the US move at present in very different directions. The traditionally sceptical attitude towards religious influence on politics in Europe—as has been pointed out—had been largely due to the heritage of a confrontation between a powerful church and a state trying to assert its secular legitimacy against that power. For a long time, therefore, politics and religion seemed to be a formula for ecclesiastical attempts to dominate the political sphere and the state's need to defend it. At a time, when the final remnants of that mighty institution of yore seem to be losing their grip on European societies, those societies begin to realise the one-sidedness of that confrontational perspective. They suddenly come to understand that religion is, as JOHANNES ZACHHUBER argues in his contribution to this book, fundamentally a power forming people's character and directing their lives, a source of the most deeply rooted values. Precisely those virtues, however, are needed badly within the political realm too. Societies lacking people with strong convictions and stable value systems become spiritually and morally poor, however economically rich they may still be. The need for such people is increasingly being felt in Germany and elsewhere. The vast number of people, who lack such a compass, heightens our appreciation of those who possess it—however difficult they may be. The astonishing respect and admiration which

9 The Pew Forum on Religion and Public Life, Religion and Politics: Contention and Consensus, 24 July 2003; online at: http://pewforum.org/docs/index.php?DocID=26.

the world—including Western Europe—has shown towards the late pope, a man whose views, more often than not, were inconvenient and frequently also out of kilter with his time may have been the most distinct, recent indication of this tendency. This same tendency is seen also in the fact, much more directly relevant for politics and religion, that in a country such as Germany, where religious affiliation overall is declining, the number of committed Christians among politicians is steady, by some counts even increasing—on this see, once again, KARSTEN VOIGT'S account as well as the detailed argument in NILS OLE OERMANN'S chapter. This divergence is most apparent (and actually most amazing) in the so-called ›new lands‹, former East Germany. This anomaly may find its explanation once one realises that religion provides for one's life a steady and thus reliable basis of core values, which appear to those who hold them as binding and unchangeable. Such an attitude may ultimately be no less important for a politician than a wide range of knowledge and the mastery of certain techniques. Yet this is precisely the assumption that has always been at the centre of the American attitude towards public religion.

If, then, we may be in a better position today in Europe to understand the justification of the American position towards religion in public life, the partial justification of the more sceptical attitude of the Europeans may have become evident at the same time. One of the insights to which 9/11 has alerted us, is the fact the religion *can also* be destructive, violent and antisocial. This insight is obscured, unfortunately, by the current misperception both in the US and elsewhere, that it is in particular Islam which is the cause of such dangers. This clearly is an oversimplification. The somewhat uncomfortable truth is that the strong value-orientation, which we find desirable in a believer, and a fundamentalist religiosity grow on the same stem. They are both forms of religion, of a power that dominates human beings from the deepest core of their selves, demanding to determine the ultimate direction of their thoughts and actions. Religion, then, is an ambiguous phenomenon, which may bring about constructive as well as destructive consequences—on the potential for the latter KARSTEN FISCHER'S analysis is particularly pertaining. Its results can be civilized or uncivilized, social as well as antisocial. Religion can be fundamentalist, and if it is, it turns into the danger for communal life as which traditional European politics has perceived it.

What follows from this insight? Religion, it appears, needs cultivation. In other words, it needs to be subjected to the same kind of treatment which we apply to phenomena that are similarly important, similarly fundamental, and similarly ambiguous. The strongest ideas that work on the human mind, such as freedom, love, or justice, are of the same fundamental and ambiguous nature. They all have the capacity to achieve enormous good, but the damage they may work if misapplied is equally enormous. In none of those cases, however, we respond by simply rejecting them. What we do (or certainly what we ought to do) is to work on those forces so crucial for human life and for human motivation to cultivate them by means of education, by means of integration, and by means of dialogue—on various aspects of which some light is shed in the contributions to this book by DAGMAR PRUIN, JEFF PECK, ROLF SCHIEDER, and BRUCE GRELLE.

It would appear that in the light of current threats to democracy and freedom emanating from fundamentalist varieties of religion, including the danger of an ideological deformation of political decision making, this kind of ›religious education‹, which combines an appreciation of religion with an insight in its ambiguous character, might be a legitimate political concern of democratic societies on both sides of the Atlantic.

All but two of the texts assembled in this book derive from papers and responses delivered at two conferences organised by the editors in collaboration with the American Institute for Contemporary German Studies (AICGS) in Washington DC. Both events, as well as the production of this book, were generously supported by a grant of the *Deutsches Programm für transatlantische Begegnung (Transatlantik-Programm)*, which draws on funds from the European Recovery Program (ERP) of the German Federal Ministry of Economics and Technology (BMWI). At the request of the editors, Patrick Deneen and Marcia Pally kindly contributed papers they had read at related, but different events.

The editors are grateful to various individuals for their help and for various contributions towards this book. Karsten D. Voigt and Irmgard Maria Fellner encouraged and supported the present editors from early on to work on this topic; over time they offered invaluable advice on all levels of the project. Cathleen Fisher and her colleagues at the AICGS, especially Karen Johnston and Kerstin Jäger, were true partners in a mutually beneficial and enriching co-operation without which the breadth of this volume, spanning disciplines and, indeed, continents, could not have been achieved. Frau Ulrike Kaiser and Frau Maria Loew-Gonnert of the KfW Bankengruppe were reliably and consistently helpful on the intricacies of financial administration. Tanja Pilger, Rosa Coco Schinagl, and Martin Schuster were inestimable in organising the two conferences; Tanja Pilger and Jonathan Zachhuber worked on the preparation of the manuscript excising a plethora of errors and perfecting the layout. The editors are acutely aware of how much the present volume owes to the efforts of all those named, and of many others. Any remaining shortcomings of it are, of course, entirely their own responsibility.

Berlin and Oxford, May 2007
Johannes Zachhuber
Dagmar Pruin, Rolf Schieder

# Religion und Politik
# Ein Vergleich zwischen der Situation in Deutschland und den USA

Karsten D. Voigt

Politik und Religion haben nach dem Zweiten Weltkrieg in Deutschland ihre wechselseitige Unabhängigkeit respektiert und zugleich durch einen engen Dialog miteinander die geistigen und ethischen Grundlagen unserer Demokratie gefördert. Zwischen Ethik einerseits und Macht und Interessen andererseits besteht kein antagonistischer Widerspruch sondern ein unaufhebbares Spannungsverhältnis. Dieses Spannungsverhältnis sollten wir nicht leugnen sondern als Anstoß für kognitive Prozesse nutzen.

Jeder, der sich ein Leben lang in der Politik engagiert, hat immer wieder schwierige ethische Abwägungen zu treffen. Bei diesen ethischen Abwägungen spielen bei vielen Politikern und ihren Wählern nicht nur in den USA sondern auch in Europa religiöse Überzeugungen und Prägungen eine wichtige Rolle. Bei aller Gemeinsamkeit der transatlantischen Interessen und Ziele haben in der Vergangenheit bei Fragen von Krieg und Frieden unterschiedliche historische Erfahrungen und eine unterschiedliche geostrategische Lage häufiger zu unterschiedlichen Politikansätzen geführt. Deshalb werden die Diskussionen zwischen Deutschen und Amerikanern nicht nur von Interessen sondern auch von ethischen Abwägungen beeinflusst.

Wie sich das transatlantische Verhältnis in Zukunft entwickelt, wie wir die Chance für einen neuen Atlantizismus gestalten, wird zwar auch weiterhin in hohem Maße von außen- und sicherheitspolitischen Gemeinsamkeiten abhängen, aber auch davon, wie wir in Europa und wie unsere amerikanischen Partner mit kulturellen, gesellschaftspolitischen und wirtschaftlichen Herausforderungen umgehen.

Wer sich auf das Thema der kulturellen und religiösen Gemeinsamkeiten und Unterschiede zwischen Europa und den USA konzentriert, könnte durch diese Konzentration auf einen einzelnen Aspekt der amerikanischen Politik den Eindruck erwecken, als ob dieser wichtige Faktor ein alles dominierender Faktor sei. Dies ist nicht beabsichtigt. Eine solche monokausale Erklärung der amerikanischen Politik wäre auch falsch.

Kulturelle und religiöse Unterschiede zwischen beiden Seiten des Atlantiks sind gegenwärtig mit einer Gefahr der Entfremdung verbunden. Ich meine damit das Risiko des Auseinanderdriftens der Weltsichten zwischen einem von der religiösen Rechten beeinflussten Umfeld der gegenwärtigen US-Administration und den von der Säkularisierung geprägten Gesellschaften in Europa. In Europa vermitteln die evangelischen Kirchen im Vergleich zur evangelikalen Rechten in den USA eine zum Teil diametral entgegengesetzte gesellschaftspolitische Orientierung.

Angesichts der fortschreitenden Säkularisierung der europäischen Gesellschaften neigen deutsche und europäische Intellektuelle dazu, den gegenwärtigen Einfluss einer vom persönlichen Glaubenserlebnis geprägten evangelikalen Rechten in den USA zu verkennen. Diese Unterschätzung und Missachtung einer wichtigen Komponente der US-Gesellschaft ergibt sich umso leichter als in den Kontakten der europäischen Intellektuellen zu den USA die Beziehungen zu säkularisierten Kreisen an der Ost- und Westküste dominieren.

Die Evangelikalen aber finden insbesondere im Süden der USA, im sogenannten Bible Belt Unterstützung. Viele dieser christlichen Gruppen sind in den letzten Jahren politisch aktiv geworden, viele missionieren aktiv. Nicht alle würden für sich die Bezeichnung ›evangelikal‹ akzeptieren. Gemeinsam ist den Anhängern der verschiedenen Strömungen der Evangelikalen, dass sie die Schriften der Bibel nicht wie die in Deutschland vorherrschende Theologie in Erkenntnisse der historisch-kritischen Wissenschaften einbetten. Eine historisch-textkritische Theologie empfinden sie als Relativierung des ›Wortes Gottes‹. Viele glauben an ein nahes Ende der Welt, an die baldige Wiederkehr des Messias und ein Jüngstes Gericht, in dem die Menschheit in Gut und Böse eingeteilt und dementsprechend verdammt oder errettet wird. Bücher, die Geschichten aus dem Leben nach dem Jüngsten Gericht berichten, sind—wie die Serie »Left behind«—auf den US-Bestsellerlisten zu finden. Die Zahlen erstaunen Europäer: 66% aller Amerikaner haben keine Zweifel an der Existenz Gottes. Nur 5% sind Atheisten, die glauben, dass es nichts jenseits der physikalisch wahrnehmbaren Welt gibt. Immerhin fast jeder zweite US-Amerikaner zählt sich zu den ›wiedergeborenen Christen‹, mehr als jeder Dritte denkt laut TIME-Umfrage regelmäßig über das Ende der Welt nach und fast 60% der US-Bürger glauben an den in der Offenbarung des Johannes beschriebenen Zusammenhang zwischen Apokalypse und Apotheose.

Viele Intellektuelle in Europa neigen dazu, die Existenz und die Überzeugungen der christlichen Konservativen mit einer leicht herablassenden Attitüde in einem Atemzug mit Glauben an Außerirdische und anderen Kuriositäten zu nennen und somit als Überreste vorwissenschaftlichen Denkens abzutun. Vorausgesetzt wird dabei die global gesehen nicht haltbare These, dass zwischen Modernisierung und Säkularisierung ein unauflösbarer Zusammenhang besteht. Es wäre ebenfalls eine Fehleinschätzung, anzunehmen, dass die Evangelikalen sich lediglich auf die Schicht armer und schlecht ausgebildeter Amerikaner beschränken.

Welches politische Potential hinter dieser Gruppe steht, haben in jedem Fall die engsten Berater des US-Präsidenten, allen voran Chefberater Karl Rove, erkannt. Ihre Forderungen werden vom Präsidenten ernstgenommen. Auch im Wahlkampf wurde auf sie Rücksicht genommen.

Der Stimmenanteil der Angehörigen der Evangelikalen ist laut einer Pew-Studie von rund 19% im Jahr 1987 auf 23% an den Gesamtstimmen im Jahr 2004 und 24% im Jahr 2006 gestiegen. In der Amtszeit Jimmy Carters gab es noch viele Evangelikale, die die Demokraten wählten. Heute tendiert die überwiegende Mehrheit dieser potentiellen Wähler klar zum republikanischen Lager: Die religiös Konservativen sind zunehmend zu einem wichtigen Faktor der gesellschaftlichen und kulturellen Koalition geworden, die die Wahlsiege der Republikaner begünstigt. 2004 wählten 78% der weißen Evangelikalen (Im Jahr 2006 waren es 72%), 52% der Katholiken und immerhin 64% der wöchentlichen Kirchenbesucher aller christlichen Konfessionen republikanisch. Im Gegensatz hierzu wählten 2002 55% derjenigen, die nie einen Gottesdienst besuchen und 50% derjenigen, die selten zur Kirche gehen, die demokratischen Abgeordneten ins Repräsentantenhaus. Im Jahre 2006 stieg dieser Prozentsatz auf 67 bzw. 60%. Im Gegensatz hierzu wählten 62% derjenigen, die nie einen Gottesdienst besuchen, den demokratischen Kandidaten Kerry. Der Anteil und gerade auch das politische Engagement der Evangelikalen zugunsten der Republikaner sind seit dem Ende der 60er Jahre mit Unterbrechungen kontinuierlich gestiegen: Im Jahr 1964 gaben lediglich 42% der engagierten Evangelikalen und 48% der sonstigen Protestanten an, republikanisch zu wählen. In Ohio und Pennsylvania gelang es demokratischen Bewerbern für den Senat mit einer gezielten Ansprache religiös gebundener Wähler, einen Teil der Katholiken und der Protestanten, die 2004 noch die Republikaner gewählt hatten, im Jahre 2006 zur Wahl des demokratischen Kandidaten zu gewinnen. Diese christlichen Konservativen haben heutzutage in 36% aller Staaten die Mehrheit in den Gremien der republikanischen Partei, in 81% der restlichen Staaten stellen sie starke Minderheiten. Das bedeutet eine Verdoppelung ihres Anteils im letzten Jahrzehnt. Auf kultureller Ebene kann man heute von einer Wertedifferenz zwischen Republikanern und Demokraten sprechen.

Die zweite Hälfte der 60er Jahre war die Zeit des großen politischen Aufbruchs der Evangelikalen, die Zeit des *Battle for America*. In ihr wurde der Grundstein für den Aufbau der sog. ›elektronischen Kirche‹ und die Integration der einzelnen Zweige ihres christlichen Netzwerkes gelegt. Nach dem Abebben der Kommunistenjagd in der McCarthy-Zeit und einer ersten Protestbewegung anlässlich der Abschaffung des Schulgebetes kristallisierten sich die Schlüsselthemen von Abtreibung, der Rolle der Frau, der Bürgerrechtsbewegung, von Schwulen und Lesben, Umweltschutz- und Abrüstungsbewegung als Projektionsfläche für ein neues Feindbild heraus. Diese Themen trieben die Evangelikalen im Sinne einer *moral majority* auf die Barrikaden zur Verteidigung ihrer traditionell christlichen Werte. An diesen Themen verläuft bis heute die kulturelle Demarkationslinie zwischen Liberalen und Konservativen. Diese Themen erlauben es aber auch, konfessionsübergreifend politische Allianzen zu schmieden und auch bei parteilich nicht von vornherein zu den Rechten tendierenden gemäßigteren Christen für die Republikaner zu werben.

Der US-Präsident bemüht sich in Politik und Rhetorik, die Erwartungen der Evangelikalen nicht zu enttäuschen. Als überzeugter und wiedergeborener Christ scheut er sich nicht, Themen wie das Sexualverhalten von Jugendlichen und Erwachsenen in die politische Debatte einzuführen und das Land durch eine Neudefinition des Verhältnisses zwischen Staat und religiösen Gemeinschaften zu polarisieren, indem er in Abkehr von der bisherigen Praxis *faith based programs* staatlich fördert. In seinen Reden sind Gut und Böse in klaren Alternativen gegeneinander gestellt, wobei er und seine Politik für das ›Gute‹ stehen. Diese manichäische Weltsicht ist allerdings nicht auf Präsident Bush und auch nicht auf republikanische Präsidenten beschränkt.

Viele Europäer und auch Amerikaner befremdet es, wenn sich Präsident Bush durch die Berufung seiner Politik auf Gott zu einer Art säkularisierter politischer Predigerfigur zu stilisieren scheint. Als ich 2005 in Washington am *prayer breakfast* teilnahm, wurde Präsident Bush—ohne dass die Anwesenden Befremden zeigten—als *spiritual leader* vorgestellt. Diese Symbolik und diese Rhetorik werden von vielen Europäern und nicht wenigen Amerikanern als problematische Sakralisierung der öffentlichen Sphäre angesehen. Dabei darf man allerdings nicht vergessen, dass diese spezifisch amerikanische Ausprägung einer zur Zivilreligion überhöhten Politik auch positiv zum Zusammenhalt einer aus unterschiedlichster Herkunft sich ständig neu konstituierenden Nation beigetragen hat.

Im Gegensatz zu Europa findet es ein hoher Prozentsatz von Amerikanern völlig normal, wenn Politiker sich in ihren Reden auf ihre religiösen Überzeugungen berufen. Dagegen sind Vorbehalte in den USA weitverbreitet, wenn Kirchen sich zu politischen Fragen äußern. In Deutschland besteht demgegenüber eine große Skepsis, wenn Politiker sich in ihren Handlungen auf ihren persönlichen Glauben berufen, während gleichzeitig mehr als die Hälfte aller Deutschen Stellungnahmen der Kirche zu politischen Fragen für akzeptabel hält.

Der 11. September 2001 bot dem Präsidenten die Chance, sich als starke Führungspersönlichkeit zu bewähren und die Nation hinter sich zu vereinigen. Der Versuch einiger christlicher Konservativer, den 11. September als Strafe Gottes für moralische Verfehlungen der Amerikaner zu deuten, scheiterte. So wetterte etwa Jerry Falwell am 13. September 2001 gegen Heiden, Alternative, Feministinnen, Schwule, Lesben und andere, die nicht der *moral majority* angehören: »Ich zeige mit dem Finger auf sie und sage es ihnen ins Gesicht—Ihr habt dazu beigetragen«. Eine nationale Protestwelle unterband diese Schuldzuweisung.

Der Kampf gegen den Terrorismus wurde von vielen Amerikanern—aus meiner Sicht zwar vereinfacht, aber nicht völlig unberechtigt—als die neue große Herausforderung des Guten durch das Böse gesehen. Richard Perle und David Frum, der Redenschreiber, der den biblisch inspirierten Begriff *Axis of Evil* geprägt hat, pointierten dies so: »Der Krieg gegen den extremistischen Islam ist ein ideologischerer Krieg als es der Kalte Krieg je sein konnte.« Gleichzeitig wurden in der Auseinandersetzung mit dem internationalen Terrorismus die USA—wiederum nicht völlig zu Unrecht—als *last resort of freedom*, also die wichtigste Macht des Guten gegen das Böse in dieser Welt begriffen. Diese Selbstdefinition der USA hat seit ihrer Gründung zur Identitätsstiftung unter Amerikanern beigetragen. Gerade vor diesem Selbstverständnis waren viele Amerikaner angesichts der Folterbilder aus dem Irak noch mehr als manche Europäer schockiert. Angesichts des hohen Anspruches an die eigene Nation schlug die Zuversicht, für das Gute zu stehen, in Selbstkritik und Beschämung um. Damit verband sich gleichzeitig die Hoffnung, dass sich in der Bereitschaft zur Selbstkritik und juristischen Korrektur das für die amerikanische Demokratie grundlegende System der *Checks and Balances* erneut bestätigen würde.

Welches Fazit ziehen wir aus diesen Überlegungen? Europa und die USA bleiben durch gemeinsame Werte miteinander verbunden. Aber die Differenzen zwischen Europa und den USA in religiösen Fragen sind groß. Das Pew Center analysierte im Juni 2003: »Amerikaner und Europäer haben Differenzen in der Außenpolitik und bei anderen Themen, aber diese Meinungsunterschiede verblassen im Vergleich zur transatlantischen Kluft in religiösen und moralischen Fragen«. Von den USA sagt man, dass sie eine »nation with the soul of a church« sei (G. K. Chesterton). Anders als nach dem Zweiten Weltkrieg konnte man von der evangelischen Kirche in Deutschland zumindest bis zum Ende des Ersten Weltkrieges sagen, dass sie eine »church with a soul of nation« war.

Hüben wie drüben ist bei breiten Bevölkerungsschichten bisher weder das Grundwissen noch die Bereitschaft da, sich in die Denkschemata des anderen einzufühlen. Nur durch Bemühen um Verständnis—was keineswegs mit Einverständnis gleichzusetzen ist—bleibt eine gemeinsame Diskursgrundlage erhalten. Wo Menschen nicht mehr miteinander kommunizieren, leidet über kurz oder lang das Verhältnis insgesamt. Der Rekurs auf Stereotypen im transatlantischen Verhältnis ist ohnehin bereits jetzt bei vielen eher die Regel als die Ausnahme. Dabei wäre es gerade angesichts von religiös begründetem Extremismus und Terrorismus wichtig, den transatlantischen Dialog über religiöse, philosophische und ethische Grundlagen demokratischer Gesellschaften zu vertiefen.

Aus meiner Sicht gibt es vor allem drei Gründe dafür, dass in der Diskussion zwischen den transatlantischen Partnern die Beschäftigung mit dem Verhältnis von Religion und Politik wichtiger geworden ist:

1. Alle europäischen Staaten und insbesondere Deutschland haben heute eine quasi-innenpolitische Beziehung zu den USA.
2. Die religiösen Landschaften in den USA und Europa verändern sich.
3. Die außenpolitische Relevanz religiöser Fragen nimmt zu.

Zu 1. Innenpolitische Orientierungen und Entscheidungen in den USA beeinflussen die Innenpolitik Europas. Aber die zu uns gelangenden Nachrichten werden vor dem Hintergrund unserer unterschiedlichen Traditionen wahrgenommen und bewertet. Das gilt auch für religiöse Themen.

In den USA werden die deutsche Botschaft und unsere Generalkonsulate mit Beschwerden religiöser Gruppen konfrontiert, die sich gegen das Verbot von Homeschooling in Deutschland wenden. Sie sehen in diesem Verbot eine Einschränkung ihrer Religionsfreiheit. Im Europa des 18. und 19. Jahrhundert wurden Kinder des Adels und der Reichen häufig zu Hause unterrichtet, während Kinder der Unterschicht keine oder nur eine mangelhafte Schulausbildung erhielten. Vor diesem Kontext sehen wir in Deutschland die Pflicht zum Besuch staatlich anerkannter Schulen als einen demokratischen Fortschritt an. Das Bundesverfassungsgericht hat sich im Juni 2006 grundsätzlich dagegen ausgesprochen, dass Kinder aus religiösen Gründen von der Schulpflicht befreit werden können. Trotz dieses Grundsatzes versuchen die für die Schulpolitik allein zuständigen Bundesländer im Einzelfall Rücksicht auf die religiösen Überzeugungen der Eltern zu nehmen: So hat das Land Bayern mit der christlichen Religionsgemeinschaft »Zwölf Stämme« einen Kompromiss ausgehandelt, dem zufolge die Kinder zwar auf dem Gelände in einem der Religionsgemeinschaft gehörenden ehemaligen Kloster unterrichtet werden können. Der Unterricht muss aber entsprechend den offiziellen Lehrplänen durchgeführt werden. Wenn die Evolutionstheorie Darwins unterrichtet wird, darf zugleich von der Schöpfung Gottes die Rede sein. In Hamburg hat ein Landgericht demgegenüber den Antrag von Eltern, die Kinder statt im öffentlichen Schulunterricht zu Hause unterrichten zu können, abgewiesen, weil eine religiöse Gemeinschaft der Eltern nicht glaubhaft nachgewiesen wurde. Angesichts der Neigung einer Minderheit von islamischen Einwanderern, sich der Schulpflicht zu entziehen, bleibt ihre Aufrechterhaltung aus meiner Sicht ein auch weiterhin unverzichtbares Element der sozialen Integration.

Anders als in den USA ist in Deutschland nicht erst das Handeln, sondern bereits das Propagieren von Hass gegen andere Religionen und andere Weltanschauungen strafbar. Die Religionsfreiheit schützt auch dann nicht vor einer

Bestrafung, wenn derartige Hass-Reden in einer Kirche, einer Synagoge oder einer Mosche gehalten werden. Die USA und Deutschland bekennen sich gleichermaßen zu den Grundwerten der Meinungsfreiheit und der Religionsfreiheit. Vor dem Hintergrund unserer historischen Erfahrungen aber praktizieren wir im Konflikt zwischen unterschiedlichen demokratischen Grundwerten eine andere Hierarchie als die USA.

In der US-Presse wird das Verbot des Tragens von Kopftüchern an Schulen in einigen europäischen Staaten (darunter auch der Türkei) häufig als Ausdruck mangelnder Toleranz gegenüber den Traditionen islamischer Einwanderer interpretiert. In Europa gilt dies Verbot vielen als logische Konsequenz aus der Trennung von Staat und Religion. Wobei es übrigens interessante Unterschiede zwischen Frankreich und Deutschland gibt: In Frankreich dürfen auch Schülerinnen kein Kopftuch tragen, weil die Schule insgesamt als staatlicher und damit säkularer Bereich gilt. In Deutschland gilt dies Verbot (wobei einzelne Bundesländer dies unterschiedlich handhaben) nur für die Lehrer, nicht aber für Schüler. Die Begründung hierfür ist, dass die Lehrer als Autoritätspersonen in öffentlicher Funktion auch in ihrer Kleidung die Neutralität des Staates gegenüber den Religionen zu respektieren haben.

Die Unterschiede zwischen Deutschland einerseits und Frankreich wie den USA andererseits ist deutlich bei der staatlichen Unterstützung von kirchlichen Bildungseinrichtungen. Im Bundesland Berlin, welches von einer Koalition aus SPD und PDS regiert wird, werden 90% der Kosten der katholischen, evangelischen und jüdischen Schulen vom Bundesland finanziert, d.h. aus Steuergeldern, sofern diese religiösen Schulen gewisse allgemeine Landesvorschriften erfüllen. Die Zahl der religiösen Schulen nimmt zurzeit zu. Berlin hat letztes Jahr eine Reihe von Kindergärten privatisiert, einige von ihnen wurden religiösen Organisationen übertragen. Die Kindergartenbeiträge werden aus öffentlichen Mitteln subventioniert. Eine theologische Fakultät gibt es an einer der drei öffentlichen Universitäten Berlins. Der 2005 gewählte Präsident der traditionsreichen Humboldt-Universität zu Berlin ist Theologieprofessor.

In Deutschland ist, anders als in den USA, das Angebot von Religionsunterricht an öffentlichen Schulen (und eine grundsätzlich freiwillige Teilnahme der Schüler an ihm) weit verbreitet. Wir sehen hierin keine Verletzung der durch unsere Verfassung gebotenen Neutralität des Staates gegenüber den unterschiedlichen Religionen. Logischerweise wird deshalb auch zunehmend islamischer Religionsunterricht an öffentlichen Schulen angeboten. An der Universität Osnabrück im Land Niedersachsen werden heute bereits Lehrer ausgebildet, die später an staatlichen Schulen in deutscher Sprache Islamunterricht erteilen sollen. Dieser Studiengang an staatlichen Universitäten wird von den muslimischen Gemeinden anerkannt.

Die Befürworter von Religionsunterricht an öffentlichen Schulen betonen die Chance und die Notwendigkeit, dass den Kindern in diesem Unterricht wichtige Werte vermittelt werden, auf denen ein demokratischer Staat beruht, dessen Vermittlung ein säkularer Staat aber nicht selber leisten kann.

Als vor kurzem das von einer SPD/PDS-Koalition regierte Land Berlin entschied, einen verbindlichen Ethikunterricht an den Schulen einzuführen, gleichzeitig aber den Religionsunterricht nur außerhalb der verbindlichen Unterrichtszeit auf der Basis einer freiwilligen Teilnahme anbot, erhob sich bei den Berliner Oppositionsparteien und auch innerhalb der SPD Protest. Bundeskanzler Schröder, der SPD-Parteivorsitzende Müntefering und die Staatsministerin für Kultur im Bundeskanzleramt distanzierten sich von diesen Plänen der Berliner SPD. Sie traten für die freie Wahlmöglichkeit zwischen einem Pflichtfach Ethik und einem Pflichtfach Religion an. Nachdem anfangs eine klare Mehrheit der Berliner dem Vorschlag des Senats zuzuneigen schien, traten laut Umfrage der BERLINER ZEITUNG vom 18. 04. 2005 56% der Berliner für eine freie Wahl zwischen einem Pflichtfach Ethik und einem Pflichtfach Religion und nur noch 39% für die von den Berliner Regierungsparteien beschlossene Lösung ein. In den USA wird demgegenüber ein Religionsunterricht an staatlichen Schulen nur von einer Minderheit, insbesondere der religiösen Rechten gefordert. Die Mehrheit der Amerikaner sieht hierin, anders als die deutsche Politik, einen Verstoß gegen die Trennung von Staat und Kirche.

Wenn ich diese Tatsachen in den USA berichte, stoße ich bei den Liberalen auf Erstaunen und bei religiösen Rechten auf Interesse.

Andererseits ist die Verbindung von Religion und Politik, die in den USA zur Entwicklung einer Art ›Zivilreligion‹ geführt hat, für Europa befremdlich. Viele Europäer empfinden die weitverbreitete religiöse Rhetorik amerikanischer Politiker als einen Missbrauch der Religion für politische Zwecke. Typisch hierfür ist ein Artikel des katholischen Bischofs von Trier, Reinhard Marx, am 23. Februar 2006 in der FRANKFURTER ALLGEMEINEN ZEITUNG:

> Mission hat oft etwas mit Religion zu tun, und George W. Bush verbirgt dies nicht. Seine Politik kommt aus seinem Glauben. Gerade der Versuch, die Menschenrechte durchzusetzen, zeigt aber: Wer ein hohes Gut erstrebt, ist auf dem Weg dahin selbst schon an dessen innere Struktur, an dessen Regeln gebunden. Glaube und Glaubwürdigkeit lassen sich nicht voneinander trennen. Mir gibt es derzeit gerade in der amerikanischen Politik einen Schuss zuviel Gläubigkeit und eine Prise zuwenig Glaubwürdigkeit! Bekenntnisse sind schnell geäußert, Religion ist kein öffentliches Tabuthema, aber worauf es ankommt, ist die Umsetzung des Bekenntnisses. Ja, wir dürfen und sollen Gott öffentlich ins Spiel bringen, aber er ist kein Instrument in unserer Hand. Wer von Gott spricht, muss demütig werden. Im zweiten Gebot heißt es: Du sollst den Namen Gottes nicht missbrauchen! Also Vorsicht, nicht Leisetreterei! Zeugnis des Glaubens, aber Konsequenz im Handeln!

In der Präambel des Grundgesetzes wird auf Gott Bezug genommen. Es gibt ein verfassungsmäßig verankertes Recht der Religionsgemeinschaften, die Körperschaften des öffentlichen Rechts sind, Steuern zu erheben. Das sind zurzeit die evangelische und die katholische Kirche und die jüdischen Gemeinden, das können in Zukunft aber auch islamische Gemeinschaften sein. Der Staat finanziert die Militärseelsorge. Es gibt einen Rechtsanspruch der Religionsgemeinschaften auf Sendezeiten im öffentlichen Rundfunk und Fernsehen. Die Beziehungen zwischen Staat und Religionsgemeinschaften werden in zahlreichen Verträgen geregelt. All dies wäre in den Vereinigten Staaten mit ihrer strikten Trennung von Staat und Kirche undenkbar.

Im neugebauten deutschen Parlament in Berlin gibt es selbstverständlich einen Gebetsraum. Über 100 Mitglieder des Bundestages rechnen sich der Prayer-Breakfast-Vereinigung zu. Die Zahl der Bundestagsabgeordneten, die sich in ihren Lebensläufen öffentlich als Mitglieder einer Religionsgemeinschaft bekennen, hat in den vergangenen 20 Jahren kontinuierlich zugenommen. Rund 15 Bundestagsabgeordnete sind vollakademisch ausgebildete Theologen, die natürlich auch Hebräisch, Griechisch und Latein gelernt haben. Hinzu kommen einige Religionslehrer. In der vergangenen Legislaturperiode des Bundestages hatten zwei der vier Vizepräsidenten des Bundestages im Nebenfach Theologie studiert. Der Präsident des Bundestages war zugleich Mitglied im Zentralkomitee der Katholiken. Da die Sozialdemokratische Partei in der ehemaligen DDR insbesondere von Pfarrern und Aktiven der evangelischen Kirche gegründet wurde, gibt es im Bundestag zurzeit mehr Theologen auf der linken als auf der konservativen Seite des Parlaments. Es ist zum festen Bestandteil der kollektiven Erinnerung aller Deutschen geworden, dass ohne das Engagement der evangelischen Kirche die friedliche Revolution im Jahre 1989 nicht so friedlich verlaufen wäre. Die Christen als Minderheit in der DDR wirkten am Ende des Kalten Krieges im Sinne des Neuen Testaments als das Salz der Erde. Ihr Geist wirkt sich, trotz einer weitgehenden Entkirchlichung, noch heute auf die politische Kultur in Ostdeutschland aus.

Es gibt zwar in der evangelischen Kirche Strömungen, die theologisch evangelikale Positionen vertreten. Strömungen, die politisch mit denen der religiösen Rechten in den USA verglichen werden können, sind mir jedoch aus dem Bundestag nicht bekannt. Sie spielen in der deutschen Gesellschaft auch faktisch keine Rolle. Trotzdem geht die bundesdeutsche Wirklichkeit zum Teil weit über das hinaus, was Teile der religiösen Rechten in den USA als politische und finanzielle Unterstützung durch den Staat für religiöse Gruppen fordern.

Amerikaner sehen den Einfluss von Religion in der Gesellschaft überwiegend positiv, in erster Linie aufgrund der positiven Auswirkungen auf das Verhalten und die Aktivitäten des Einzelnen. Da die Amerikaner derzeit sehr besorgt über den Moralzerfall in der amerikanischen Gesellschaft sind, wird Religion als positiver Einfluss erachtet. Viele glauben, dass ein religiöser Einfluss dazu an-leitet, ein besseres Leben zu führen, wie z.B. die Übernahme von Ehrenämtern und Wohltätigkeitsarbeit und die bessere Erfüllung der Elternrolle, die Abnahme von Kriminalität und den Rückgang von Gier und Materialismus. In einem Artikel in der USA-TODAY am 10.01.2006 unter der Überschrift »Is God dead in Europe?« wird zwischen dem Abstieg Europas, seinem moralischen Verfall, seiner sinkenden Geburtenraten und der abnehmenden Religiosität der Europäer ein unmittelbarer Bezug hergestellt. So wie die Europäer irren, die unterstellen, dass zwischen Modernisierung und Säkularisierung ein unauflösbarer Gleichklang bestehe, irren die Amerikaner, die voraussetzen, dass ein unmittelbarer Zusammenhang zwischen Religiosität und moralischem Verhalten bestünde.

Politisch und kulturell kann man sich kaum größere Unterschiede vorstellen als zwischen der religiösen Rechten der USA und der säkularisierten oder der christlichen Linken in Deutschland. Bei der ethischen Bewertung des Klonens und der Nutzung von Stammzellen gibt es aber erstaunliche Übereinstimmungen von Teilen der deutschen Linken mit Teilen der amerikanischen religiösen Rechten: dies ist auf ein gleichermaßen ethisch motiviertes aber entweder religiös oder säkular begründetes Bedürfnis nach dem Schutz der ›Schöpfung‹ zurückzuführen. Bei Teilen der Evangelikalen—wie z. B. dem prominenten Vertreter der ›Christian Coalition‹, Rev. Joel Hunter—führt dieses Eintreten für den Schutz der Schöpfung inzwischen auch zu einer Bejahung des christlichen Engagements für den Umweltschutz.

Einen wesentlichen Anlass für das Entstehen und die politische Mobilisierung der religiösen Rechten bilden die Urteile des Supreme Court zur Abtreibung. Das Bundesverfassungsgericht ging demgegenüber einen—aus Sicht eines Amerikaners—konservativeren Weg: Die deutsche Verfassung bekennt sich zum Recht auf Leben und zu seinem Schutz. Als eine Mehrheit des Parlaments mit meiner Stimme die Abtreibung in den ersten drei Monaten generell für straffrei erklärte, schränkte das Bundesverfassungsgericht im Jahre 1993 diese Regelung unter Hinweis auf den in der Verfassung gebotenen Schutz des Lebens ein.

Einen ähnlich pragmatischen Kompromiss zwischen prinzipiellen Normen und der Lebenswirklichkeit praktiziert Deutschland in der Frage der Homosexualität. Homosexuelle Paare sind zwar faktisch und rechtlich heterosexuellen Lebensgemeinschaften weitgehend gleichgestellt. Im normativen Sinne handelt es sich dabei aber nicht um Ehen. Die im Grundgesetz geschützte Ehe ist verfassungsrechtlich auf die Gründung einer Familie angelegt und steht damit gleichgeschlechtlichen Paaren nicht offen. Einige Pastoren segnen gleichgeschlechtliche Paare. Sie vollziehen aber formell keine kirchlichen Trauungen. In den USA gingen die Einzelstaaten sehr unterschiedliche Wege. Im Wahlkampf 2004 wurde von Konservativen immer wieder hervorgehoben, dass in Massachusetts, dem Heimatstaat des demokratischen Präsidentschaftskandidaten Kerry, die Ehe gleichgeschlechtlicher Paare zulässig sei. Die anglikanische Kirche wird vom Thema Homosexualität tief zerrissen.

Was aber bleibt ist folgender Eindruck: Aufgrund der jahrelangen kontroversen Diskussionen in den usa glauben, wie die meisten Europäer auch die meisten Deutschen, dass sie in der Frage der Homosexualität viel liberaler als die Amerikaner und insbesondere als die religiöse Rechte in den usa sind. Dieser Eindruck ist in einigen Regionen der usa berechtigt, gilt aber für San Francisco sicher nicht.

Zu 2. In den meisten europäischen Ländern nimmt die Bindung an christliche Kirchen und die von ihnen vertretenen Glaubensinhalte ab, und der Besuch von Gottesdiensten geht zurück. Dieser Prozess der Entkirchlichung ist in den verschiedenen Regionen Europas unterschiedlich stark ausgeprägt. In Deutschland gehört etwa ein Drittel der Bevölkerung der katholischen Kirche an, ein Drittel ist evangelisch und ungefähr ein Drittel ist konfessionslos. Dabei gibt es allerdings große Unterschiede zwischen Ost und West: Im Westen gehören ca. 76% einer der beiden christlichen Kirchen an. Auf dem Gebiet der ehemaligen ddr sind nur noch ca. 28% der Bevölkerung Mitglieder von Kirchen. Neuere Daten deuten in Deutschland allerdings auf ein Abklingen dieser Entkirchlichung hin. Auf Dauer halte ich eine Trendumkehr nicht für ausgeschlossen. Hierfür spricht, dass der Anteil der Deutschen, die ihre religiöse Überzeugung als für sie selber sehr wesentlich halten, seit 1986 von 22% auf 27% gestiegen ist (in Ostdeutschland stieg seit 1993 der Prozentsatz von 14 auf 23%). Laut einer Umfrage des Meinungsforschungsinstitut Allensbach im Jahre 2006 sind ein Viertel der Eltern der Meinung, dass Kinder im Elternhaus eine feste religiöse Bindung erwerben sollten. 1991 waren es noch 13%. Trotz des Prozesses der Entkirchlichung werden der evangelischen und der katholischen Kirche weit über den Kreis der Gläubigen hinaus eine hohe Glaubwürdigkeit zuerkannt, wenn sie sich ethisch begründet äußern, u.a. zu Fragen von Krieg und Frieden, der Entwicklungs- und Einwanderungspolitik, aber auch zu sozialen Fragen und ethischen Aspekten der Technologiepolitik. Die gleiche Glaubwürdigkeit besitzt der Zentralrat der Juden, wenn er z.B. Stellungnahmen zur demokratischen Kultur in Deutschland abgibt.

Die usa sind im Vergleich zu diesen europäischen Entwicklungen ein Land der Gläubigen und der Gottesdienstbesucher. 43% aller Amerikaner behaupten, wöchentlich die Kirche, Synagoge oder Moschee zu besuchen, 75% mindestens einmal im halben Jahr. Die meisten Amerikaner geben an, dass sie zumindest gelegentlich Gebetshäuser aufsuchen. In Deutschland besuchen dagegen weniger als 15% wöchentlich den Gottesdienst. Eine Mehrheit der Amerikaner betet täglich. Weniger als 5% beten nie. Ca. 35% der Amerikaner sind Kreationisten, d.h. sie glauben die Erschaffung der Welt, so wie sie in der biblischen Schöpfungsgeschichte dargestellt wird. Auch die Formen, in denen sich religiöser Glaube ausdrückt, und die dabei vertretenen Inhalte entwickeln sich auseinander. Nur etwa 1,3 der 26 Millionen Protestanten in Deutschland können in ihren theologischen Auffassungen den Evangelikalen zugerechnet werden. Die Feststellung Bischof Hubers, »der Protestantismus ist aus streng theologischen Gründen auf die enge Verbindung von Glauben und Vernunft angewiesen. Das gilt um des Glaubens willen, der subjektiv angeeignet, also verstanden werden will; und es gilt um der Vernunft willen, für die der Stachel kritischer Selbstreflexion unentbehrlich ist, damit sie ihre Endlichkeit weder vergisst noch verleugnet«, würde bei den Evangelikalen auf entschiedenen Widerstand stoßen. Desgleichen wohl seine These: »Ein nicht durch die Vernunft aufgehellter Glaube aber trägt die Gefahr in sich, barbarisch und gewalttätig zu werden. Stattdessen ist es nötig, die wechselseitige Verwiesenheit von Vernunft und Glaube immer wieder neu zu entfalten« (Buch-Zitat aus ›Glaube und Vernunft‹, 30.10.06). Die in Europa dominierende Theologie verortet ihren Glauben nicht im Widerspruch zur Aufklärung und auch nicht im Widerspruch zu den naturwissenschaftlichen Erkenntnissen über die Entwicklung der Erde und der Menschheit. In einem Satz zusammengefasst: In Europa dominiert eine Theologie, die sich als Schwester der Philosophie versteht. Dies gilt auch für zahlreiche christliche Gemeinden in den USA. Die Kontakte der deutschen Kirchen zu den amerikanischen Evangelikalen sind vergleichsweise spärlich.

Auf dem amerikanischen Markt der Religionen vollzieht sich der Wettbewerb in Formen, die uns Europäer an den Wettbewerb zwischen verschiedenen Markenprodukten in der Marktwirtschaft erinnern. Gerade diejenigen Gemeinden, die wir als Ausdruck eines christlichen Fundamentalismus wahrnehmen oder die sogar als religiöse ›Wellness‹-Bewegung diskreditiert werden, haben den größten Zulauf zulasten traditioneller eher ›europäischer‹ Kirchen. Dieser Trend geht einher mit einer wachsenden Bereitschaft, seine religiöse Zugehörigkeit zu wechseln. Noch 1955 waren laut *Gallup* nur 4% der Amerikaner bereit, die Religion ihrer Kindheit zu ändern. In der Mitte der achtziger Jahre zeigte eine erneute Gallup-Umfrage, dass bereits ein Drittel aller Amerikaner die religiöse Zugehörigkeit ihrer Jugend aufgegeben hatte und zu anderen Kirchen und Gemeinden gewechselt war. Etwa ein Drittel der Hispanics gehört heute protestantischen Gemeinden an. Dabei ist ein Übertritt von Hispanics zu evangelikalen Gruppen überproportional häufig.

In einem Vortrag im Juni 2004 hat der Vorsitzende des Rats der Evangelischen Kirche in Deutschland, Bischof Huber, dargelegt, mit welcher Religionskultur der USA sich die meisten Deutschen identifizieren können und wo sie zur politischen Entfremdung beiträgt. Ich zitiere ihn deshalb ausführlich:

> Die religiöse Berufung dazu, eine bessere Welt herbeizuführen, nahm in der jüngeren Geschichte der USA sehr unterschiedliche Formen an. Die Vision, aus dem Geist des christlichen Glaubens eine bessere Zukunft

herbeizuführen, bündelte sich beispielsweise im Jahr 1963 in einem einzigen kurzen Satz: ›I have a dream—Ich habe einen Traum‹. In der Rede, die sich um diesen Satz rankt, beschwor der baptistische Geistliche Dr. Martin Luther King damals seinen Traum von Freiheit und Gleichheit der Menschen. Dieser Traum verband sich nicht mit einem besonderen Herrschaftsanspruch, sondern mit der Forderung nach Gleichberechtigung der bisher Unterdrückten. Die besondere religiöse Berufung, die er geltend machte, mündete auch nicht in eine Rechtfertigung der Gewalt, sondern in den Appell zu gewaltfreiem Widerstand. Eine Vision wurde laut, die die Kontinente, ja sogar die Religionen überspannt. Mahatma Gandhi und Dietrich Bonhoeffer kann man unter die geistigen Vorläufer dieses Traums rechnen.

Deshalb erweist sich dieser Traum auch bis zum heutigen Tag als eine lebendige Brücke über den Atlantik. An kaum einem Punkt gibt es eine größere Nähe zwischen den USA und Deutschland, den USA und Europa. Und es ist sicherlich kein Zufall, dass hier der christliche Glaube in besonderer Weise ins Spiel kommt. Der Gedanke der Gleichheit aller Menschen vor Gott ist der entscheidende Bezugspunkt, aus dem sich der Kampf gegen die Diskriminierung aus Gründen der Rassenzugehörigkeit genauso ergibt wie die Absage an den Einsatz tötender Gewalt als politisches Mittel.

In Martin Luther Kings Version kommt die christliche Prägung des amerikanischen Traums mit besonderem Nachdruck zum Klingen. Sie macht eindringlich deutlich, dass der amerikanische Traum ein christlicher Traum ist. Die ganze Tradition seit der Mayflower und den Pilgervätern klingt in dieser Rede vom amerikanischen Traum mit. Ein baptistischer Prediger stellt sich im Kampf um die Bürgerrechte der Schwarzen bewusst in diese Tradition.

Zugleich tritt freilich auch eine mögliche Umkehrung in den Blick, die dann sagen würde: Der christliche Traum ist ein amerikanischer Traum. Wo sich eine solche Umkehrung vollzieht, mündet der amerikanische Traum in die Vorstellung einer amerikanischen Überlegenheit im christlichen Namen. Die Ironie der amerikanischen Geschichte wird dann negiert. Das besondere Berufungsbewusstsein dieser Nation wird dann zur Rechtfertigung eines politischen Überlegenheitsanspruchs.

Gemeinsam mit vielen Amerikanerinnen und Amerikanern wird man dagegen festhalten: Der christliche Traum ist kein amerikanischer Traum. Er wäre aber auch kein deutscher Traum, obwohl das in unserer eigenen Geschichte bisweilen gedacht wurde. Er hat überhaupt keinen nationalen Charakter, sondern überspannt die Menschheit.

Die weitverbreitete Verbindung zwischen Religion und Patriotismus in den USA stößt in Europa nicht nur auf Unverständnis sondern auf Erschrecken und Ablehnung. Diese Verbindung weckt andere negative Erinnerungen—in Deutschland aufgrund unserer Geschichte, in der Menschen wegen ihrer Religionszugehörigkeit verbannt und vernichtet wurden—sowie in ganz Europa wegen einer Geschichte, in der immer wieder versucht wurde, Kriege und Eroberungen mit der religiösen Überzeugung zu legitimieren.

Die auf beiden Seiten des Atlantiks zu den demokratischen Grundprinzipien gehörende Unterscheidung zwischen Staat und Religion und das Verfassungsgebot einer säkularen Rechtsordnung wurzelt in einer 2000 Jahre langen

Geschichte. Sie wurde sehr früh und sehr präzis durch die Lehre von Augustinus von den beiden Reichen, der *civitas Dei* und der *civitas terrena* dargelegt. Sowohl die amerikanische wie auch die französische Revolution fußen auf diesen Traditionen. Beide ziehen daraus aber unterschiedliche Konsequenzen für die Regelung des Verhältnisses von Staat und Kirche. Das deutsche Verfassungsrecht und die deutsche Praxis unterscheiden sich wiederum sowohl von der amerikanischen wie auch der französischen.

Für die Begründer des Islam bildeten Religion, Politik und Recht eine Einheit. Dies erklärt, warum nicht nur islamische Extremisten sondern auch islamische Traditionalisten einer Übertragung unserer Verfassungs- und Rechtstraditionen auf islamische Staaten widersprechen. Dass einige islamische Staaten die Konversion eines Anhängers des Islam zu einer anderen Religion strafrechtlich ahnden, ist mit unserem Verständnis der weltweit gültigen Menschenrechte nicht zu vereinbaren.

Innerhalb der transatlantischen Gemeinschaft stellt die Einwanderung aus islamischen Staaten uns vor neue Herausforderungen.

In den USA dominiert die Auffassung, dass die Amerikaner bei der Integration auch von islamischen Einwanderern erfolgreicher als die Europäer sind. Die Fehler der Europäer bei der Integration islamischer Einwanderer seien einer der Gründe für die Zunahme eines islamischen Extremismus und bei einer kleinen Gruppe von islamischen Einwanderern seien diese Fehler bei der Integration sogar die Ursache für deren Sympathie für terroristische Aktivitäten.

Sicher ist: Diese Einwanderung wird beide Seiten des Atlantiks und auch die Einwanderer selbst verändern. Welche Richtung diese unvermeidlichen Veränderungen nehmen sollen und wo die Grenzen dieser Veränderung liegen, ist umstritten. Die unterschiedlichen Wege, die die einzelnen Bundesländer bei der Einbeziehung des islamischen Religionsunterrichts an öffentlichen Schulen gehen, sind hierfür ein Beleg; die Kontroversen über die Voraussetzungen für den Erwerb der deutschen Staatsbürgerschaft ein weiterer. Aufgrund unserer unterschiedlichen Traditionen unterscheiden sich vielfach auch die Antworten auf beiden Seiten des Atlantiks. Trotzdem sollten wir noch viel mehr als bisher bereit sein, von unseren jeweiligen Erfahrungen zu lernen.

Zu 3. Konflikte und Krisen in zahlreichen Ländern mit überwiegend muslimischer Bevölkerung haben negative außenpolitische Auswirkungen. Die weite Verbreitung antiwestlicher und insbesondere antiamerikanischer Stimmungen beunruhigt Europäer und Amerikaner gleichermaßen. Diese Stimmungen als irrationaler Ausdruck rationaler sowie ökonomischer Probleme in der islamischen Welt zu sehen, ist unzureichend. Eine solche Sichtweise ließe die kulturelle Aufladung von Konflikten zwischen dem Westen und der islamischen Welt außer acht. Es muss vielmehr zur Kenntnis genommen werden, dass zunehmend die islamische Religion zur ideologischen Form geworden ist, in der relevante Teile der Bevölkerung in der islamischen Welt ihre Konflikte mit der westlichen Welt ausdrücken. Die weitaus überwiegende Mehrheit der Muslime lehnt den Terrorismus als dem Wesen des Islam widersprechend ab. Dies gilt auch für die überwältigende Mehrheit der über drei Millionen Anhänger des Islam in Deutschland. Aber Tatsache bleibt auch, dass zahlreiche terroristische Gruppen sich selber auf den Islam zur ideologischen Legitimation ihrer Gewalt berufen. Dies hat negative Auswirkungen auf das Ansehen des Islam auf beiden Seiten des Atlantiks.

Amerikaner und Europäer treten gemeinsam für mehr Demokratie, mehr Rechtsstaatlichkeit und einen besseren Schutz der Menschenrechte weltweit und damit auch in der islamischen Welt ein. Bei entsprechenden Initiativen im Nahen und Mittleren Osten arbeiten wir zusammen. Trotz dieser Gemeinsamkeiten in den Zielen gibt es Unterschiede in unserer Sichtweise und in unseren Methoden.

Die USA haben in ihrer Geschichte nie die Erfahrung gemacht, dass religiöse Überzeugungen und Gruppierungen eine Gefahr für ihre Demokratie darstellten. Im Gegenteil. Sie neigen deshalb dazu, ihre positiven Erfahrungen auf die islamische Welt zu übertragen und Risiken für demokratische Traditionen nicht in religiösen Traditionen sondern in Tyrannen, autoritären politischen Führungen und undemokratischen Institutionen zu sehen. Diese lassen sich relativ schnell, im Notfall auch unter Einsatz von militärischer Gewalt, beseitigen. Hinzu kommt, dass viele Amerikaner dazu neigen, dem Menschen ein in seiner Natur liegendes Streben nach Freiheit und Demokratie zuzuschreiben. Die Europäer stimmen mit den Amerikanern in ihren demokratischen Werten und Zielen überein, neigen aber zu einer skeptischeren Sichtweise der Natur des Menschen.

Die europäische Erfahrung unterscheidet sich von der amerikanischen. Auch in Europa gab es zahlreiche Christen und Juden, die sich aktiv gegen Diktatur und für Demokratie und Menschenrechte einsetzten. In zahlreichen europäischen Ländern aber stellten lange Zeit die dominierenden religiösen Traditionen und Institutionen ein Hindernis bei der Demokratisierung dar. Es bedurfte einer Neudefinition der politischen Kultur durch die Kirchen selber, bevor sie verlässliche und aktive Stützen einer demokratischen Entwicklung wurden. In einigen europäischen Staaten dauerte dieser Prozess bis ins 20. Jahrhundert hinein an. Eine solche positive Neudefinition der religiösen Traditionen hat sich noch lange nicht in allen islamischen Gesellschaften durchgesetzt. Sie braucht Zeit. Diese Zeit ist wahrscheinlich in zahlreichen Staaten nicht in Jahren sondern in Jahrzehnten zu bemessen. Der Vorstellung, dieser notwendige und mögliche Prozess der geistigen und religiösen Reform in der islamischen Welt ließe sich durch Anwendung militärischer Gewalt beschleunigen, stehen die meisten Europäer skeptisch gegenüber.

In der europäischen Geschichte wurden zahlreiche Kriege im Namen der Religion geführt. Im 30-jährigen Krieg vor rund 350 Jahren, in dem sich die Kriegsgegner beider Seiten auf die Werte des Christentums beriefen, starb in vielen Regionen Deutschlands die Hälfte aller Einwohner. Im Ersten Weltkrieg stand auf den Koppeln der Gürtel der deutschen Soldaten »Gott mit uns«. Gut war immer die eigene Seite, böse die der anderen. Vor diesem historischen Hintergrund erinnert die in den USA weitverbreitete Verbindung von Patriotismus und Religion uns Europäer heute an frühere Zeiten unserer Geschichte, die überwunden zu haben wir uns heute glücklich schätzen. In Deutschland wird man—anders als in den USA—in kaum einer Kirche heute noch eine Nationalflagge sehen.

Das positive Verhältnis der Evangelikalen zu Israel trägt zur proisraelischen Haltung der US-Bevölkerung bei. Im Jahr 2004 sagten in den USA 75% der Juden, 52% der Evangelikalen, 33% der Mainline-Protestanten, 24% der schwarzen Protestanten, 25% der katholischen Latinos, dass Israel mehr als die Palästinenser unterstützt werden sollte. Für sie hat sich mit Gründung des Staates Israel 1948 eine Prophezeiung der Bibel erfüllt, nämlich die Rückkehr der Juden ins Gelobte Land. Die New York Times fragt im November 2006, ob diese proisraelische Haltung der Evangelikalen mehr von der Theologie oder mehr von der Politik beeinflusst sei. Viele amerikanische Juden sehen den Eifer der Evangelikalen mit gemischten Gefühlen. Wer den evangelikalen Glauben vom nahen Ende der Welt teilt, ist häufig auch geneigt, eine christliche Missionstätigkeit unter Juden zu billigen. Diese Konvertiten zum Christentum, die sogenannten messianischen Juden, sind aber in Israel—und nicht nur dort—umstritten. Die deutschen Kirchen verzichten—anders als ein Teil der Evangelikalen in den USA—ausdrücklich auf eine Mission unter Juden.

Der Anspruch Israels auf die besetzten Territorien—in der Bibel entspricht dies Judäa und Samaria—ist in den Augen vieler Evangelikaler legitim. Einen territorialen Interessensausgleich zwischen Palästinensern und Israelis lehnen sie ab. Viele Politiker in Israel sehen aus realpolitischen Gründen in den Evangelikalen Bündnispartner. Es gibt mittlerweile sogar eine Koordinationsstelle in der Knesset, den *Christian Allies Caucus*, die den Kontakt zu den evangelikalen Partnern pflegt. Der amerikanische TV-Prediger Robertson erhielt vor einiger Zeit eine Auszeichnung des Tourismusministers, weil er durch seinen Aufruf zu Reisen in das Heilige Land der israelischen Tourismusindustrie über 400.000 Pilger bescherte. Während zahlreiche europäische und amerikanische Kirchen Projekte der Dialoge und der Versöhnung zwischen Israelis und Palästinensern fördern, gewähren die evangelikalen *Christian Friends of Israel* israelischen Siedlern in den palästinensischen Gebieten Unterstützung.

Trotz dieser gewichtigen Strömungen in der republikanischen Wählerschaft wäre es aber eine falsche Analyse, der Bush-Administration die Fähigkeit zu einer realistischen Politik im Konflikt zwischen Israel und Palästinensern absprechen zu wollen. Erst recht wäre es eine falsche Analyse, die proisraelische Haltung der gegenwärtigen Administration auf einen überproportionalen Einfluss der amerikanischen Juden auf die Republikaner zurückzuführen: Nur 25% der amerikanischen Juden haben für Bush, dagegen 74% für Kerry gestimmt.

Wegen der Verfolgung christlicher Minderheiten in China und im Sudan versuchen christliche Gruppen Einfluss auf die amerikanische Politik gegenüber diesen Staaten zu nehmen. Dabei gehen sie—und dies ist sehr typisch für die amerikanische Politik—ad hoc-Koalitionen mit Gruppen mit ähnlichen Zielen aber anderen Motiven ein.

Auf beiden Seiten des Atlantiks dominieren gemeinsame Interessen, Werte, politische und religiöse Traditionen. Aber es gibt auch Unterschiede. Diese Unterschiede sollten wir nicht in den Vordergrund stellen, aber auch nicht leugnen. Wir sollten versuchen, uns auch in unseren Unterschieden zu verstehen und zu respektieren. Manchmal könnte die Erkenntnis von Unterschieden sogar den Anstoß von gemeinsamen Lernprozessen bilden.

Wenn es eine Lektion gibt, die wir nach dem 11. September 2001 gelernt haben, dann die, dass wir gute und stabile transatlantische Beziehungen nicht einfach als gegeben hinnehmen dürfen. In erster Linie gilt es, sich angesichts der Herausforderungen durch eine veränderte geopolitische Lage und angesichts der vielschichtigen und sich verändernden Gesellschaftsstrukturen auf beiden Seiten des Atlantiks profundes Wissen übereinander und damit die Verständnisgrundlage füreinander zu bewahren. Dies gilt nicht nur aber auch für die Auseinandersetzung und den Dialog mit den christlichen Evangelikalen, um Vorurteilen und Stereotypen entgegenzuwirken.

# Religion and Politics in the United States: Implications for Transatlantic Relations

CATHLEEN S. FISHER

## Introduction

From all appearances, religion has become a new fault-line in transatlantic relations. By turns, Europeans appear to be both fascinated and repelled by Americans and their old-fashioned religiosity. »To Europeans,« *The Economist's* editors wrote in 2003, »Religion is the strangest and most disturbing feature of American exceptionalism.« In a similar vein, at a 2005 gathering of European foreign policy experts, a respected long-time German observer of American politics singled out religion as a major source of difference between the United States and Germany. European fascination with evangelicals and American religiosity more generally gives way to fear, however, when it comes to the purported influence of religion on presidential decisions and US foreign policy. As Daniel Keohane of the Centre for European Reform put it, »It's not that most Europeans have a problem with religion per se. It's more whether they suspect that religion affects a politician's choice on policy.«[1]

How different are Americans, in fact, when it comes to the role of religion in public and political life? What explains the apparent Americans' exceptionalism relative to most European countries? Finally, do or should these differences matter either to Europe or in transatlantic relations?

This paper examines the complex relationship between religion, public life, and politics in the United States, and its implications for transatlantic relations. The paper begins with an overview of the influence of religion in American public life and, conversely, of the ›politicization‹ of religion for partisan ends, concluding with a discussion of future trends in light of the 2006 election results. The paper then considers the relevance of religion and politics in the United States for transatlantic relations, with particular focus on European fears about religion and US foreign policy. The paper concludes with some observations regarding common challenges facing Europeans and Americans as they confront a world in which religion is becoming more, not less, salient.

[1] Quoted in A. Kohut/B. Stokes, America Against the World. How We Are Different and Why We Are Disliked, New York 2006, 99.

## Religion in American Politics

When it comes to the role of religion in public life, the United States is often considered the ›deviant‹ case among post-industrial states. In contrast to Europe, many Americans retain traditional religious beliefs and remain involved in institutionalized religion. Six out of ten Americans, for example, say that religion is very important to them. Most Americans report that they attend a house of worship on an occasional basis, while four out of ten claim to attend a house of worship weekly.[2] In their analysis of the World Values Survey data, Norris and Inglehart conclude that »the United States remains one of the most religious in the club of rich countries, alongside Ireland and Italy. (...) This makes America one of the most religious countries in the world.«[3]

Americans are not only more traditional than many Europeans in their adherence to religious beliefs and behaviors; they are also willing to grant religion a more significant role in public life. Americans have a largely positive view of the role of religion in society, primarily because of its purportedly salutary impact on an individual's conduct and activities. At a time when many Americans are concerned about the decline of morality in American society—manifested in the breakdown of families, materialism, and other societal problems—many believe that religion can lead individuals to lead better lives, contributing in turn to greater volunteerism and charity work, improved parenting, decreased crime, and a decline in greed and materialism.[4]

The positive influence of religion is believed to extend to the political realm. In an August 2004 survey conducted by the Pew Research Center, seven out of ten Americans said that they want the president to have strong religious beliefs. Americans are generally comfortable with public references to personal faith by their politicians, and only 26 percent of respondents say that politicians »mention religious faith and prayer too much.«[5] And Americans largely defend the right of religious groups and leaders to be engaged in contemporary political debates, though they are wary of endorsements of specific political

---

[2]Pew Research Center, Mapping the Political Landscape 2005, Washington DC, 16. Some analysts argue that Americans in fact tend to overreport church attendance, because of the positive normative value associated with church-going. By the same token, some suggest that Europeans actually under-report their attendance at houses of worship, reflecting a very different normative context.

[3]P. Norris/R. Inglehart, Sellers or Buyers in Religious Markets? The supply and demand of religion in the US and Western Europe, in: The New Religious Pluralism and Democracy, Washington DC, April 21-22, 2005, 7.

[4]For Goodness' Sake. Why So Many Want Religion to Play a Greater Role in American Life, report from Public Agenda prepared for The Pew Charitable Trusts, 2001, 10-12.

[5]Cf. Pew Forum on Religion and Public Life, ›GOP the Religion-Friendly Party, But Stem Cell Issue May Help Democrats,‹ 24 August 2004, 2. http://pewforum.org/publications/surveys/religion-politics2.pdf.

candidates from the pulpit.[6] Such practices as the use of church membership rosters by parties or voter guides issued by churches—both practices in the 2004 presidential election—remain controversial, moreover.

In a more abstract sense, religious elements figure prominently in shared narratives about America's founding and national identity. Generations of Americans have been raised with the notion that their forefathers and -mothers, as well as many who came after, traveled to the new continent in search of religious freedom. From the early days of the republic, individual freedom of conscience, combined with the fact of religious diversity in a land of immigration, have necessitated the institutional separation of church and state, as codified in the US Constitution.

Paradoxically, however, the constitutional »wall of separation« between church and state has come to coexist with the infusion of religious influences into American political and public life. Elements of American Protestantism have become intertwined with national symbols and rites (e. g. the »pledge of allegiance,« the invocation of »in God we trust« on US currency, etc.) in a ›civil religion‹—a kind of national/religious political culture that seeks to unify and integrate a diverse society and ensure the nation a moral foundation.

On the other hand, the balance between religion and politics remains contested. Opinion polls show that Americans are about evenly split over whether the Christian Right has gone too far in advancing its conservative agenda. As on other issues, Republicans tend to view the Christian Right more favorably, with Democrats tending toward negative views.[7] The continuing tension between religion and politics is also seen in American debates on ›hot button‹ social issues, such as abortion, same-sex marriage, stem cell research, end-of-life, and the teaching of creationism or ›intelligent design‹ in public schools. On all of these issues, Americans remain divided.[8] For example, on the issue of abortion, a majority of Americans still oppose making it more difficult for a woman to obtain an abortion, with the numbers of those favoring more restrictions much higher among Republican-leaning groups. On stem cell research, support appears to grow as people learn more about the issue. End-of-life issues

[6]In a July 2005 Pew poll, 51 percent of respondents said houses of worship should express their views on political and social issues (the numbers were higher for white evangelicals and black Protestants), but 63 percent said that clergy should not endorse candidates or issues. Cf. Pew Forum on Religion and Public Life, Religion a Strength and Weakness for Both Parties, 30 August 2005, 13.

[7]Cf. op. cit., 6.

[8]While Christian conservatives succeeded in pushing the US Congress to vote to allow the parents of Terri Schiavo to take their case to a federal court, a majority of the American people were critical of the federal government's involvement in deciding the Florida woman's fate. According to an ABC News Poll conducted at the time, 63 percent of respondents supported removal of Ms. Schiavo's feeding tube, while 70 percent opposed Congressional involvement. Cf. Mapping the Political Landscape 2005, 35-38 (n. 2).

are also divisive, as more and more ›baby boomers‹ confront difficult choices having to do with aging parents or other loved ones.

## The Politics in American Religion

Yet, while America is characterized by much greater religiosity than much of Europe, the story of religion and politics in the United States is also about politics. Specifically, it is about the instrumentalization of religion to form winning coalitions, and religion as identity politics.

As numerous polls and analyses have documented, the American electorate is politically polarized and very closely divided. In the past decades, the Republican Party has gathered strength in numbers, achieving rough parity with the Democrats. At the same time, the number of voters identifying themselves as independent of either party has increased. The two major political parties are themselves divided into competing factions. Additionally, the ideological wings of both parties have gained influence, due to refinements in the practice of ›gerrymandering‹ (the drawing of congressional district boundaries to create more homogeneous and therefore ›safe‹ seats), which have created a more partisan and ideological Congress.

In this political landscape, both parties have to appeal to a large swath of groups and factions within the party tent in order to form a winning coalition. The analogy one could draw is to ›coalition politics.‹ In the American case, however, the coalitions have to be formed within, rather than between, political parties.[9] For example, in the 2004 presidential election, President Bush and the Republican Party could count on support from about 40 percent of Americans (this included solidly Republican-oriented groups and others who tended Republican). The challenge for Republican strategists was twofold: to turn out the ›base‹ and to secure support from an additional 8-10 percent of the electorate.

This is where religion often entered the equation. In 2004, evangelicals—an estimated 23-24 percent of the population—were essential to a Republican winning coalition, but they had to turn out to vote. And in 2004, evangelicals did turn out. According to exit polls, 78 percent of white evangelicals voted for Bush, »making them by far the single most potent voting bloc in the electorate« according to a Pew study.[10] The evangelicals in some ways acted as ›king

[9]In contrast to Europe, American political parties are heterogeneous, catch-all constructions or alliances of separate groups and interests. This is true for the Democratic as well as the Republican Party, with moderate factions in both parties sometimes complaining about the influence of liberals or conservatives, respectively.

[10]The Pew Forum on Religion and Public Life, Religion and Public Life: A Faith-Based Partisan Divide, Washington DC, January 2005, 7. The Republicans also went after other religious voters, making inroads with Catholics and black Protestants.

makers‹—not unlike the smaller parties in a parliamentary coalition system, a role that grants them influence disproportionate to their size.

But if Republican strategists have been eager to make common cause with evangelicals to win elections, many evangelicals have been just as enthusiastic about entering the political arena to advance a conservative agenda. As in other parts of the world, the number of self-identified evangelicals in the United States has grown steadily in past decades, while mainstream churches have lost adherents. The rise in the numbers of evangelicals has been accompanied by the proliferation of conservative Christian organizations working hard to elect sympathetic candidates, take control of local- or state-level party organizations, and advance a conservative social agenda in support of traditional sexual morality, religion in education, traditional gender roles, and a presence for Christianity in public life.[11] They have been backed by substantial resources and excellent organizational networks and have reportedly enjoyed »unparalleled access to the White House« under the Bush administration.[12]

Republican Party strategists have used a combination of targeted political communication and initiatives to cement the bond with evangelicals. For example, President Bush's speech writers have routinely injected biblical allusions and paraphrasing that is unintelligible to secularists, but signals to the faithful through a kind of religious code that the president is »one of their own« and therefore to be trusted in advancing the conservative Christian agenda. A similar function has been served by President Bush's support of a constitutional amendment defining marriage as between a man and a woman or his unbending opposition to stem cell research. Such language and practices may well reflect President Bush's personal world view and religious beliefs; they also demonstrate effective use of identity politics for partisan ends.

## The Future of ›Religionized Politics‹: The Meaning of the 2006 Mid-Term Elections

It is unclear whether this pattern of ›religionized politics‹ and ›politicized religion‹ can or will be sustained. The outcome of the 2006 mid-term elections sent conflicting messages in this regard. Despite concerted efforts by both parties to integrate religion and values into their appeals, in the end the 2006 election was a national referendum, in which voters expressed their frustration with an unpopular president, the Iraq war, and corruption in the Republican-led Congress. Democratic efforts to reach out to religious voters helped secure

[11] C. Wilcox, The Christian Right in American Politics. Conquering Force or Exploited Faction? in: Understanding the ›God Gap‹. Religion, Politics, and Policy in the United States and Germany, Washington DC 2005, 16-21.

[12] Cf. N. Munro/C. Hegland, The Faithful, in: National Journal, 4 December 2004, 3589.

victories in several state races but, in contrast to 2004, the ›culture wars‹ played a relatively minor role in the 2006 election campaign. Additionally, Americans sent conflicting messages on abortion, stem-cell research, minimum wage, and same-sex marraige.

The election results suggest that the debate about religion in American politics is becoming more complex and unpredictable. This is due to several factors. First, Democratic leaders, such as freshman Democratic Senator and party hopeful Barack Obama, are making conscious efforts to talk about their religious faith and to reach out to religious voters. To this end, the Democratic Party in 2005 recruited several conservative candidates that would appeal to religious voters to run in a number of state races.[13] Second, parallel to these party initiatives, some progressive Christians are trying to reframe the debate about religion and American politics. Religious leaders such as the Reverend Jim Wallis or the Reverend Paul Sherry, the national director of the »Let Justice Roll Living Wage Campaign,« have sought to mobilize a ›Christian Left‹ to support a progressive agenda in service of greater social justice (e. g. the minimum wage initiative), stem cell research, protection of the environment and climate, and peace.

Third, the close alliance between the Republican Party and the Christian Right has come under closer scrutiny by both the party faithful and faithful Christians.[14] In his book, *Faith and Politics*, former Senator, Ambassador, and Episcopalian minister John Danforth has criticized the Christian Right's influence in the Republican Party and argues that religion has become a divisive and destructive force in American politics, transforming the Republican Party into a sectarian party.[15] In a book published in October 2006, David Kuo, an evangelical who served in the Bush White House office of faith-based initiatives, called for evangelical Christian to begin a ›fast‹ from politics.[16] Kuo's criticism reflects the disappointment of some evangelicals in a party that, in

[13]For example, Bob Casey, the Democratic challenger to Republican Senator Rick Santorum (Pennsylvania), a standard bearer for the Christian Right in the US Congress, is a Catholic who opposes abortion. Similarly, the Democratic candidate for a Tennessee Senate seat, Harold Ford, opposed abortion and same-sex marriage, as did Democratic candidate for governor in Ohio Ted Strickland, an ordained Methodist minister.

[14]In 2005-6, a series of books, critical of religion in American politics, were published. They include, for example: M. Lerner, The Left Hand of God. Taking Back Our Country From the Religious Right, San Francisco 2006; J. Wallis, God's Politics. Why the Right Gets in Wrong and the Left Doesn't Get It, San Francisco 2005; J. Carter, Our Endangered Values. America's Moral Crisis, New York 2005; and K. Phillips, American Theocracy, New York 2006.

[15]Senator J. Danforth, Faith and Politics. How the ›Moral Values‹ Debate Divides America and How to Move Forward Together, New York 2006.

[16]D. Kuo, Tempting Faith. An Inside Story of Political Seduction, New York 2006.

their view, has failed to fully deliver on a conservative political agenda, despite evangelicals' steadfast support for Republican candidates in repeated elections.

The 2006 election outcome did not end the debate over the appropriate role for religion and religious groups in American politics. The success of more conservative Democratic candidates and passage of several progressive initiatives in the 2006 elections is likely to encourage those seeking to break the GOP's hold on religiously-motivated voters. Yet, for now, the ›Christian Left‹ remains more theory than reality. Further, progressive religious voters are more diverse in outlook than white evangelicals, who remain a relatively cohesive and powerful political block, despite some defections in the 2006 elections. On the other hand, the close alliance between the Christian Right and the Republican Party is certain to be the topic of much debate both within the party and among evangelicals. The resurgence of moderate voters in 2006 is seen by some as a repudiation of ›base‹ politics and the fundamentalists' increased influence in the Republican party. Evangelicals may be challenged as well to consider whether greater involvement in partisan politics has been wise or effective.

If these trends continue, voters who are strongly motivated by religious or ethical concerns may face difficult and confusing choices at the ballot box. In 2006, the most important issue for some ›values voters‹ indeed may have been the Iraq war itself. One Minnesota Republican leader captured the dilemma summarily: »If you're pro-life and mad about the war, where do you go?«[17] In the future, white evangelicals may remain focused on the life and family values agenda, while Christian ethnic minorities (e. g. African Americans and Latinos) demonstrate greater concern about social justice issues or immigration. Protection of the environment may also find more support among religious voters, both progressive and conservative. In a climate of competing moral messages and priorities, religiously-motivated voters may find it more difficult to clearly identify which party will advance their particular values and moral concerns. In any event, while it may be reframed or more diffuse in nature, the debate about religion in American politics and the politics of religion is likely to continue.

## Religion and Politics in America: Implications for German-American and Transatlantic Relations

Compared to most European countries, the United States *is* exceptional in its religiosity. Religion, moreover, is a more salient factor in American public life and politics than in much of Europe, although this may have as much to do with winning elections in a polarized America as it does with spiritual beliefs

[17] Rep. J. Abeler, quoted in: GOP's Hold on Evangelicals Weakening, WASHINGTON POST, 6 October 2006.

and the historical origins of church-state relations in the United States. But do or should these differences matter to Europeans and transatlantic relations?

### *Perceptions and Misperceptions*

In theory, Europeans should be little concerned about whether or how American domestic political debates about abortion, stem-cell research, or same-sex marriage unfold. Such debates lie, after all, firmly in the realm of domestic politics and have their parallels in many European countries. Yet, in the transatlantic echo chamber, purely domestic American political debates reverberate across the Atlantic, where Europeans often lack the cultural or historical cipher to ›decode‹ American political discourse and its hidden motivations. In the absence of an accurate cipher, the religious tones that weave through American political debates are interpreted as further evidence of a values divide between the United States and Europe, justifying and deepening a sense of alienation from a ›culturally foreign‹ America. The problem is exacerbated by a tendency, both in media portrayals and in the collective conscious, to filter out information about the divisions *within* American society over religion and politics (e. g. many Americans are firm secularists) and to neglect an American tradition that links progressive causes to religious influences in US politics.

The ›perception problem‹ is related as well to the fact that American religiosity has come to be seen as part and parcel of an US administration and an American president that are strongly disliked in much of Europe. For the duration of his term in office, President Bush is the face of American religiosity. That makes American religion inherently problematic and divisive.

### *Religion and American Foreign Policy*

American scholars differ over the relative influence of religion on US foreign policy. In their book-long analysis of public opinion and how Americans differ from the rest of the world, Andrew Kohut and Bruce Stokes argue that religion plays an insignificant role in shaping Americans' views on foreign policy. Other factors—media, education, personal experience—are more influential, the authors argue. Kohut and Stokes conclude:

> Certainly religion and morality play a larger role in American life than in most other Western nations. (...) But the vision held by many Europeans and other non-Americans of a United States run by religious fanatics is a caricature that distorts the American religious experience. (...) Whatever their own religious views, most Americans have no interest in imposing their faith on others and, with the exception of policy toward Israel, religion has little bearing on how they think about international affairs.[18]

[18] A. Kohut/B. Stokes, op. cit. (n. 1), 94.

A very different conclusion is drawn by Walter Russell Mead of the Council on Foreign Relations, who argues:

> Religion has always been a major force in US politics, policy, identity, and culture. Religion shapes the nation's character, helps form Americans' ideas about the world, and influences the ways Americans respond to events beyond their borders. Religion explains both Americans' sense of themselves as a chosen people and their belief that they have a duty to spread their values throughout the world. (...) The ideas exercise profound influence over the country's behavior abroad and at home.[19]

Who is right about the influence of religion on American foreign policy? How, if at all, does religion influence US foreign policy? And are Europeans justified in their perceived fears of a religiously-driven America?

The answers depend in part on the assumptions one makes regarding the principal drivers of a nation's foreign policy (the levels of analysis problem in international relations theory). These factors include the global structure of power, risks, and threats; the world views, belief systems, and personalities of individual leaders and decision-makers; and a myriad of domestic factors—institutions, decision-making structures and processes, societal and cultural influences.

There is little doubt that systemic factors have a powerful influence on US foreign policy. US presidents routinely paint glowing visions of a new world order. But underlying such visions and ideals are calculations of power and interest in a broader global strategic environment, a dichotomy that is clearly understood outside of the United States, as seen, for example, in the SPIEGEL cover at time of the Iraq war (»Blut für Öl«).

When it comes to individual US leaders, President George W. Bush's religious views remain a topic of much dispute and debate. The president attests to a religious conversion, says publicly that he prays, and has participated in Bible studies. It is nevertheless unclear whether Bush in fact is an evangelical. Moreover, while the impact of the president's beliefs and world view doubtless are important to consider, as a series of revelatory books about the Bush administration demonstrate, international events (e.g. 9/11) and an often dysfunctional structure of policymaking and White House decision-making have shaped US foreign policy decisively.

The principal religious influences on US foreign policy would appear to be related to domestic political and cultural factors. First, evangelicals have influenced foreign policy through their role in electing a Republican majority in the House and Senate and a Republican president to the White House. Moreover, on the issue of Israel, evangelicals have made common cause with pro-Israeli

[19] W. R. Mead, Foreign Affairs, Sept./October 2006, http://www.foreignaffairs.org/.20060901faessay85504/walter-russell-mead/god-s-country.html.

groups and Jewish organizations to press the administration to steadfastly support Israel. To a large extent, however, the alliance between evangelicals and pro-Israel groups only strengthens a pre-existing tendency in US policy.

At a broader cultural level, religious elements are present in the way that Americans view the world and their place in it, as Mead argues. Though American foreign policy is characterized by competing traditions, it is underpinned by an enduring and collectively shared sense of the United States as an exceptional, ›chosen‹ nation destined to fulfill a transformative mission, through example or deed. American presidents often appeal to these collectively shared understandings of a nation's role and ›foreign policy identity‹ to win public support for specific foreign policy actions. For example, President George W. Bush spoke to Americans' sense of themselves as a nation chosen to be a ›city on a hill‹ when, speaking on the eve of the Iraq war, he declared »the cause we serve is right, because it is the cause of all mankind.« Indeed, a religiously-infused, cultural sense of mission may have been particularly influential in the Bush administration's foreign policy and world view.[20]

In the final analysis, however, cultural factors compete with many other factors in shaping US foreign policy. Moreover, the causal connections between collective beliefs and foreign policy are complex and only dimly understood. As Leon Fuerth, who served as national security advisor to former Vice President Gore, recently observed: »As a nation, we reason from religion to ethics and from ethics to a sense of the American identity, and from that sense of American identity to the question of right conduct, including right conduct in the world and what was expected of us, and only from there to foreign policy.«[21]

## Transatlantic Commonalities

In addition to overstating the dangers of a religiously-driven US foreign policy, many Europeans also tend to ignore the fact that both Americans and Europeans are coping with similar domestic and foreign policy problems with religious dimensions as a consequence of globalization.

The United States faces a dual challenge related to religion, society, and identity: as a result of immigration, America has become a more religiously diverse society; at the same time, it is witnessing a period of resurgent religiosity particularly among Christian evangelicals. Both phenomena place the traditional institutional relationship between church and state under strain. Americans are grappling with these challenges, moreover, in a climate of greater soci-

[20] J. Judis, The Chosen Nation. The Influence of Religion on US Foreign Policy, in: Policy Brief 37, Carnegie Endowment for International Peace, March 2005.

[21] Pew Forum on Religion and Public Life, Event Transcript, in: God's Country. Evangelicals and US Foreign Policy, Washington DC, September 2006.

etal insecurity and vulnerability—physical insecurity through terrorist threats; economic insecurity through outsourcing, dislocation, and the fear of unemployment or loss of medical insurance; and what Luis Lugo of the Pew Center for Religion and Public Life has termed »cultural insecurity« generated by growing pluralism of values and perspectives due to immigration and global communications.

Germans and Europeans are having their own set of debates related to religion, society, and identity. As in the United States, globalization is fueling feelings of insecurity and vulnerability, though the manifestations are different: opposition to further expansion of the EU; growing concern about Muslim minorities in European countries; and fear of losing the cultural certainties and the ways of life that have defined European societies.

In addition to the domestic challenges related to greater religious diversity at home, neither the United States nor Europe will be able to ignore religion in their relations with countries outside their borders.

Rather than marching steadily toward secularization, much of the world is experiencing a resurgence of religion and religious influences, due to the spread of democracy and rapid-fire growth of Pentecostal and charismatic Christianity. In many developing countries, when opportunities for democratic participation arise, religious groups are often the best organized and able to mobilize. As Timothy Shah of the Pew Forum on Religion and Public Life and Monica Duffy Toft have observed: »Religion was supposed to fade away as globalization and freedom spread. Instead it's booming around the world (...). Democracy is giving people a voice, and more and more, they want to talk about God.«[22] Viewed in this global context, it is German and European secularism, rather than American religiosity, that appears the aberration.

Indeed, the United States and Europe are already confronting policy issues and choices at the nexus of religion and politics, including:

### *Muslim Integration and Islamic Terrorism*

Some American and also European observers worry that the failure of Germany and other European countries to integrate their Muslim populations may be fueling Islamist extremism in Europe, posing a threat both to these societies and to the United States. The respective ability of both Europe and the United States to integrate Muslim populations successfully could have direct bearing on the threats they face from radicalized Islamists, both from within their borders and internationally.

[22] T.S. Shah/M.D. Toft, Why God Is Winning, in: Foreign Policy (July/August 2006) 39.

*Turkey and the European Union*

The role of religion in determining Europe's identity and cultural and political boundaries is also an important, if often unarticulated, subtext of the debate about Turkey's eventual accession to the European Union. Most Europeans appear to cling to a complex and unarticulated notion of Europeanness that mixes secularism and a Christian cultural identity. This conflation, some argue, will make it difficult for Europe to come to any consensus on its outermost borders or the internal cultural identity of the European Union. A rejection of Turkey on cultural (religious) grounds could strengthen nationalist sentiment in Turkey and those forces who would prefer other alignments that with the EU and/or provoke new demands for minority rights by the Turkish minority in Germany.

*Globalizing Islam*

As the Danish cartoon controversy and other public debates over religious symbols and references have demonstrated, the domestic and foreign dimensions of the West's relations with Islam can overlap in unexpected ways and with unanticipated consequences. Coping with the phenomenon of a globalizing Islam constitutes a shared challenge for Europe and the United States.

## Conclusion

To confront these common challenges effectively, Americans and Europeans would benefit from a better understanding of the impact of history, culture and institutions on their respective views of the relationship between religion, politics, and modernity across the Atlantic and around the world.

Americans have never equated modernity with secularization. Contrary to the predictions of secularization theory, the United States has modernized, but religion remains a vital part of private belief, values, and behavior, and of American public life.[23] In other words, the United States is modern, secular, and religious; there is no perceived contradiction among the three.

In Germany and much of Europe, a different normative context exists. Many Germans and Europeans equate religion in public or political life with strife and bloody conflict. Religion for most is largely a private matter. Moreover, most Germans and Europeans assume that modernity in fact will and should lead to a declining role for religion in public life. Although many Germans and other Europeans may turn to the national churches to perform important life rituals, as sociologist José Casanova has observed, they nonethe-

[23]Secularization theory posits that modernization will inevitably lead to the irreversible decline of religious beliefs and traditions as well as the control of religious institutions and norms in society.

less believe that a modern and enlightened European is a secular one.[24] This is also the normative prism through which Europeans view American religiosity, which in this normative context appears pre-modern and irrational, and therefore dangerous.

Yet, in many ways, Americans and Europeans are *both* exceptional in their relationship to religion. American religiosity is ›deviant‹ when measured against growing secularism in much of Europe but is fully in line with trends in many other parts of the world. And although many European countries have become more secular, religion as a cultural influence retains political salience even in Europe as seen in contemporary debates about the place of Muslims in national and European public and political life. In this sense, the ›religion gap‹ would appear to be less a fault-line dividing America from Europe than a persistent source of tension within and across these diverse, globalized societies.

[24]On the normative expectations governing American and European views of religion and modernity, see José Casanova, Immigration and the New Religious Pluralism. A EU/US Comparison, Discussion draft for conference on conference on ›The New Religious Pluralism and Democracy,‹ April 21-22, 2005, Washington DC, Georgetown University's Initiative on Religion, Politics, and Peace; and Id., Der Ort der Religion im säkularem Europa, Transit-Europäische Revue 27 (2004).

# Religion Expressed, Religion Submerged Evangelicalism's Historical Influence on the Deep Structure of US Foreign Policy

MARCIA PALLY

> There is no country in the world where the Christian religion retains greater influence over the souls of men than in America. – Alexis de Tocqueville

> There is no nation which has an attitude so pure that they cannot be bettered by self-examination – John Foster Dulles, 1946

America, in the 17th century, was not a bastion of individual liberty, rights or freedom of conscience. Following the European traditions with which they were familiar, most colonials did not separate civil jurisdiction from religious control. They assumed instead the *cuius regio, eius religio*, by which the ruler of a region determines its religion. Yet over the next two centuries, America became a place both individualistic and progressive for the time—a representative democracy grounded on Enlightenment ideals with a strong focus on individual freedom as defined as absence of economic and political restraints, and with a strong streak of anti-authoritarian, self-reliant optimism. In short, a society which valued liberty and liberalism, and assumed the world worked best guided by them. Much in the geography, patterns of immigration, and survival conditions brought about this shift, and much from British cultural heritage as well. The remaining factor was evangelical Christianity, which was radically progressive and America's dominant religion from the colonial period to the First World War.

This essay on evangelicalism's impact on the deep structure of US foreign policy begins with two premises: one, that the values and assumptions of a people form the ground from which foreign policy emerges, and two, that the preponderance of policy over time—what is done after all the debates are over—is the best guide to the range of possibilities likely in the future. From the first premise, assumptions are the articulated or unarticulated beliefs about how the world works—for instance, that liberty means absence of restraint rather than freedom to join or participate. Values are what is considered worth making an effort to gain or preserve—for instance, that absence of restraint is of prime political importance and thus, worth fighting for.

In the American case, both its values and assumptions were fed early on by evangelicalism. Thus, while democracy supporters in Europe have prided themselves on being ›unmusikalisch‹ regarding religion, understanding American politics requires an ›ear‹ for the evangelical strains that run through it. The evangelical influence remains potent in US politics—submerged or implicit in America's values and assumptions—regardless of its overt presence or who is in power. The first premise then involves not a two-step argument from evangelical doctrine to foreign policy, but a three-step argument, from evangelicalism to American values and assumptions, to foreign policy.

The second premise suggests that, in anticipating future US foreign policy, the *longue durée* of past policy needs to be studied, along with the values and assumptions that underlie it. What do we know about America's assumptions, values, and history that will help us understand its future foreign polices regardless of who is in the White House? This study is critical to Europe in making policy of its own. With a realistic assessment of the likely range of US policies, Europe can prepare for eventualities within that span. Without it, Europe will ever be left reactive. This is the case not only for trans-Atlantic relations but policy in any place where Europe might interact with US interests and conduct. And that is rather a lot.

What's more, it's the entire range that must be anticipated, not the slice feared or hoped for. Much of Europe was relieved that the Democrats won Congress in 2006 and expressed hope that a new administration in 2009 will return America to certain policies more to Europe's liking. But this is an ahistorical view. For one thing, Democratic foreign policy has not departed much from Republican, as a *longue durée* study reveals. That is, the approach of G.W. Bush in substance is not the outlier often claimed and not very different from the preponderance of foreign policy, made by both parties. Democrats are not likely to depart from this usual range, as it is in part their own. For another, the idea that US policy will return to something better assumes it was superior in some past, usually taken to be the postwar period. This time of institution-building is seen as the American norm (and it is America's violation of these norms that so disappoints admirers of US leadership). Indeed, US foreign policy in Western Europe postwar was brilliant. Yet, however productive for that half-continent, it was neither a norm nor a model to which America can return under a new administration.

In investigating the deep structure of US foreign policy—the values and assumptions which are shared, as Thorstein Veblen noted, by society's various classes and subgroups—I will focus on the evangelical contribution to it. The story of British cultural heritage, immigration, and the frontier is well known, and the popularity of fundamentalism worldwide has provoked the attention of democrats and pluralists. How did American evangelicalism depart from its European parent, and how did its tenets become American values and assumptions?

American evangelicalism emerged in the 18th century from the enthusiast aspects of the Calvinist and the Anglican churches, and from the pietistic and Moravian movements especially in Germany. The search of the evangelicals was for an inner Christianity, a move of the heart toward a personal, living relationship with Jesus. Their main emphases were:

- Personal, individual acceptance of Jesus' gift of salvation;
- Crucicentrism or the centrality of the crucifixion as that gift of redemption;
- Conversion to a personal relationship with Jesus that would be holistic and life-transforming;
- The mission to bring others to that life-changing conversion;
- The inerrancy of the Bible and the authority of the literal words of Scripture, rather than ecclesiastical or interpretive traditions;
- Individualist Bible reading by ordinary men and woman;
- The priesthood of all believers rather than reliance on a specially-trained priestly class. As the colonials saw the New World as the New Jerusalem and each fragile settlement as a covenant community (like that of Israel of old), each person, they held, had a personal covenant with God.[1] Each person was His priest, and hierarchies were unneeded.

These last few are already anti-authoritarian, but in America, evangelicalism moved further towards both individualism and anti-authoritarianism. This stands in contrast to Europe, where the dominant religions were part of the authority structures of *ancien regime* as political, military and police powers. Even Luther mandated obedience to the upper estates, and his instructions to the princes to put down the peasant uprising of 1525 cost thousands their lives. From 1648 until World War I, Europe's established churches supported monarchist, conservative and militarist parties. As a consequence, the democratizing forces of Europe's Enlightenment contained a strong anti-clerical critique. Democratic reforms were linked with secularism and an abhorrence of the irrational, of doctrinal absolutes, and of Manichaean worldviews. In America, by contrast, the churches opposed British rule and became even more radically democratic and anti-authoritarian through the 19th century. Thus, the American Enlightenment had little anti-clerical critique. Enlightenment

[1] Cf. R. Schieder, Wieviel Religion verträgt Deutschland? Frankfurt/M. 2001, 98.

and evangelicalism were pulling not against each other but together. As the Baptist John Leland wrote, »Rebellion to tyrants is obedience to God.«[2]

Starting in the 18th century, three key areas of support for democratic development emerged among American evangelicals: first, by the mid-18th century, American churches embraced republican self-rule in the British tradition: mixed government (head of state, elite leadership, popular participation), checks and balances, and the idea that man's law follow natural law, which declared man free. The Presbyterian Benjamin Rush in 1791 wrote to the Baptist minister Elhanan Winchester saying, »Republican forms of government are the best repositories of the Gospel.«[3] Second, America's evangelicals embraced the Commonsense Moral Philosophy of the Scottish Sentimentalists, with its emphasis on the common man's ability to make moral and political judgments, and thus govern himself. Third, America's evangelicals considered the New World to be the New Jerusalem, whose special mission was to be model and purveyor of freedom the world over. Economic freedom was conflated with political, and much of the dispute with London involved the right of government to deprive people of their property (in taxation) without their consent (in the form of political representation)—an infringement on rights which the Americans considered political tyranny as well as economically hobbling. The Rev. John Winthrop's famous saying in 1630 is an American cornerstone, »For we must consider that we shall be as a City upon a Hill, the eyes of all people are upon us.«[4] One hundred and fifty years later, the revolution was seen as »the good fight« for liberty, blessed by Jesus.

These three ideas—republicanism, Commonsense Moral Philosophy, and God's blessing for America's liberating efforts—were readily absorbed by Americans of every stripe. Indeed, the rough conditions in the sparse colonies made individual liberty and initiative, self-reliance and self-governance a matter of survival. The mutual influence of the evangelicals and the democratizers became one of the great, hand-in-glove stories in history. From their synergy came a set of assumptions and values, which has been called America's ›civil religion‹ and has both religious and secular expression.

[2]W. Cutler/J. Cutler, Life, Journals and Correspondence of Rev. Manasseh Cutler, 2 vols., Cincinnati 1888, vol. 2, 66-67.

[3]B. Rush, Letter of Nov. 12, 1791, in: L.H. Butterfield (ed.), Letters of Benjamin Rush, 2 vols., Princeton 1951, vol. 1, 6111.

[4]F. Bremer/J. Winthrop, America's Forgotten Founding Father, New York 2003, 180.

| **Secular:** | **Religious:** |
|---|---|
| • Individual self-reliance in economics and politics | • The importance of the individual's acceptance of Jesus, as the path of salvation |
| • The value of the initiative and common sense of the ordinary man in business and politics; anti-intellectualism | • Belief in the common man's ability to understand the Bible and to obey its precepts by his own initiative and will; literalist readings of the Bible (taking little from scholarly interpretive traditions) |
| • Freedom from illiberal tyranny in this world, economic and political | • Freedom from the tyranny of the devil/temptation |
| • Liberty as absence of restraint in economics and politics | • Liberty as freedom of conscience unrestrained by ecclesiastical or political leaders |
| • Anti-Authoritarianism and suspicion of government; anti-elitism | • Anti-papism and suspicion of church authorities; anti-clericalism |
| • The belief in the perfectibility of man and thus in future-orientedness, optimism and can-do-ism | • Belief that man may not only be forgiven for his sins but become free of sin; the perfectibility of man |
| • Belief in America as the model and purveyor of economic and political freedom—the American mission | • Belief in America and the model of purveyor freedom, which Jesus blesses over tyranny—the American mission blessed by God |

Where European Calvinism did not hold to these beliefs, evangelicalism evolved then, especially in America, with interesting consequences.

First, through the 18th and early 19th centuries, evangelicalism shifted from an emphasis on God's grace—something God does—to the *individual's* role in salvation—something man does. This God-to-man shift was emphasized especially in Arminianism, popularized in America by the preachers John and Charles Wesley and which later became the basis for Methodism, America's most popular denomination of the 19th century. Through Methodism, this God-to-man shift boosted the individualism, self-reliance and can-do-ism already characteristic of the nation. For Americans were learning, both from their frontier and religious experiences, that matters of importance were theirs—not King or God's—to accomplish.

This God-to-man shift also had an important effect on America's relationship to doubt, which in turn set the tone for US foreign policy. European Calvinism held to the doctrine of »eternal security«, where those who hold their faith in Jesus until death are saved. Yet this left believers tormented, worried whether they had the sort of true faith. Among Americans, confident in their commonsense reason, worry lightened. They knew they believed in Jesus, and Commonsense Moral Philosophy told them they could be secure in that knowledge. Thus they knew they were redeemed. This made the ›elect‹ inclusive and democratized salvation, which sat well with Americans who found hierarchies repugnant and who were in any case making all the decisions—to revolt against the British, to elect their own government, and run much of daily life. The maxim »God helps those who help themselves« are the words of Ben Franklin. Today, 75% of Americans believe they are the words of Jesus.[5] That is, they believe Jesus is the author of the mandate to self-reliance.

Second, also rising in importance in optimistic America was the idea that man can be not only forgiven for sin but free from sin—that is, belief in the perfectibility of man. The Calvinist obligation on each man to develop a system of lifelong moral behavior, noted by Max Weber in *The Protestant Ethic and the Spirit of Capitalism,* became the Pilgrim's Progress—not only progression but improvement. Add to this America's faith in individual initiative one finds the ground for America's belief in its obligation to help perfect him.

Third, the assumption of God's blessing for the War of Independence meant that America was not only a purveyor of liberty but one whose use of force was also blessed. The nation's continental borders too were extended through force, against the Amer-Indians, French, Mexicans, and British. The New Jerusalem was maturing in a nation with a positive experience of aggression. Note that the obligation to extend liberty does not entail what we now call nation building. The value of liberty and the obviousness of God's blessing upon those who bring it were thought so evident that none in this world could refuse them. The arrival of liberty as America understood it, like the arrival of the gospel, would surely be recognized as Good the world over.

[5] Cf.: America's Religious Right. You Ain't Seen Nothing Yet, in: The Economist, 23 June 2005.

In sum, by the early 19th century, the American experience and its churches had formed mythopoetics of self-reliant, liberating obligation. Indeed, it is hard to know whether individualistic, anti-authoritarian, missionary Calvinism captured America or whether America captured its religions for its self-reliant, anti-elitist, optimistic can-do-ism. Ironically, the Constitutional separation of church and state boosted rather than weakened American religiosity. By keeping churches out of government, the Constitution guaranteed that religion would continue to be seen as a force for good, untainted by the corruptions and hypocrisies of politics, and associated with republican anti-authoritarian optimism. Religion in America thus remains in power while administrations come and go.

The synergy between evangelicalism and progressive forces in America continued through the 19th century. Evangelicals were anti-Federalist, Jeffersonian, supported land reform and cheered on the populist Jacksonian revolution in the 1830s. The more radical churches were, the more popular they became, supporting women preachers and black churches. The number of Methodist churches rose from 20 in 1770 to 19,883 in 1860.[6] By the middle of the 19th century, the evangelical Methodist and Baptist churches accounted for two thirds of Protestants in the US and were subdividing into scores of radical communities. Reading the Bible individually and taking the text literally increasing became the norm for the many Americans isolated on the frontier and without training in interpretive traditions. Mid-19th century, two Kentucky evangelicals, R. Marshall and J. Thompson, said,

> We are not personally acquainted with the writings of John Calvin, nor are we certain how nearly we agree with his views of divine truth; neither do we care.[7]

Evangelical churches were the backbone of American civic life; many of the associations praised by Tocqueville were run by their members, who were busy perfecting man at home—in the public school movement, in temperance campaigns—before they got busy perfecting him overseas. After the Civil War and through industrialization, the evangelical Social Gospel spearheaded efforts to aid the urban poor and moved so far as to develop a thorough-going critique of capitalism.

The turn to conservatism from this progressive, even radical, history involved Germany as a key player. At the turn of the 20th century, a schism emerged within evangelicalism between the Social Gospel and conservatives, who felt the churches should focus less on social projects aiding the poor and

[6] Cf. F. Mills, Mentors of Methodism, 1784-1844, in: Methodist History 12 (1973), 43; A. Stevens, A Compendious History of American Methodism, New York 1867, 528; W. Sweet, Religion on the American Frontier, 1783-1840, vol. 4, The Methodists, Chicago 1946, 45-46.

[7] N. Hatch, The Democratization of American Christianity, New Haven 1989, 174.

more on saving souls. Making matters worse, on the conservatives' view, were imports of the scholarly, New Bible criticism from Germany, which they took to be both elitist and elastic. Where this new scholarship relied on educated men to interpret the Bible, America had relied on the readings of ordinary citizens; where the new scholarship was a literary and archeological interpretive approach, America had relied on literalist Bible-reading that had served the American common man so well. When World War I broke out, Americans were inclined to think, no wonder Germany was the evil enemy—look at how they treated the Bible!

Confronted by this New German scholarship, scandalized by the ›immoral‹ Jazz Age and by the godless Bolshevik revolution, conservative evangelicals insisted on their simple, homegrown Christianity and, for the first time, became fundamentalist. The term was coined by oil magnates Lyman and Milton Stewart, who founded the Bible College in Los Angeles and who, between 1910 and 1915, published the pamphlet series, *The Fundamentals*, distributed en masse and free to preachers. The characteristics of piety's new defenders were typical of worldwide fundamentalism: in-group purification and asceticism, an eschatological, apocalyptic emphasis, and an intellectual absolutism which provides »ontological security«[8] by answering existential and cosmological questions and by providing a path for right-living.

A similar backlash was responsible for the coalition between evangelicals and Republicans beginning in the 1960s. The nation faced international communism, the black Civil Rights movement, the youth counterculture, the anti-Vietnam war movement, the women's movement, and the gay rights movement. In response, many rediscovered nativist sentiments quiescent since America's ascension to global leadership post World War II. Evangelicals and the Republican Party made common cause. The New Right coalition would take the country back from the hippies, from welfare advocates, from ›special pleaders‹ for blacks and women, and from those who were ›soft on communism‹—in short, from all those who had abandoned America's tradition of individualist self-reliance and its mission to fight illiberal tyrannies the world over. They were joined in the 1970s by neo-Conservatives, World War II liberals who believed the lesson of the 20th century was never to appease tyranny—now the communists—as Hitler had been appeased.

Key to the New Right's success was an alignment of Republican policies with the American worldview. Classic Republican business-interests in unregulated markets and ›small government‹ were understood as self-reliance, optimistic perfectibility, and personal liberty; foreign policy was understood as having a government big enough to fell illiberal regimes overseas. In the 1980s, the

[8] M. Marty/R.S. Appleby (eds.), Fundamentalism Comprehended. The Fundamentalism Project, Chicago 1991-95, 835.

Republican economic platform became even more attractive, as the middle classes, labor unions, and pension programs began investing assets in the stock market, giving millions a ›business interest.‹ Note that the evangelicals had not changed their views. But in the post-60s political context, when self-reliance and US responsibility abroad seemed lost to the Democrats, mired in Vietnam and the indulgent counterculture, the radical liberalism of early evangelicalism had become Republican.

What has this outlook—individualist self-reliance, belief in economic and political liberty, in man's perfectibility, and in America's obligation to perfect him—meant for US foreign policy? As a deep structure for US conduct abroad, it forms the outer limits of the possible—what politicians can envision and what the people are willing to support regardless of the party in power. To be sure, domestic policies have seen more shifts historically—in civil liberties; in questions of the government's role in the market, health care, and environmental protection; in the social ›wedge‹ issues of abortion, stem cell research, and homosexuality; and in the relationship of church to state. But foreign policy has shifted less—remarkably, considering the money, passion, and careers given to competing theories and strategies. Democrats and Republicans have shared a foreign policy tradition grounded in these values and assumptions.

Since independence, the US has been expansionist for the purpose of domestic enrichment. It has also been suspicious of international agreements, what Th. Jefferson called »entangling alliances«, except when it has a controlling influence over them—as it did not after World War I, but as it did after World War II, and as it does not in the ICC, Kyoto Protocols, and among others that have been rejected. After all, why should the New Jerusalem—as America has thought of itself since Winthrop's »City on the Hill« sermon—bind itself by the rest of the woebegone world? Yet mistrust of agreements has not hobbled expansive economic and geopolitical endeavors.

This is unremarkable; European and Asian powers did the same in their day. But just to get an idea of what was involved: to protect its trade, as an infant nation, the US fought France and Britain (1790-1815), and by the Civil War the US had sent its navy or troops to the Marquesas Islands (1813), Tripoli and Algiers (1815), Caribbean and Pacific (1822), South America (1826), Sumatra and West Africa (1830s), Liberia and Canton (1840s). In Mid-Civil War, the North had resources enough to send its navy to Japan and China; in 1898 the US fought Spain for its first overseas territories. Among Wilson's reasons for entering World War I was protection of US loans to the Allies and a seat at the peace table, where he'd have an influence in structuring Europe's postwar economies to US advantage. Between 1898 and 1924, Latin America saw 21 military interventions by the US, which also began oil explorations in the Mideast.

These policies were not unsuccessful. In 1919, US direct foreign investment was $94 million, by 1929 $602 million.[9]

Yet these expansionist policies were undertaken not only pragmatically but also under the rubric of liberty and liberalism—founded on the nation's traditional, optimistic worldview where man is perfectible, and self-reliant America is obligated to perfect him. Economic freedom is thought to bring political liberty, if not immediately then eventually. Both are assumed to bring peace, which abets commerce, closing the circle. In 1959, Seymour Lipset described this virtuous circle in his modernization theory:[10] once a certain level of economic development was achieved through liberal markets, a liberal civil society and government would emerge.[11] Conversely, economic illiberalism overseas has been seen as diminishing liberty both abroad and within the US. On this view, as overseas markets and raw materials were lost to the US, domestic production would fall, leading to depression and political unrest, which could be addressed only by illiberal economic planning and illiberal police control. In 1947, Secretary of State George Marshall—of the Marshall Plan—noted,

> the cumulative loss of foreign markets and sources of supply would unquestionably have a depressing influence on our domestic economy and would drive us to increased measures of government control.[12]

In foreign policy, the liberalism/liberty virtuous circle has meant, liberalize the economies of the world as much as possible and liberate where necessary—wherever a piece of the liberal global economy looked to fall to socialist or autarkic alternatives. And not only areas economically key to America but, in chain-link fashion, areas connected to them. In the effort to liberate, force has not been precluded. Having won its independence and continental borders through war, aggression retains its positive valence. Should liberation require war, proxy war or covert operations, these have been seen as protective of American interests and liberty abroad—that is, as saving weaker nations from worse alternatives. The slow process of nation-building, by contrast, has not often been included in US foreign policy on the assumption that liberty and liberalization are Goods that none would resist.

This way of understanding the world, this mix of economic pragmatism and liberating idealism, was evident from the nation's beginning. In 1785, Th. Jefferson noted the clamor for overseas trade in a letter to John Jay, »Our people

[9] Cf. W.A. Williams, The Tragedy of American Diplomacy, New York 1959, 148.

[10] Cf. S.M. Lipset, Some Social Requisites of Democracy. Economic Development and Political Legitimacy, in: American Political Science Review 53 (1959), 69-105.

[11] This did not turn out not to be the case: rising standards of living stabilize democracies that have already formed but do not lead necessarily to democratization. See A. Przeworski/M. Alvarez/J. Cheibub/F. Limongi, Democracy and Development. Political Institutions and Well-Being in the World, 1950-1990, New York 2000.

[12] Williams, op. cit. (n. 9), 271.

are decided in the opinion that it is necessary for us to take a share in the occupation of the ocean«,[13] and he worried such an occupation would lead to wars with other nations. It did. Madison maintained that westward expansion was necessary to prevent economic competition and thus political faction from disrupting the cohesion of the country. Yet at the same time, American continental expansion was seen as enlarging the experiment in democracy—it »extended the area of freedom« in the words of Andrew Jackson.[14] The depressions of the 1870s and 1890s reinforced the consensus that foreign markets were key to the domestic economy—a consensus including farm and labor movements as well as the National Association of Manufacturers. Yet Secretary of State John Hay's Open Door policy (1899-1900) was, in his words, both to

> safeguard for the world the principle of equal and impartial trade with all parts of the Chinese Empire and to bring about permanent safety and peace to China.[15]

The 1898 war with Spain got America its first overseas territories. But for most Americans, Cuba's attempt to expel Spain recalled their own war of independence, and after watching the island struggle for three years, they were ready to intervene. To be sure, economic motives were central to America's interest in World War I—US share of world exports went from 13.5% in 1913 to over 25% in 1920.[16] Yet the nation's belief that the war was, as Wilson said, »to do justice and assert the rights of mankind«[17] was earnest.

Wilson's words are as good a summary as any of America's liberalize/liberate aims:

> The attainment of a liberal capitalist world order (...) safe both from traditional imperialism and revolutionary socialism, within whose stable liberal confines a missionary America could find moral and economic pre-eminence.[18]

In World War II, the idea that American forces were the »missionaries of capitalism and democracy« had caught the national imagination.[19] This was not

[13] Th. Jefferson, Letter to John Jay, August 23, 1785. Online at: http://www.yale.edu/lawweb/avalon/jefflett/let32.htm.

[14] Cf. M. Rogin, Recolonizing America, in: American Literary History 2 (1990), 144-149, here: 146. Online at: http://links.jstor.org/sici?sici=0896-7148(199021)2%3A1%3C144%3ARA%3E2.0.CO%3B2-E.

[15] Cf. Papers Relating to the Foreign Relations of the United States, Washington DC 1899, 129f. Online at: http://www.pinzler.com/ushistory/opendoorsupp.html.

[16] Cf. E. Parsons, Why the British reduced the flow of American troops to Europe in August-October 1918, Canadian Historical Review III (1977), 178.

[17] Cf. R. McElvaine, Woodrow Wilson's Burden, Bush's—And Ours, George Mason University's History News Network, 14 February 2005. Cf.: http://www.hnn.us/articles/10108.html.

[18] N.G. Jr. Levin, Woodrow Wilson and World Politics. America's Response to War and Revolution, Oxford 1968.

[19] Cf. Williams, op. cit. (n. 9), 231.

cynical but a profound faith in the virtuous circle of economic and political liberalism.

In the global restructuring of the postwar period, US internationalism and institution-building came to be seen as the norm for American foreign policy. Today it is regarded as a template to which the US may return. But this ahistorical view is Eurocentric. US policy on that Western half-continent was smart but *sui generis.* The *logic* was consistent with the liberate/liberalize intentions of the US; that is, the US aimed at liberating Europe from Nazism, pre-empting communism, and building an integrated liberal economic system. The policies implemented, however, were unusual, owing to the region's unique role as a buffer against the Soviets and as a market for US products.

As the GIs came home, war plants closed, and fear of depression grew. America became alarmed at having a smaller percentage of world exports than it had had in 1928 (when government loans and grants are subtracted).[20] In testimony to Congress, Secretary of State Dean Acheson said,

> You could probably fix it so that everything produced here would be consumed here, but that would completely change our Constitution, our relations to property, human liberty, our very conceptions of law. And nobody contemplates that. Therefore, you find you must look to other markets and those markets are abroad.[21]

Labor was in support. A United Auto Workers Union statement in 1945 held that »we cannot possibly maintain full production and full employment unless we have a world pool of free and prosperous consumers.«[22]

Europe had been a first-world market which, along with its colonies, was buying 77% of US exports by World War I.[23] No other region could be expected so quickly to develop a market large enough to buy up US goods. The Marshall Plan was funded in this context. The US worked to rebuild strong liberal economic *and* political institutions, which it thought feasible as Western Europe had had them before the war—and had had the principles since the 18th century.[24] Japan too served as a trading partner and buffer against the Soviets and Chinese—though the US retained greater political controls for a longer time in part because Japan had a history of liberal markets but not liberal politics.

---

[20] Cf. Williams, op. cit. (n. 9), 232.

[21] R. Keohane, Hobbes's Dilemma and Institutional Change in World Politics. Sovereignty in International Society, in: H. Holm/G. Sorensen (eds.), Whose World Order? Uneven Globalization and the End of the Cold War, Bolder/CO 1995, 166.

[22] Williams, op. cit. (n. 9), 238.

[23] Cf. Williams, op. cit. (n. 9), 87.

[24] And even with the aim of a liberal politics, the US was not so liberal as to tolerate the French and Italian communist parties, whose participation in postwar elections was undermined and whose organization, offices and members were attacked by Italian scab labor and American union men flown it by the US government. In 1947 the French and Italian governments were told to dismiss their communist ministers or suffer a cessation of food aid.

Finally, to support these goals and prevent its trading partners from melting down in another world war, the US negotiated international institutions, from Bretton Woods to NATO and the UN, as it had a determining influence on their mandates and management.

These conditions existed nowhere else and nowhere else has the US repeated its postwar performance—neither in the Asian ›Tigers‹ of South Korea and Taiwan, where the US supported dictatorships into the 1990s,[25] nor elsewhere in the developing world. There, economic liberalism and political *stability* were valued, as they guaranteed access to raw materials, blocked Communist access, and kept strategic areas from slipping out of the global economy. Democracy in the developing world was not a priority if elected governments had goals other than these. With these concerns at the fore, a broad range of socialist and autarkic policies were misread as existential threats to the global economy and thus to America's prosperity and liberty alike. Or at least at critical points, distinctions were not made between threats that were existential and those that were not. Indeed, the US was not in a position to make such distinctions. Beliefs about the domestic and universal benefits of liberal and global trade, and faith in the progress from liberal economics to liberal democracy, precluded making them. Even in the 1940s, as the US was establishing democratic, multilateral institutions in Europe, democracy was undermined in Indochina as Truman aided the French in its re-colonization efforts. Ho Chi Minh, an admirer of the US, began the Vietnamese Declaration of Independence with words from America's »All men are created Equal. They are endowed by their creator... «[26] Yet, fearing not only that the independence movement was communist-backed but that such backing would close Indochina's resources to Japan and the West, Truman ignored Ho's eight letters asking that the US, USSR, China and Britain bring Indochina's status to the UN for a mediated settlement.[27]

Through the Cold War, democracy and political self-determination fell victim to US policies in Indonesia, Iran, Ghana, South Africa, Southeast Asia, Chile and throughout Latin America—the whole list of direct and proxy wars, covert efforts and coups d'état meant to liberate developing nations from what were seen as worse, illiberal alternatives. The only instance of this that sparked major protest in the US was Vietnam, not least of all because of the draft. Developing-world democracy has been supported under two conditions: where autocratic regimes cease to cooperate with the US (Iran's mullahs, Saddam Hussein after 1990, Panama's Manuel Noriega) or where they are losing control of

[25]Carter sent US troops to help suppress the student-worker uprising in Kwangju, Korea in 1980.

[26]For the Vietnamese Declaration of Independence, 2 September 1945, cf. online at: `http://coombs.anu.edu.au/~vern/van_kien/declar.html`.

[27]Cf.: The Pentagon Papers, 1971, 4.5.8.26.

their unsatisfied populations (Saudi Arabia, China)—in short, where political liberation rather than *status-quo* stability may be better at guaranteeing economic liberalization.

The shift from replacing an uncooperative leader to replacing an illiberal political system with democracy at first glance appears a significant change in both goals and strategies. It has been more simply a tactical shift, as the US has always thought it was bringing in a better system. When the US has ousted one leader and supported another, it has done so because it believed its preferred candidate was not only a stabilizer but a liberalizer whose free markets would lead to rising living standards and eventually liberal politics. Both tactics—the coup d'état/regime change and encouraging democracy—have aimed at liberal goals. The difference between them in US foreign policy has been one of timing and local contingencies. Support for democracy aims at letting the population have its say relatively quickly, when that population is impatient and provoking local instability (China, Saudi Arabia). Political reforms become a means toward stability and establishing the liberal system considered best in any case. Support for economically liberal but politically illiberal leaders relies on a different time frame: stability now (to keep unwanted groups out of government); liberal politics will flow later, from liberal economics, as it did in Korea and Taiwan, and as is hoped for in Egypt and Pakistan.

In sum, the postwar approach in Europe and Japan was not America's norm *for itself* in foreign policy, and it remains rare in the post-Cold War era, beginning with Bill Clinton. While operations in Bosnia and Kosovo had humanitarian dimensions, Clinton intervened there also to give NATO its ›out of area‹ mission, thus maintaining its *raison d'être* in Europe. »If we're going to have a strong economic relationship that includes our ability to sell around the world«, he said, »Europe has got to be a key (...). That's what this Kosovo thing is all about.«[28] NATO remains under US leadership. Clinton continued America's long influence over Latin America in implementing NAFTA, and extended China's Most Favored Nation status in spite of its human rights abuses. He negotiated with the Taliban for a trans-Afghan pipeline to be built by the American oil company, Unocal.

It was not Bush's 2002 National Security Strategy that first announced US intentions to maintain global military superiority. The 1950 National Security Council 68 advocated American military superiority globally[29] as did the Pentagon's 1997 *Quadrennial Defense Review*[30] under Clinton. As for international agreements, which Bush too bends, the Clinton-era 1995 Decision Directive 39

[28]Bill Clinton, Remarks to AFSCME Biennial Convention, Omni Shoreham Hotel, Washington DC, 23 March 1999; http://www.leftbusinessobserver.com/Kosovo.html.

[29]Cf.: National Security Council 68, FRUS 1950, 1: 252-253.272-274.

[30]Cf.: Report of the Quadrennial Defense Review, 1997, 5.

on terrorism states: »Return of suspects by force may be affected without the cooperation of the host government.«[31] Finally, the shift from a reactive to a pre-emptive military policy began not with Bush but with Calvin Coolidge's 1924 and 1926 interventions in Honduras and Nicaragua, and with Clinton's 1998 bombing of Bin Laden's Afghanistan camp.

US foreign policy under G.W. Bush, in light of this history, was unradical. He promoted a liberal economy in bilateral trade agreements, the WTO, and NAFTA. NATO remains under US direction, and Europe and Japan remain key political and trading partners. Bush expected them to cooperate in the war on terror—as they have done, from intelligence-sharing to extraordinary rendition. He objected when Europe distinguished itself from US policy politically (the Iraq war) or economically (the Boeing-Airbus and 2002 steel controversies)—as America has objected since World War II. Bush balanced US interests in Russia and China as a market/place of investment against their growth as geopolitical and economic competitors. US concern that these countries democratize stems from fear that illiberal politics there is apt to restrict a liberal economy or provoke commerce-disrupting unrest. Bush had no interest in North Korea other than containing nuclear armament, so he expended only diplomacy there. Sub-Saharan Africa is no more forgotten than usual, save in discussions of overseas aid, which Bush in 2004 increased to $19 billion, up from less than $7 billion in 1997, under Clinton.[32]

Since September 11th, as Robert Kagan noted,

> America did not change (...). It only became more itself (...). It is an objective fact that Americans have been expanding their power and influence in ever-widening arc since even before they founded their own independent nation.[33]

Over a century earlier, the historian Frederick Jackson Turner, in an 1896 *Atlantic Monthly* article, said it this way: »For really three centuries the dominant fact of American life has been expansion« and

> The demands for a vigorous foreign policy, for an inter-oceanic canal, for a revival of our power on the seas, and for the extension of American influence to outlying islands and adjoining countries are indications that the movement will continue.[34]

[31] Cf.: the washington post, 5 February 1997, 28.

[32] Cf. W. Mead, God's Country? Foreign affairs, Sept./Oct. 2006. http://www.foreignaffairs.org/mead_reading.

[33] R. Kagan, Of Paradise and Power. America and Europe in the New World Order, New York 2003, 85-86.

[34] F.J. Turner, The Problem of the West, in: Atlantic Monthly 78 (1896), 289-297. Online at: http://www.theatlantic.com/issues/95sep/ets/turn.htm.

Bush's understanding of the world and his decision to invade Iraq were within this American range. The results of Bush's approach to terrorism, Iraq and Iran may differ from previous interventions in the developing world, but results often differ—consider Korea, Vietnam, and Nicaragua. The approach itself is unnovel. Bush had an interest in a liberal economy in the Mideast and Central Asia that allows the US access to a key resource and to infrastructure development opportunities. He supported economically liberal and politically stable (if illiberal) states, and sought to liberate where an autocratic leader, Saddam Hussein, became uncooperative. He would not negotiate with Iran regarding its nuclear program unless it ceased its development, though he participated in multi-party talks with resourceless North Korea even after it had exploded a nuclear device—negotiations which in February 2007 led to a cessation of the North Korean weapons program in return for international aid.

Interestingly, Americans who opposed the war shared the belief in liberty and self-determination of those who advocated it. The opposition to the 2003 Iraq war was concerned about the effect of war on liberty and about the rectitude of America imposing its will on Iraqis postwar. Advocates of the war were concerned about the effect of Saddam on liberty and believed that a US-organized postwar would bring liberty through liberalism.

Historically at least, from among the voices on the political landscape, intervention for the sake of resources and a liberal economy has prevailed, as it did unremarkably in Iraq. Arguably, the 2003 war in Iraq was more justified than many US operations of the preceding 50 years, as at least a torturing tyrant was removed there. Moreover, as we've seen, neither an insistence on global military superiority nor pre-emptive strikes are unique to Bush nor does his use of torture exceed other US practices. In Europe, the most long-lasting of these was Operation Gladio, the covert ›stay-behind‹ armies created in the 1940s under the CIA and NATO to sabotage communist and socialist parties. Violent measures including bombings and possibly assassination were used in Germany, Italy, Turkey, France, Spain, Portugal, Belgium, and Sweden.[35] Gladio had US support until its existence was acknowledged by Italy's head of state, Giulio Andreotti, in 1990; it was then investigated by the EU.[36]

In the developing world, the US Office of Public Safety, through its International Police Academy, supplied and trained over one million Third World policemen in interrogation including torture, intelligence gathering, crowd control, and assassination. The School of the Americans continues today to train Latin American military and police in these activities. When in 1996, un-

[35] Cf. D. Ganser, NATO's Secret Armies. Operation Gladio and Terrorism in Western Europe, London 2005.

[36] Cf.: ETH Zurich research project on Gladio, »Terrorism in Western Europe. An Approach to NATO's Secret Stay-Behind Armies.« Daniele Ganser, Director. Online at: `http://diplomacy.shu.edu/journal/new/pdf/VolVINo1/08_Ganser27.pdf`.

der pressure from watchdog groups, the Pentagon made SOA training manuals public, editors at the NEW YORK TIMES wrote,

> Americans can now read for themselves some of the noxious lessons the United States Army taught to thousands of Latin American military and police officers at the School of the Americans during the 1980s (...) interrogation techniques like torture, execution, blackmail and arresting the relatives of those being questioned.[37]

The present administration continues even the tradition of manipulating intelligence. Indeed, the effort to use a people's assumptions to further political ends—in this case, ends the nation wanted (in oil and a stable Mideast)—cannot be said to be exceptional to Bush or to the US. This is not to excuse government duplicity but to make the obvious point that a list of such misbehavior would be long. One could look to Bismarck's famously distorted Ems telegram, which goaded the French to war in 1870-71, though the proposal to place the Prussian Hohenzollern Prince Leopold on the throne of Spain—unacceptable to France—had been withdrawn by Leopold himself. Or one could look to any government which must, in Noam Chomsky's efficient phrase, »manufacture consent« for its policies.

But to stay with the US example: In 1947, a Congressional investigative committee concluded, »Government propaganda distorts facts with such authority that the person becomes prejudiced or biased in the direction which the government propaganda wish to lead national thinking.«[38] In 1957, General Douglas MacArthur, a Republican hawk and hero of the War in the Pacific, protested that,

> Our government has kept us in a perpetual state of fear—kept us in a continuous stampede of patriotic fervor—with the cry of a grave national emergency (...). Yet in retrospect, these disasters seem never to have happened, seem never to have been quite real.[39]

Lyndon Johnson escalated US involvement in Vietnam under rigged intelligence in the 1964 Gulf of Tonkin scandal. It was under both parties that, from the 1950s to the 1970s, the FBI illegally obtained information on US citizens, leading to the 1978 law prohibiting such activity, which Bush last year again violated.[40]

[37] School of the Dictators, NEW YORK TIMES, 28 September 1996, 22.

[38] C. Johnson, The Sorrow of Empire. Militarism, Secrecy and the End of the Republic, New York 2004. Military Training, Hearing Before the Committee on Armed Services. (1948, March, 17, 18, 22-25, 29-31, April 1-3), 744.

[39] For the quote see: http://www.quotedb.com/quotes/2731; cf. also, T. Risse-Kappen, Cooperation Among Democracies. The European Influence on US Foreign Policy, Princeton 1995.

[40] G.W. Bush's National Security Agency compiled information on citizens, through wiretapping, searching computer records, etc., without legally mandated court orders.

Also unnovel is Bush's rhetoric, which I would not dismiss as PR, as it reflects the way much of the nation understands US policies and what motivates it to action. Indeed, as all leaders, Democrat and Republican, have chosen words they believed the nation would embrace, the language suggests as much about the audiences as about the speakers. The counter-argument, that it reflects nothing about America's leaders, who use this language cynically to hoodwink the people, overlooks that American politicians have no need to be cynical. Americans are not uncomfortable with the economic motive for foreign policy because of the assumption of a productive progress from economic to political liberalism. There is little need to hide or prettify what is believed to be not only a good but a global good. Bush's language, like that of other leaders, tells us about the motives and expectations of both government and people.

While being »missionaries of capitalism and democracy« was a slogan of World War II, Bush, in his Second Inaugural Address, said, »America's vital interests [capitalist markets] and our deepest beliefs [democracy] are now one.«[41] Expressing America's optimistic Manichaenism (optimistic because America plunges ahead into certain victory), Bush in October 2005 described the war on terror as »facing a radical ideology with unalterable objectives: to enslave whole nations and intimidate the world.«[42] In 1946 George Kennan described the Soviets:

> We have here a political force committed to the belief that with the US there can be no permanent *modus vivendi*, that it is desirable and necessary that the internal harmony of our society be disrupted, our traditional way of life destroyed, the international authority of our state be broken.[43]

The pragmatic/idealistic worldview that prompted Wilson's »liberal capitalist world order« where »America could find moral and economic pre-eminence« finds itself again in Bush's 2006 State of the Union Address,

> We will choose to build our prosperity by leading the world economically (...) the only way to secure the peace, the only way to control our destiny is by our leadership. So the United States of America will continue to lead.[44]

[41]G.W. Bush, Second Inaugural Address, online at: http://www.whitehouse.gov/inaugural/.

[42]The White House, Press Release on 6 October 2005, online at: http://www.whitehouse.gov/news/releases/2005/10/20051006-3.html.

[43]T. Etzold/J. Gaddis (eds.), Containment. Documents on American Foreign Policy and Strategy, 1945-1950, New York 1978. Kennan both advocated containment of the Soviets and was involved in the 1948 US National Security Council 20/4 covert campaign to oust the Soviets from Europe and »to eliminate the Soviet threat altogether«. Cf. G. Mitrovich, Undermining the Kremlin, 1947-1956, Ithaca/NY 2000.

[44]President Bush Delivers State of the Union Address, Press Release on 31 January 2006; online at: http://www.whitehouse.gov/news/releases/2006/01/20060131-10.html.

Bush's religious rhetoric too was less an outlier than thought. The frequent use of religious imagery throughout US history emerges not from confessional similarities among America's leaders but because the values and assumptions undergirding our politics have roots in the nation's liberal, individualistic evangelicalism. Moreover, both the lack of an anti-clerical Enlightenment and the extra-state position of America's churches conspired to preserve religion's positive valence. It remains associated with liberty, freedom of conscience, anti-authoritarianism, and the good fight against illiberal tyranny. America's political language did not become religious; it has never been otherwise.

The Deist Thomas Jefferson said in his Second Inaugural Address, »I shall need, too, the favor of that Being in whose hands we are, who led our forefathers, as Israel of old (...).«[45] During the war of 1812, Frances Scott Key wrote the national anthem with the certainty that God was on America's side: »conquer we must when our cause is just.«[46] Both Lincoln and the Confederate president Jefferson Davis prayed to God for victory in the Civil War. Lincoln called his Emancipation Proclamation freeing America's slaves »A promise to my maker«[47] and in 1862 wrote Meditations on Divine Will; the nation outside the White House thrummed to »The Battle Hymn of the Republic«, America's ›second‹ national anthem, written during the Civil War by Julia Ward Howe. A sample of its explicitly Trinitarian and militaristic tones,

> In the beauty of the lilies Christ was born across the sea,
> With a glory in His bosom that transfigures you and me:
> As He died to make men holy, let us die to make men free,
> While God is marching on.
> Glory! Hallelujah![48]

At the beginning of America's international expansion in 1898, William McKinely said,

> There was nothing left for us to do but to take them all and to educate the Filipinos and uplift and civilize and Christianize them, and by God's grace do the very best we could by them, as our fellow men for whom Christ also died.[49]

[45] Th. Jefferson, Second Inaugural Address; online at: http://www.yale.edu/lawweb/avalon/presiden/inaug/jefinau2.htm.

[46] F.S. Key, The Star-Spangled Banner; online at: http://www.francisscottkey.org/.

[47] W. Wolf, The Almost Chosen People. A study of the Religion of Abraham Lincoln, New York 1959, 18-19.

[48] J. Ward Howe, Battle Hymn of the Republic, in: The Atlantic Monthly (1862). Online at: http://www.theatlantic.com/issues/1862feb/batthym.htm.

[49] T. Donnelly, The Past as Prologue. An Imperial Manual, Foreign Affairs, July/August 2002; online at: http://www.foreignaffairs.org/20020701fareviewessay8529/thomas-donnelly/the-past-as-prologue.html.

McKinley was not distracted by the Filipinos' 300-year Catholicism. On America's entrance into World War I in 1917, at the same time that Wilson strategized about expanding America's share of world exports, he echoed Luther's words at the Diet of Worms (1521: »I stand here; I can do no other«) saying, »God helping her, she [America] can do no other.«[50]

Franklin D. Roosevelt in 1942 used Hitler's words to explain US entrance into the war. Roosevelt said the world is »too small to provide adequate *Lebensraum* for both Hitler and God.«[51] On D-Day, his address to the nation was a prayer in its entirety:

> Almighty God: Our sons, pride of our nation, this day have set upon a mighty endeavor, a struggle to preserve our Republic, our religion, our civilization, and set free a suffering humanity (...) They [our soldiers] fight to liberate (...). With Thy blessing, we shall prevail over the unholy forces of our enemy (...). Thy will be done. Amen.[52]

The Manichaean ›evil empire‹ was the invention of the Democrat Harry Truman, implementer of the Marshall Plan. In his first speech to Congress on assuming the presidency after Roosevelt's death, Truman said,

> At this moment, I have in my heart a prayer. As I have assumed my duties, I humbly pray Almighty God, in the words of King Solomon (...). I ask only to be a good and faithful servant of my Lord and my people.[53]

In his Inaugural Address John Kennedy called out, »The trumpet summons us again (...). Let us go forth to lead the land we love, asking His blessing and His help«.[54] During the Iran hostage crisis, a NEW YORK TIMES cover showed Jimmy Carter on his knees in the Oval Office, surrounded by advisors. Under the photo were the words: »President Carter and his cabinet pray for the release of American hostages.«

All those cited since McKinley have been Democrats. Thus, that G.W. Bush irritated US allies abroad with his religious references was curious, as so many American leaders have used them. Indeed, assessed against the American tradition, the religious refrains in Bush's speeches are not only usual but

[50] W. Wilson, War Message, 2 April 1917; online at: `http://net.lib.byu.edu/~rdh7/wwi/1917/wilswarm.html`.

[51] F.D. Roosevelt, State of the Union Address, 6 January 1942, at: J. Woolley/G. Peters, The American Presidency Project [online]. Santa Barbara, CA: University of California (hosted), Gerhard Peters (database). Available from World Wide Web: (`http://www.presidency.ucsb.edu/ws/print.php?pid=16253`).

[52] F.D. Roosevelt, Prayer on D-Day, 6 June 1944, at: J. Woolley/G. Peters, op. cit. (n. 49), `http://www.presidency.ucsb.edu/ws/index.php?pid=16515`.

[53] H.S. Truman, Address before a Joint Session of the Congress, 16 April 1945; online at: `http://www.trumanlibrary.org/ww2/stofunio.htm`.

[54] J.F. Kennedy, Inaugural Address, 20 January 1961, online at: `http://www.yale.edu/lawweb/avalon/presiden/inaug/kennedy.htm`.

similar to those of Truman, a Democrat who presided over the postwar foreign policy that is today seen as so different from Bush's approach. While Bush, on September 20, 2001 announced his war to save the »civilized world« from terrorists,[55] in 1947, Democrat Truman too had split the world into two camps, the free world and the communists. When Bush provocatively declared, »you are with us or against us« he was echoing Matthew 12: 30, »He that is not with me is against me.« Truman also judged that the world had come to a turning point where parties must take sides.[56] In January 1949, Truman thrummed,

> Now, I am confident that the Divine Power which has guided us to this time of fateful responsibility and glorious opportunity will not desert us now. With that help from Almighty God which we have humbly acknowledged at every turning point in our national life, we shall be able to perform the great tasks which He now sets before us.[57]

In 2006, Bush's popularity fell and America put Democratic majorities in both houses of Congress because he was not succeeding at his wars. Yet even after conditions in Iraq deteriorated, 62% of Americans believed the US has a special role in the world and that pre-emptive war is justified.[58] America's rejection of the Republican Party was not a rejection of its ideals but of Bush's inability to effect them—not a change in traditional values but an embrace of them, and repudiation of policies that fail to realize them. America did not turn its head from one side of a philosophical divide to another, like a spectator watching a tennis match. Rather it stared straight ahead while the Republicans walked off its screen for incompetence, at least for a time. US efforts in Iraq ceased to look like a liberating mission, much as efforts in Vietnam had after 15 years of involvement there. Absent the larger, compelling framework of the Cold War, the nation was quicker to react in 2006 to the loss of its self-image as redeemer. That the war in Iraq was not a proxy war but one in which American youths were dying sped this process, as Americans are willing to die but not cynically, without a cause.

---

[55] Cf.: G.W. Bush, Address to a Joint Session of Congress and the American People, 20 September 2001; online at: `http://www.whitehouse.gov/news/releases/2001/09/20010920-8.html`.

[56] Cf. for Bush: President Welcomes President Chirac to White House, Press Release on 6 November 2001; online at: `http://www.whitehouse.gov/news/releases/2001/11/20011106-4.html`; for Truman: Special Message to the Congress on Greece and Turkey: The Truman Doctrine, 12 March 1947; online at: `http://www.trumanlibrary.org/publicpapers/index.php?pid=2189&st=&st1=`.

[57] H.S. Truman, Annual Message to the Congress on the State of the Union, 5 January 1949, at: J. Woolley/G. Peters, op. cit. (n. 49), `http://www.presidency.ucsb.edu/ws/index.php?pid=13293`.

[58] Cf. J. Guth/J. Green/L. Kellstedt/C. Smidt, Faith and Foreign Policy. A View from the Pews, in: The Review of Faith & International Affairs, Fall 2005.

Had the postwar been somewhat more successful, Americans would have complained neither about keeping the military in Iraq nor about the dubious intelligence that brought the war about. For a stable Iraq cooperative in commerce would have allowed America to see itself as the liberator it believes it should be. And Iraqi democracy would be assumed to follow.

There is no argument here that Bush's approach was good or bad policy, only that it was not exceptional policy. Bush, like those before him, prosecuted America's politics—and had the nation's support—out of faith in the liberalism and liberty which emerged from America's secular and religious experience. That the world works best under liberal economics and politics may be wrong or right, but in anticipating future policy, the point is this: *what has been possible under the liberalizing/liberating obligation remains possible* US *foreign policy.* On January 20, 2004, John Le Carre told the INTERNATIONAL HERALD TRIBUNE that he is »waiting for the real Americans to come back.« Yet there are no ›real‹ Americans to come back. What Samuel Huntington has called the American Creed—liberty, egalitarianism, individualism, laissez-faire economics and ›progress‹—and what the British writer Anatol Lieven calls Jacksonian nationalism—defensive, violent, self-absorbed, intolerant[59]—are tethered at the source, at the 350-year-old tradition of self-reliant, liberal, anti-authoritarian, missionary can-do-ism. This core sets the limit of the possible.

At this point, I should briefly address two objections to my idea. One is that America is divided between the people and greedy, hypocritical politicians who impose policy upon them—that is, policy does not emerge from the values and assumptions of the nation but from a domineering class whose interests differ from those of the people. The second is that America is divided between two sorts of people: the real (good) Americans and the evil. Both ways of imagining America divided are unuseful.

First, the idea that politicians conduct their own, alien policies ›packaged‹ as American values to trick the public is overly optimistic. For it assumes that if Americans could only rid themselves of politicians—nefarious creatures unlike themselves—they would behave well and justly. This is generous to the American people, but unlikely. They are not duped but share the assumptions of their leaders, who after all, come from the same culture. Those assumptions may be individualistic, liberal, entrepreneurial, pragmatic and bourgeois, but they are held both by politicians and those who elect them across the socio-economic spectrum. Unlike even more hierarchical democracies such as France, the American political class is changeable and does not cull only from an elite. Truman (D), Nixon (R), Reagan (R) and Clinton (D), to mention just a few, were all middle class—Nixon, Reagan and Clinton, lower middle class. Indeed,

[59] Cf. A. Lieven, America Right or Wrong, New York 2004.

leaders over the last century who were born into money—Franklin Roosevelt, John Kennedy—tended to be Democrat, not business-Republicans, as a class-interest analysis would suggest.

The wicked-politician idea also assumes that mendacious leaders know they do evil—as their own constituencies believe lying, cheating and manipulation are wrong—but do it anyway. This too is optimistic. More likely is that most believe their policies are the way the world works best, and their constituencies elect them because they agree: this is what power is for and far better that we be the ones using it for, overall, we use it for better purposes than other political actors do. This is not a cynical packaging of wrongdoing in the language of values but an understanding of the best path in a difficult world.

The second way of imagining America divided, between the real (good) Americans and evil ones, is equally unhelpful. Not only do most Americans share assumptions and values at the level of deep structure, but even at a superficial level, Americans fail to fall into distinct groups. Neither economic conservatism nor party affiliation predicts social conservatism. Views on government's role in domestic politics do not predict those on foreign policy. Even at the 2004 presidential election when the nation was supposedly polarized into ›red‹ and ›blue‹ states, the Pew Research Center for the People and Press found no clear division,

> The typology study's finding of significant cleavages within parties not only runs counter to the widespread impression of a nation increasingly divided into two unified camps, but also raises questions about political alignments in the future.[60]

One might make the narrower claim that an economic elite (presumed to be evil) has captured the government through the influence of money on electoral politics. This assumes that, if Americans only rid themselves of capitalists or the rich—wicked people unlike themselves—they would behave generously overseas. Again, this is kind but unlikely. The values and assumptions that ground conduct abroad, however liberal, capitalist or individualistic, are not those of an economic elite but of the nation. One could go to many places for evidence but why not to that great poet of American thought, Ralph Waldo Emerson, who in his essay »Self-Reliance« (1841) wrote,

> Are they my poor? I tell thee, thou foolish philanthropist, that I grudge the dollar, the dime, the cent I give to such men as do not belong to me and to whom I do not belong.[61]

[60] Pew Research Center for the People and the Press, Beyond Red vs. Blue. Republicans Divided About Role of Government—Democrats by Social and Personal Values, 10 May 2005; online at: `http://people-press.org/reports/display.php3?ReportID=242`.

[61] R.W. Emerson, Self-Reliance, in: id. Emerson's Essays, New York 1981, 31-66, here: 37; online at: `http://www.emersoncentral.com/selfreliance.htm`.

This unembarrassed sentiment cannot be credited to Ronald Reagan or George W. Bush; it has been associated for two centuries with self-responsible, risk-taking entrepreneurialism, not only accepted but prized. Policies that abet this go-for-it economic behavior make sense to most Americans most of the time. Moreover, owing to the widespread value of self-reliance, the rich are seen as self-responsible risk-takers and are little resented. There was little citizens' protest, for instance, against Bush's regressive 2001 and 2003 tax cuts, which according to the government's own documentation gave roughly 32% of the cuts to the richest 1% of Americans and 53% of the cuts to the top 10%.[62] Indeed, most Americans believe their own risks might turn out well, too. (Did not Bill Gates drop out of college to play with zeroes and ones?) In 2002, in the shock of 9/11 and recession, 19% of Americans nonetheless believed they were in the wealthiest 1%; another 20% believed they would be there soon; 81% of college students said they would be richer than their parents and 59% said they would become millionaires.[63] Obvious instances of the rich hijacking government may irritate America's sense of equality of opportunity and provoke its ever-ready anti-authoritarianism. But overall the nation's embrace of individual liberty and self-reliant can-do-ism make Americans slow to identify such a hijack as the source of their woes.

In sum, America is divisible into good and evil neither at the level of political and social affiliation nor at the level of value and assumption. The nexus of liberal beliefs discussed here motivate both Creed and Nationalism. A substantive shift away from them and the foreign policy they support appears unlikely at present. To begin with, the assumptions and values from which America's political conduct emerges change only slowly. On a more practical level, the US would have to overcome the ›hegemon's temptation‹ to use or even overstretch its military to preserve its reputation, and this is difficult for any power. Finally, self-interest is inherent in foreign policy.

Given the likely persistence of America's traditional foreign policy range, is it a problem? After all, the values and assumptions that moved America to ›save‹ Southeast Asia and Latin America from communism, which Europeans call hubristic folly, also moved America to storm Omaha Beach and rebuild postwar Europe. The mix of pragmatism, idealism, and fix-it-ism that brought the 2003 war in Iraq also brought the Marshall Plan, UN, Bretton Woods, OECD, and NATO. For many Americans, the effort in Iraq was of the same liberating can-do-ism that made America airlift a blockaded Berlin and take

[62] Cf. P. Krugman, Weapons of Math Destruction, in: NEW YORK TIMES, 14 April 2006, Section 1, 21; online at: http://www.nytimes.com.

[63] Cf. D. Brooks, The Triumph of Hope Over Self-Interest, in: NEW YORK TIMES, 12 January 2003, Section 4, 15; online at: http://www.nytimes.com; Survey, in: The Economist, 9 October 2004, 13; J. Leland, Faith in the Future. Why America Sees the Silver Lining, in: NEW YORK TIMES, 13 June 2004, Section 4, 1.

Inchon Harbor. Perhaps a flawed American hegemon is on the whole more productive and peaceful for the world than one without liberal economic and political values, such as China or Putin's Russia.

Having made an argument for a certain consistency in US foreign policy, I'd like to briefly address five challenges to my case—that is, five possibilities for change. One, raised especially since the 2006 Republican defeat in Congress, is whether the protest voices in America—against expansionist foreign policy, or at least expansionism by force—could be the ground for a different sort of conduct overseas. To date, these movements, however meaningful for their participants, have had little effect on foreign policy—none on World War I, some on Vietnam and possibly Iraq, but only when the army was losing with significant US casualties for no clear ideal. They have been ineffective because they have had the support of a minority of the public; most Americans have agreed on their country's global role and because of the self-interest inherent in foreign policy. That is, a voluntary withdrawal from economic and geopolitical expansionism lacks historical precedents by any power in any economic system. Moreover, such a withdrawal contravenes America's long-held belief in liberal overseas markets as necessary for economic and political liberty *at home*. Restraint goes against the grain of America's can-do initiative, and such long-term thinking runs against the quick-fixism that comes from energetic, self-reliant pragmatism. Though the self-image of being the world's liberator runs deep in America, the idea of doing so by acting less—rather than more—does not.

What then, of the isolationist and realist traditions in US foreign policy? Could they be a second and third source of foreign policy change? The first is a sentiment without a practice, the second, a practice without sentiments. Even in times of frequent isolationist rhetoric, isolationism has had small impact on foreign policy—not even in the infant nation, as we've seen in the rapid overview of US naval and military efforts above. While *protectionist* trade policy has enriched manufacturers and made populists since William Jennings Bryan attractive in sectors vulnerable to unemployment, it rarely impeded interventionism abroad. One might say it the other way: it is remarkable how confident America has been of its interventionism against the notion that the New Jerusalem should remain untainted by the follies of the rest of the woebegone world. Even in the so-called isolationist 1920s, America broadened its economic presence beyond anything that had come before, becoming, for the first time, a significant threat to Britain's financial hegemony.[64]

Realists in practice have followed the expansionist lines of US foreign policy. In the 19th century, they were frank colonialists; after World War II, they were Cold Warriors, prosecuting direct and proxy wars. The geopolitical focus

[64]Cf. P. Cain/A. Hopkins, British Imperialism 1688-2000, Harlow 1993, 479.

of the Ur-realist Henry Kissinger did not keep the US out of Southeast Asia, Latin America, the Soviet bloc (where possible), or the Mideast. Moreover, by realist accounting, the end of the Cold War should have allowed the US to reduce its presence globally, as America's illiberal arch-enemy collapsed. Yet Kissinger did not advise America to do so. Rather, he encouraged confidence in America's influence and reach. »At the dawn of the new millennium«, he said in his characteristically modest prose, »the United States is enjoying a pre-eminence unrivaled by even the greatest empires of the past.«[65]

Realists do not keep America from its expansive foreign policy. They in fact propose one, but one that implements only what they see as the pragmatic interests of the country—half the double purpose of America's traditional foreign policy. That is, they insufficiently attend to the interplay between America's economic and political values, and to the extent that they do, their proposals lose the support of the nation. In the 1950s, Eisenhower could not reduce US troops in Europe, the realist option, though he was the hero of World War II and Korea. The nation believed in America's indispensable role in safeguarding liberty and economic liberalism in Europe.

Once the Iraq postwar turned into civil war, the US invasion began to be called an idealist (neo-con) misadventure that had to be corrected by the realist fix-it man of the Reagan and both Bush administrations, James Baker. In 2006, he headed the Iraq Study Group to propose a new approach. Yet, this misreads the war. Wresting Iraq's oil and weapons from a volatile dictator was not an idealist project; it was a classic blend of realist liberalization and liberation. The Bush family, Cheney, Rice and Republican leadership in 2002 and 2003 were business and geopolitical pragmatists; the secretaries of the navy and army were long-time executives in the defense industry. The war would not have gone forward unless they held it to be of benefit. Nor did Baker's committee propose a new realist plan. It recommended an increase in troops to try (again) to stabilize Iraq, an eventual military withdrawal, securing corporate ownership of Iraq's oil industry, and a cessation of oil subsidies to the Iraqi people.[66] There is little here that has not been in the mainstream of US foreign policy for over a century.

In withdrawing support for the Iraq war, the nation may have rejected failure and a betrayal of its ideals. But this is quite different from abandoning ideals themselves for something more ›realist.‹ The country is no more likely to pursue its pragmatic interests absent a liberating understanding of its actions than to pursue idealistic aims without a pragmatic interest.

[65] H. Kissinger, Does America Need a Foreign Policy? New York 2001, 17.

[66] US Institute of Peace, The Iraq Study Group Report; online at: `http://www.usip.org/isg/iraq_study_group_report/report/1206/index.html`.

A fourth possibility for change lies in the potential shift to renewable energies. That oil independence will have profound impact on the environment and geopolitics is indisputable, but in what direction will that impact push us? A world run on renewable energy will increase economic duress in the oil-producing countries of the Mideast, Central Asia, and Africa, likely creating more anger and violence. In such a case, these regions would have the geopolitical weighting of today's non-oil-producing, developing countries—Afghanistan, for instance, where in 2001-2002, the US spent $13 billion on the war effort and $10 million on humanitarian aid. In 2004, the US spent $1.1 billion on reconstruction and $1 billion per month maintaining its armed forces.[67] It is not clear that a region *lacking* resources of interest to the US will cause a shift in America's traditional approach to the developing world.

Fifth, the US might be forced to change its foreign policies by other actors. China, India, Russia, and the group of smaller economies led by Venezuela and Brazil singly might put the US in changed circumstances. Or as an ensemble they might, bringing geopolitics to a dispersal of power not seen since World War I. Additionally, threatening or violent actions by any state or non-state group with a significant weapons cache will provoke a response from the US. Iran and North Korea are two states that come to mind as of this writing, but this is a club with an expanding membership.

Two things are not clear in these cases. One cannot assume that a change in the policies of other actors will yield a change in the US response. America might hold that its policies remain productive even in changed circumstances. Or its values and assumptions—long and dearly held, and so productive for the nation—might preclude seeing alternatives. The second interesting question is how much Europe will be one of those actors which, by its vision and actions, change world circumstances.

[67] Cf. A. Rashid, The Mess in Afghanistan, in: The New York Review of Books, 12 February 2004, 26.

# Religion and Public Education in the United States Politics, Ethics, Law, Pedagogy[1]

BRUCE GRELLE

My goal in this paper is to present an ethical, legal, and pedagogical framework for thinking about religion and public education in the United States. This framework is rooted in the first two clauses of the First Amendment to the US Constitution, which state that »Congress shall make no law respecting an establishment of religion, or prohibiting the free exercise thereof (...)« I will have more to say about these ›religious liberty‹ clauses of the First Amendment in just a moment, but first we must consider the larger political and cultural contexts in which the topic of religion and public education presents itself, namely, the American experiment in pluralistic democracy. By reflecting on the nature of this experiment in pluralistic democracy, we can better understand what is at stake in discussions of religion and public education.

## American Politics and Contemporary ›Culture Wars‹

From its beginning more than two hundred years ago, the United States of America has been a *pluralistic* society. It is now, and always has been, constituted by many different religious, political, racial, ethnic, and cultural groups, though of course the nature and degree of this diversity has shifted over time. As a *democracy*, the United States is committed to the idea that all citizens should have a meaningful opportunity to participate in the governance of their lives together as members of society. Regardless of whether one judges the day-to-day life and practice of contemporary American politics to be more or less democratic, most will acknowledge that democracy—government of the people, by the people, and for the people—is a definitive *ideal* (even though not always a definitive reality) of American history.

By describing America's pluralistic democracy as an ›experiment‹, we remind ourselves that our lives and histories are tenuous and open-ended. For just over two-hundred years America has been experimenting with the idea that free people from diverse religious, cultural, ethnic, and racial backgrounds

[1] A slightly revised version of this chapter has previously appeared as Teaching about Religions in US Public Schools: European and American Contrasts, in: PANORAMA: International Journal of Comparative Religions Education, Vol. 18, December 2006.

are capable of governing themselves and living together peacefully. But the outcome of an experiment is not guaranteed ahead of time. An experiment may succeed, or it may fail. Ultimately the success (or failure) of the American experiment in pluralistic democracy is contingent upon citizens' commitment to it and upon their ability to secure the conditions that are necessary for its survival. Among the most important of these conditions is the ability to *learn to live with our deepest differences.*

Over the past several decades, America has been wracked by ›culture wars‹ in which public debate has increasingly become reduced to anti-democratic and intolerant caricature and slander of one's political and religious opponents.[2] In many places, public schools have become battlegrounds in these culture wars. Public school students and teachers have found themselves caught up in clashes and controversies over religion in textbooks and curricula, religious holidays, sex education, and school funding, among other issues. As Charles C. Haynes has written,

> [e]xtremes have surfaced on all sides, and any notion of a common vision for the common good is often lost in the din of charge and counter-charge. As alienation and frustration deepen, public education is weakened and our future as one nation of many peoples and faiths is called into question.
>
> (...) At issue for this nation, as for much of the world, is the simple, but profound question that runs through modern experience: How will we live with our deepest differences?
>
> Nowhere is the need to address this question greater than in public education. Not only are schools the storm center of controversy involving religious differences, they are the principal institution charged with transmitting the identity and mission of the United States from one generation to the next. If we fail in our school policies and classrooms to model and to teach how to live with differences, we endanger our experiment in religious liberty and our unity as a nation.[3]

Some religious and political groups have perpetuated America's culture wars by advocating what Haynes has described as a »sacred public school.« Proponents of this model argue that public school policies and practices should prefer and transmit their own contentious and nostalgic version of America's ›Christian heritage.‹[4] Their opponents in the culture wars advocate a ›naked public school‹ where religion is entirely excluded from the curriculum and from the school environment as-a-whole in the name of the constitutional separation

---

[2] Cf. J.D. Hunter, Culture Wars. The Struggle to Define America, New York 1991; J.D. Hunter, Before the Shooting Begins. Searching for Democracy in America's Culture War, New York 1994.

[3] Ch.C. Haynes/O. Thomas (eds.), Finding Common Ground. A First Amendment Guide to Religion and Public Education, Nashville, [3]1998, 1.1.

[4] Cf. e.g. the work of David Barton and his Wallbuilders organization at `http://www.wallbuilders.com/`.

of church and state. Both of these approaches to religion and public education are based upon a misunderstanding of the First Amendment.[5]

The approach that I will outline is an alternative to these two approaches. This third model—what Haynes calls a »civil public school«—is firmly rooted in First Amendment principles, and it represents an *emerging consensus* among American citizens and educators when it comes to the topic of religion and public education. This new consensus was heralded by the 1988 publication, »Religion in the Public School Curriculum: Questions and Answers«, a statement of principles endorsed by a remarkably broad range of educational, religious, and civic organizations.[6] At this point I will turn to the ethical, legal, and pedagogical principles that underlie this new consensus.

## An Ethical Framework for Thinking about Religion and Public Education in the United States

In an effort to find common ground that will enable Americans to continue to live with their deepest differences rather than being torn apart by them, a growing number of citizens and educators have called for renewed commitment to the ethical principles on which the American experiment is based. Foremost among these principles are the three Rs of religious liberty: rights, responsibilities, and respect.[7]

›Rights‹ are the freedoms or liberties that are necessary for the expression of human dignity. Religious liberty or freedom of conscience—the freedom to believe or to disbelieve—is among the most fundamental of human rights. A society is only as just and as free as it is respectful of this right for its smallest minorities and least popular communities.

In addition to the defence of individual rights, the success of a democracy also depends upon the willingness and ability of its citizens to accept their civic responsibilities. ›Responsibilities‹ are the duties or obligations owed to oneself and to one's fellow citizens. Chief among these is the duty to guard for others those rights that we wish guarded for ourselves. In response to what many see as American society's obsession with individual rights at the expense of a sense of social responsibility, the new consensus regarding religion and public education stresses that the health of a democratic society depends upon the

[5]Cf. Ch.C. Haynes/O. Thomas, Finding Common Ground. A Guide to Religious Liberty in the Public Schools, Nashville 2001, 5-6.

[6]This consensus statement and a listing of its seventeen co-sponsors is reproduced in: Haynes, Thomas, Religious Liberty, op. cit. (n. 5), 87-92. Online at: http://www.firstamendmentcenter.org/PDF/FCGchapter7.PDF.

[7]This discussion is based on Haynes/Thomas, First Amendmend, op. cit. (n. 3) and on Haynes/Thomas, Religious Liberty, op. cit. (n. 5). For information regarding the California 3 Rs Project see http://score.rims.k12.ca.us/score_lessons/3rs/.

linkage of rights *and* responsibilities and upon the ability of citizens to balance the pursuit of self-interest with the pursuit of the common good.

The third R, ›respect‹, has to do with the manner in which we conduct ourselves in conflicts and debates with our fellow-citizens, including those fellow-citizens with whom we most seriously disagree. Conflict and debate are vital to democracy. A society where there is no vigorous debate and disagreement is probably not a very democratic society. But *how* we debate, not only *what* we debate, is critical for the health and well-being of a democracy. Respect, or civility, is a fundamental condition for maintaining the vitality and viability of our democratic experiment.

A shared commitment to the three R's of religious liberty can provide the basis upon which citizens with deep religious differences can negotiate those differences with civility and work toward the creation of »a common vision for the common good in public education.«[8] This approach to finding common ground has had remarkable success in building consensus among very disparate interest groups on a range of controversial questions that arise in public education. An outstanding example of this success is the publication of *Religious Liberty, Public Education, and the Future of American Democracy: A Statement of Principles.*[9] This five-page document was sponsored jointly by a broad coalition of educational, religious, and civic organizations. It sets forth a vision of the place of religion in public schools that is both consistent with First Amendment principles and academically sound:

> Public schools may not inculcate nor inhibit religion. They must be places where religion and religious conviction are treated with fairness and respect. Public schools uphold the First Amendment when they protect the religious liberty rights of students of all faiths or none. Schools demonstrate fairness when they ensure that the curriculum includes study *about* religion, where appropriate, as an important part of a complete education.[10]

We can better appreciate the significance of this consensus statement when we recognize that the twenty-three co-sponsors included such organizations as the Christian Coalition *and* People for the American Way, which are often bitter opponents in litigation over the place of religion in public life. That such otherwise disparate organizations can come together to co-sponsor a consensus statement relating to the role of religion and public education in American democracy is a testament to the ability of First Amendment principles of religious liberty and freedom of conscience to unite Americans across religious, ideological, and political divisions.

[8] Haynes/Thomas, First Amendment, op. cit. (n. 3), 1.7.

[9] This document is reproduced in Haynes/Thomas, Religious Liberty. op. cit. (n. 5), 9-13.

[10] Op. cit., (n. 5) 12.

## A Legal Framework for Thinking about Religion and Public Education the United States

Congress shall make no law respecting an establishment of religion, or prohibiting the free exercise thereof. – Religious Liberty Clauses of the First Amendment to the United States Constitution

The ›establishment‹ and ›free exercise‹ clauses of the First Amendment provide the constitutional basis for what Thomas Jefferson described as »a wall of separation between Church & State.«[11] In the United States, ›public‹ schools and universities are funded and administered by state and local governments. As such, they are subject to the constitutional separation of church and state and, therefore, they must remain ›neutral‹ with regard to religion.[12] Unlike ›private‹ and parochial schools, which may promote religious beliefs and practices, the ›establishment‹ clause prohibits ›public‹ schools from doing so. This prohibition was made clear in a series of famous ›school prayer‹ cases in the 1960s when the US Supreme Court ruled that school-sponsored religious exercises, such as organized group prayer and devotional Bible reading, were violations of the ›establishment‹ clause of the First Amendment.[13]

At the same time, however, the Supreme Court sought to make it clear that *learning and teaching about* religion in the public schools is perfectly consistent with constitutional principles. Indeed, as Justice Tom Clark wrote in the case of *Abington School District v. Schempp*,

> (...) it might well be said that one's education is not complete without a study of comparative religion or the history of religion and its relationship to the advancement of civilization. It certainly may be said that the Bible is worthy of study for its literary and historic qualities. Nothing we have said here indicates that such study of the Bible and of religion, when presented objectively as part of a secular program of education, may not be effected consistently with the First Amendment (...).[14]

In addition to this distinction between school-sponsored practice of religion and teaching about religion, the Supreme Court has also set forth the concept of *neutrality* as another important legal guideline for thinking about the relationship between religion and public education. To help interpret the ›establishment‹ clause of the First Amendment, the court developed a three-part test that has come to be known as the ›Lemon test.‹ In *Lemon v. Kurtzman*,

[11] Cited in: Ch.C. Haynes, Religion in American History. What to Teach and How, Association for Supervision and Curriculum Development, Alexandria/VA 1990, 48.

[12] While the First Amendment originally applied only to the federal or national government of the US, the passage of the Fourteenth Amendment guaranteeing equal protection to all US citizens and subsequent Supreme Court decisions have applied it to the State and local governments as well.

[13] Cf. Engel v. Vitale, 370 US 421, 1962; Abington School District v. Schempp, 374 US 203, 1963.

[14] Online at: http://www.oyez.org/cases/case/?case=1960-1969/1962/1962_142.

the Supreme Court set forth three tests of a constitutional State action in education:

1. It must have a secular (i.e. an educational) purpose
2. Its primary effect must neither advance nor inhibit religion
3. It must not foster excessive government entanglement with religion

Although the ›Lemon Test‹ has been subjected to criticism by several Supreme Court justices and some scholars, government neutrality toward religion has remained a guiding principle for the interpretation of the ›establishment‹ clause of the First Amendment.[15]

Despite this legal emphasis on government neutrality, during the 1960s and 1970s many Americans came to believe that the public school environment was not simply neutral toward religion but hostile toward it and that the religious liberty rights of students in the public schools were often discriminated against. In response to this perception, the US Congress passed »The Equal Access Act« in 1984. The three key principles of the Act are: *non-discrimination*; *protection of religious speech at student-initiated and student-led meetings*; and *local control*. Under the terms of the Act, secondary school students have the right to pray individually or in-groups, to read the Bible and other types of religious literature, and to form religious clubs. These activities must be initiated and led by students, not by school teachers, administrators, or outside adults, and they are subject to the same »time, place, and manner« restrictions that school officials apply to other student activities. But so long as schools allow other non-curriculum related student activities, they must not discriminate against student religious groups. Of course, schools may decide not to allow any non-curriculum related student groups to meet. In that case, student religious groups may be prohibited as well.[16] In 1990, the Supreme Court upheld the constitutionality of »The Equal Access Act« by a vote of 8-1 in the case of *Westside Community Schools v. Mergens* (496 US 226), noting that there is a

> crucial difference between government speech endorsing religion, which the Establishment clause forbids, and private speech endorsing religion, which the Free Speech and Free Exercise clauses protect.[17]

During the 1990s, President Bill Clinton and Secretary of Education Richard W. Riley issued statements which sought to make clear that *public schools are not ›religion-free zones.‹* In 1995, 1998, and again in 1999, the US Department of Education, at the direction of the President and in consultation with the

[15]Cf. Haynes/Thomas, Religious Liberty, op. cit. (n. 5), 40-44.
[16]Cf. op. cit., (n. 5) 113-124.
[17]Online at: `http://www.oyez.org/cases/case/?case=1980-1989/1989/1989_88_1597`.

Justice Department, mailed guidelines on religious expression in public schools to every school district in the country. These presidential guidelines were drawn in large part from »Religion in the Public Schools: A Joint Statement of Current Law«, issued by thirty-five religious and civil liberties groups in 1995.[18] More recently in 2003, President George W. Bush's Secretary of Education, Rod Paige, issued guidance on constitutionally protected prayer in public elementary and secondary schools. This guidance explains the responsibilities of state educational agencies and local educational agencies with respect to this aspect of the *No Child Left Behind Act* passed by Congress in 2001. This emphasis in American law on the protection of student religious speech and expression in public schools stands in obvious contrast to the more restrictive policy adopted recently in France.

## A Pedagogical Framework for Thinking about Religion and Public Education in the United States

We have seen that the courts have found public school-sponsorship of religious practices such as organized prayer to be violations of the ›establishment‹ clause of the First Amendment. We have also seen that *teaching about* religion in an academic, objective, or neutral fashion has been found acceptable by the courts. Yet until quite recently, the topic of religion has been all but absent from the public school curriculum in the United States. There are many reasons for this, including widespread misunderstandings by teachers, school administrators, and members of the general public about what is and is not legally permissible when it comes to the topic of religion in the public school classroom. This misunderstanding, combined with a desire to avoid controversy and a fear of litigation, has often led public schools to either ignore or actively avoid anything having to do with religion whenever possible.

We are thus faced with an ironic situation in which public school education about religion in the United States, widely regarded as the most ›religious‹ of the world's developed countries, has lagged far behind religious education in many European countries, which are widely regarded as among the most thoroughly secularized countries in the world. In Germany and Britain and in other parts of Europe, religious education is a well-established subject matter in the curriculum and an area of professional specialization for which teachers can become certified. In the United States, education about religion, when it happens at all, is typically incorporated within history and social studies, and most teachers in these fields have had no formal training in the academic study of religion as part of their professional preparation. History and social studies

[18]Cf. M. Beauchamp, Guidelines on Religion in Public Schools. An Historic Moment, in: Spotlight on Teaching 17 (2002), 2.4.10.

textbooks have only very recently begun to include the topic of religion and still tend to give it only minimal attention.[19]

Nonetheless, since the late 1980s momentum has been building in support of the inclusion of religion in the curriculum of American public schools. During this time, both the National Council for the Social Studies (1984) and the Association for Supervision and Curriculum Development (1988) issued statements calling for more attention to be given to religion, and a recent analysis of national and state social studies standards has documented that nearly all fifty states now include the topic in some fashion or another.[20] In California, for example, the State Board of Education adopted a curriculum in 1988 that explicitly called for more attention to be given to the study of religion and ethics. The *History-Social Science Framework for California Public Schools K-12* stresses the importance of religion in human history and states that »students must become familiar with the basic ideas of the major religions and the ethical traditions of each time and place.« It further adds:

> To understand why individuals and groups acted as they did, we must see what values and assumptions they held, what they honored, what they sought and what they feared. By studying a people's religion and philosophy as well as their folkways and traditions, we gain an understanding of their ethical and moral commitments. By reading the texts that people revere, we gain important insights into their thinking. The study of religious beliefs and other ideological commitments helps explain both cultural continuity and cultural conflict.[21]

In California, the world history curriculum for sixth, seventh, and tenth grades deals explicitly with the religions of India, China, and the Middle-East. Other grade levels deal with the role of religion in American history and society. And some general knowledge of world religions is also a necessary background for understanding many of the current events in world affairs that are discussed throughout the K-12 curriculum.

As I mentioned above, there is a growing consensus regarding the question of *why* study about religion should be incorporated within public schools. Teaching about religion in the schools makes an indispensable contribution to *historical and cultural literacy*. It is simply impossible to achieve an adequate

[19] Cf. W. Nord, Religion & American Education. Rethinking a National Dilemma, Chapel Hill 1995; and W. Nord/C. Haynes, Taking Religion Seriously Across the Curriculum. Association for Supervision and Curriculum Development, Alexandria/VA, 1998.

[20] National Council for the Social Studies, Including the Study about Religion in the Social Studies Curriculum: A Position Statement and Guidelines, NCSS, 1984. Association for Supervision and Curriculum Development, Religion in the Curriculum, ASCD, Alexandria/VA, 1984. S. Douglass, Teaching About Religion in National and State Social Studies Standards, Council on Islamic Education and the First Amendment Center, Fountain Valley/CA, 2000.

[21] California State Department of Education, History-Social Science Framework for California Public Schools Kindergarten Through Grade Twelve, Sacramento 1988, 7.13.

understanding of human history and culture (literature, art, music, philosophy, law, ethics, politics) without knowing the role that religious beliefs, practices, and communities have played and continue to play in human life. Moreover, the cross-cultural and historical study of religion is also an integral part of *education for citizenship in a pluralistic society*. As we have seen, a basic requirement of citizenship in such societies is respect for religious liberty or freedom of conscience. This respect must be extended to members of all religious communities as well as to those who are members of none. Yet such respect is often difficult to sustain without some objective knowledge of the histories, beliefs, and customs of the diverse peoples and traditions of the world. Without this knowledge, it is all too easy to caricature and trivialize the religious beliefs and practices of our fellow citizens, especially if they happen to be from a religious, racial, or ethnic community that is different from our own. A civil society cannot long survive in such a climate of ignorance and misunderstanding.

In addition to this growing consensus about *why* the topic of religion should be included in the curriculum, there is also significant agreement regarding basic pedagogical guidelines for *how* to teach about religion in public schools. These guidelines have been set forth in »A Teacher's Guide to Religion in the Public Schools«, a consensus document endorsed by nineteen disparate educational, religious, and civic organizations and included in materials distributed to every public school in the nation by the United States Department of Education during the Clinton administration.[22] According to the guidelines,

> The school's approach to religion is academic, not devotional.
>
> The school strives for student awareness of religions, but does not press for student acceptance of any religion.
>
> The school sponsors study about religion, not the practice of religion.
>
> The school may expose students to a diversity of religious views, but may not impose any particular view.
>
> The school educates about all religions, it does not promote or denigrate religion.

[22] A Teacher's Guide to Religion in the Public Schools, First Amendment Center, Nashville, 1999. For an account of the United States Department of Education's promulgation of these guidelines, see M. Beauchamp, op. cit. (n. 17), 2.4.10. For discussion of differences between the texts and the signatories of the two consensus documents: »Religion in the Public School Curriculum: Questions and Answers« and »A Teacher's Guide to Religion in the Public Schools«, see `http://www.teachingaboutreligion.org/Guidance%20for%20Teaching/consensus_documents.htm`.

> The school informs students about various beliefs; it does not seek to conform students to any particular belief.[23]

These guidelines are rooted in the religious liberty principles of the First Amendment and reflect current law regarding religion and public education. They seek to maintain a sharp distinction between teaching *about* religion in public schools on the one hand, and the promotion of religion or religious indoctrination on the other hand.

## Conclusion: American and European Contrasts

In this paper I have sketched political, ethical, legal, and pedagogical frameworks for thinking about religion and public education in the United States. It is important to notice that I have said nothing regarding possible theological, religious, spiritual, or existential frameworks for thinking about this topic. Indeed, I have not even used the phrase ›religious education‹ to describe the academic study of religion in American public schools, because this phrase often carries with it the connotation of spiritual formation or nurture and the cultivation of students' own religious identities. These topics are strictly excluded from the American consensus approach to teaching about religion in public schools for both legal and cultural reasons. The *inclusion* of a theological, religious, spiritual, or existential component of religious education throughout much of Europe and the *exclusion* of such a component in the United States is one of the most significant differences between the study of religion in European and American schools.[24]

As we have seen, the primary aim of teaching *about* religion in American public schools is to increase pupils' understanding of different religions in history and society. A closely related aim has been to increase tolerance and sensitivity toward people of different faiths as well as toward those who are affiliated with no particular religious faith. While there is considerable latitude for student religious expression in the school environment, in the context of the curriculum both students and teachers are to approach religion in an ›academic‹ fashion. That is, they are to ›bracket‹ their own personal religious identities and existential questions and strive for an objective and neutral approach to the study of religion that sets aside one's own personal presuppositions, narratives, and experiences. This approach is often presented in terms of a contrast between a historical and social scientific or ›outsider's‹ perspective versus a theological or ›insider's‹ perspective on religion.

---

[23] Teacher's Guide, op. cit. (n. 21), 3.

[24] Of course there is a growing literature in the United States on education and spirituality in the lives of students and teachers, but much of it relates to post-secondary education or to private rather than public schools.

From the standpoint of much recent European research and practice in the field of religious education, the American consensus approach's continued insistence on ›objectivity‹ and ›neutrality‹ in the study of religion and its reliance on an absolute distinction between social science and theology appears naïve and outdated. As German researcher Friedrich Schweitzer has written,

> [t]he social sciences (...) have been subjected to critical theological analysis that has raised serious doubts concerning their allegedly non-religious outlooks. (...) At the beginning of the twenty-first century, contemporary education has, at least for the most part, given up the claim to objectivity which was so characteristic for earlier education authors even some decades ago.[25]

Schweitzer believes that many of the claims to objectivity made by educational theories have been exposed as resting on a naïve understanding of truth that is unsupported by evidence and that is no longer acceptable. This has led rightly, in his view, to more attention being given to the »subjective self-understanding of children and adolescents« as well as to the »so-called naïve theories of teachers and parents.«[26] According to Schweitzer,

> [t]here is no scientific point of view and certainly no God perspective available to researchers whose interpretations of religions deserve an *a priori* preference over the self-interpretations of religious communities. Consequently, recommending an educational basis for religious education (with which I agree) does not exclude a theological basis. In a sense that at first glance may appear paradoxical, an educational basis for religious education *requires* a theological basis because education must include the interplay of the perspectives of the religious insider and of the outsider.[27]

Coming at the same issue from a different angle, British researcher Robert Jackson has written that

> [f]rom the perspective of religious education theory, the research challenges the sharp distinction generally made between religious education and religious nurture.[28]

For Jackson, religious education is not only about understanding others, it is also concerned with relating material studied in class to students' own beliefs and assumptions; it is concerned with helping young people to clarify and develop their own views and beliefs [29] and with the development of their own

[25] F. Schweitzer, Let the Captives Speak for Themselves! More Dialogue between Religious Education in England and Germany, in: British Journal of Religious Education, 28:2 (March 2006), 147-148.

[26] Op. cit., 148.

[27] Loc. cit.

[28] R. Jackson, Religious Education. An Interpretive Approach, London 1997, 4.

[29] Op. cit., 1-2.

religious or spiritual identities.[30] Asking students and teachers to ›bracket‹ their own personal religious identities and existential questions and striving for an objective and neutral approach to the study of religions that sets aside one's own presuppositions and experiences runs the risk of undermining students' sense of the relevance of the subject matter and its connection to their own lives.

Several influential European models of religious education both acknowledge and cultivate a connection between ›learning about‹ and ›learning from‹ religion, with the result that »religious understanding« becomes »simultaneously academic and personal.«[31] On this view, religious education is potentially transformative of the student's own religious self-understanding, and a good bit of attention is devoted to how religious education teachers can ›enable‹ such transformations. Engagement in ›conversations‹ with different worldviews and ways of life sometimes leads students to reassess their own worldviews and ways of life. »To be edified, in this sense, is to be taken out of one's own self. Through the challenge of ›unpacking‹ another worldview one can, in a sense, become a new person.«[32] Thus, the promotion of »religious literacy« involves efforts »to help each pupil to identify with and argue for a particular religious or non-religious position« and to help students »find their own positions within the key debates about religious plurality.«[33]

In contrast, teaching about religion in American public schools cannot be geared toward students' religious edification and nurture—even a non-traditional and pluralistic form of religious nurture—because the First Amendment *requires* public schools to be neutral toward religion. This not only means that they may not promote or denigrate any *particular* religious faith, but also that they may not promote or discourage religious faith *in general.* Apart from this legal barrier to the inclusion of ›existential‹ or ›spiritual‹ aims as a component of religious literacy, there are cultural ones as well. In this connection Warren Nord is right to suggest that while Jackson's view of the potentially transformative implications of study about religion may be acceptable when it comes to secondary schools and undergraduate education in the United States, »there would be powerful resistance to any public profession that the purpose of education in elementary schools is to redefine religious identities.«[34] My own experience has been that there is often parental resistance to such a notion even

[30] R. Jackson, Rethinking Religious Education and Plurality. Issues in Diversity and Pedagogy, London 2004, 18.

[31] A. Wright, cited in R. Jackson, op. cit. (n. 29), 85.

[32] Jackson, op. cit. (n. 25), 130-131. Cf. also Jackson, op. cit. (n. 29), 88.

[33] R. Jackson, Rethinking Religious Education and Plurality. Issues in Public Religious Education, in: Religion & Education 32:1 (2005), 6.

[34] W. Nord, Religion, Pluralism, and Public Education in America, in: Religion & Education 32:1 (2005), 13.

at the level of secondary education. Thus, in the setting of American public schools, when the term is used at all, ›religious literacy‹ most typically refers to a student's mastery of certain basic information about the world's religions, and as such it tends to be viewed as a dimension or component of a broader conception of cultural and historical literacy.

It is beyond the scope of this paper to do much more than simply note these salient differences between American and European understandings of the aims and methods that are appropriate for the study of religion in state-sponsored schools. Clearly, the consensus approach to education about religion in American public schools reflects the unique religious, cultural, political, and legal traditions and circumstances of the United States just as the prevailing models of religious education in Germany, Britain, and other parts of Europe reflect their distinctive national, political, and historical contexts. And of course, just as there are significant differences between American and European approaches to the place of religion in schools, there are significant differences between European approaches both within and between countries. As Schweitzer writes,

> [t]he German model will never fit England and Wales, and the British model does not make sense for Germany. Too many contextual factors play a role, so that we should always count on a pluralism of different models even in a limited area like the European Union.[35]

Yet even in the context of this inevitable pluralism of approaches to the study of religion, Schweitzer and others have urged the development of »minimum requirements or basic standards for religious education that should be guaranteed in all countries irrespective of their special situation.«[36] A discussion of basic standards is also getting underway in the United States, where national content standards currently exist for other subject matters but not for the study of religion. These European and American discussions of basic educational standards and related topics will undoubtedly be promoted by the ongoing internationalization of debates about religious education and the growing interest in comparative studies of different approaches to religion in the schools in different national contexts. Humboldt University's project on »Religion und Politik—transatlantische Perspektiven« is to be commended for its contribution to the advancement of these discussions.

[35]Schweitzer, op. cit. (n. 22), 149.

[36]Loc. cit. See also, F. Schweitzer, International Standards for Religious Education, in: Panorama. International Journal of Comparative Religious Education and Values 14:1 (2002), 49-56.

# Religious Education in Germany—A Model for the Future?[1]

ROLF SCHIEDER

Religious education in Germany has acquired a bad reputation. The concept seems to be too unique and too closely connected to the former ›landesherrliches Kirchenregiment‹, a structure formed in the Middle Ages under which kings or princes ruled the church and determined the religion of their subjects. Present-day religious education in Germany therefore seems anachronistic in a religio-political world in which the accepted paradigm is that of the separation of church and state and a multi-faith approach in religious education.

The differentiation between church and state is one of the most fundamental achievements of modern states. Religious freedom is guaranteed by the state. However, the notion of »separation between church and state« can easily be misinterpreted as the exclusion of religion from the public sphere. All twentieth-century totalitarian regimes that tried to reduce religion to a private function eventually learned that religion also has a claim on the public sphere that cannot be suppressed forever; religion returned when these regimes were overthrown and, in some cases, was even a catalyst for their demise. A politician does not have to be a believer in order not only to guard the free exercise of religion, but also to care about learning to use religious freedom responsibly. This requires passing down lessons—learned from one generation to the next. How do societies fulfill this obligation? Is the responsibility delegated to families and churches, or has also the state some responsibility for the religious education of its citizens?

As in the United States, church and state are separate in Germany, and the secular state is supposed to be strictly neutral in religious matters. However, in contrast to the United States, the German state practices a friendly partnership with the churches, which are important civil society associations. About 80% of German pre-schools are run by churches, as are most private schools. The churches are the most important employers in the social services field. There are many areas of cooperation between church and state in Germany, and religious education in public schools is included on the list of these areas.

Since the enforced division between the secular state and religious authorities is seen as one of the hallmarks of a modern state, to argue that religious

[1]This article first appeared in Reconciling Religion and Public Life: Essays on Pluralism and Fundamentalism in the United States and Germany. AICGS German-American Issues 07, 2007, 30-37. Reprinted with kind permission of AICGS, Washington DC.

education in Germany merits more than its outdated reputation can be viewed as a rather bold move. Nevertheless, the argument here is precisely that: the public nature of German religious education, where the church has only limited influence on religious education, is a model that builds a ›civil religion‹ that embraces multiple religious traditions and strives to teach tolerance through education. The challenge to the model today is to do for Islam what it has done for Christianity and Judaism—to provide Islam with an identifiable position within the public sphere and ensure that the practice of Islam in Germany occurs against the background of religious tolerance and the civic values that have shaped European nations.

## The Legal and Historical Frameworks of Religious Education in Germany

To argue that the German case is unique because of its history is not useful; religious education in all European countries reflect each country's particular historical context.

Take for instance France, which has had no religious education in its public schools since 1905, when the concept of ›laïcité‹ was adopted by the state. This concept understands religion as a private matter and consequently excludes religion as far as possible from the public sphere. In England, the system of religious education only works because of the country's state-church system. Austria has had Islamic religious education in public schools for decades because of the history of coexistence between Christians, Muslims, and Jews under the long-reigning Habsburg Monarchy.

Religious education in Germany is governed by Article 7 of the German Constitution and is therefore included in the list of constitutional articles (1-19) that outline the fundamental human rights (›Grundrechte‹) that the state is obligated to respect and to which every citizen has the right to appeal. Some argue that Article 7 on religious education should not be lumped together with articles pertaining to human rights. Others make the case that Article 7 in conjunction with Article 4, which guarantees religious freedom, is an expression of the state's respect of the freedom of religion and of parents' will in matters of religious education for their children. The essence of Article 7 is that the state has no right to impose religious beliefs on pupils in public schools.[2] Religious education is not a compulsory subject, but a voluntary one. Although Article 7:1 states that the school system in Germany is under the supervision of the state, religious education is a special case. Article 7:2 reserves for parents the

[2] It has to be noted however, that in the constitutions of the bigger German states, »awe of God« is still one of the constitutional aims of the public educational system, but this God has no confessional profile.

right to decide whether or not their children will take part in religious education. Article 7:3 rules that no teacher shall be forced to teach religious education and also determines that religious education must be taught in accordance with the principles of the religious communities being represented.

The prominent role of religious education in the German Constitution can best be understood within the historical context of the post-World War II era. The ›fathers and mother‹ of the German Constitution were deeply influenced by their experiences under the totalitarian Nazi regime. The Nazis established a political religion that was anti-pluralistic. It extinguished the Jewish religion, but also was anti-Christian. It intended to destroy and replace all traditional religions with worship of the nation. Consequently, post-war German politicians tried to keep the state free from religion. But the churches seemed well prepared to supply the public with some sort of religious common sense. And this is why is seemed plausible for the state to cooperate with the churches in the field of public religious education.

Post-war German politicians were also taking into account the historical experience of the religious wars of the seventeenth century. At the conclusion of these wars, France, Spain, and Italy remained Catholic, while Sweden, Denmark, and Norway became Lutheran. Germany, however, was and remained split between Catholic and Protestant. In order to ›keep the peace‹ domestically, German politics needed to avoid religious conflicts while also integrating the churches into the political system by offering them opportunities for cooperative engagement in education and social services.

One major development in religious education policies came in 1969, when the so-called ›Ersatzfach Ethik‹ (alternative ethics course) was created. In the late 1960s, large numbers of students, in the typically revolutionary attitude of the 1968 generation, made use of their right not to attend religious education courses. Religious education teachers complained that pupils were essentially choosing between religious education classes or the ice-cream parlor. In response, almost all German states established ethics classes as an alternative to voluntary religious education; those who chose not to take a religion class were required to attend an ethics class instead.

## ›Civilizing‹ Religion through Education

The German system of religious education gives the state the chance to influence the religious system without violating its secular neutrality. However, the mere fact that religion is taught in public schools and not in the churches deeply influences the practice of teaching religion. One might call this the state's strategy for creating civil religion through education. The state's rationale for investing money in religious education, therefore, is not motivated by charity. The state needs citizens who are well educated about religion because such citizens are better prepared to cope with the reality of religious plurality.

Although religious education is called »confessional religious education,« this description is misleading. Teachers of religious education are trained at public universities, teach other subjects in addition to religion, are supervised not by a church official but by the director of the school, and qualify as civil servants because they are employed by the state. Religious education in Germany is not a church event held in school classrooms; the churches' influence on religious education is limited, and religious education curricula are developed jointly by the churches and the state educational organizations. The churches are allowed to certify that teachers of religious education are members of the denomination about which they are teaching. Although empirical studies show that religious education teachers feel loyalty towards their religious denomination, they nevertheless keep a considerable distance to the church congregation to which they belong. Religious education teachers generally stress that the type of religious education given in public schools must be different from the way religion is taught in the churches.[3]

In addition to supervising the religious education of students in public schools, the state also oversees the education of religious education teachers and clergy at the university level. Theology departments are integral parts of German universities, and professors in these departments, just like professors in other university departments, are paid by the state. The theology departments are largely independent from the churches. Following in the traditions of liberal scholars such as Friedrich Schleiermacher, Adolf von Harnack, and Ernst Troeltsch, German theologians feel as indebted to the ideas of the Enlightenment as to the biblical tradition. When students of theology graduate from university, they have gone through an intense process of self-critical reflection on their traditions, beliefs, and attitudes. This is the impact of the so called ›historical-critical method‹, which puts the bibilical teachings into a historical perspective and which, by the way, triggered the fundamentalist religious reaction in the United States in the nineteenth century.

The integration of theology into established fields of scientific study at German universities guarantees that German religious education teachers will be able to respect and relate to different religious worldviews. Today, this training is more important than ever. A growing Muslim population in Germany is increasing demands that Islamic religious education be incorporated into the curriculum at German public schools, in accordance with the rights guaranteed by Article 7:3 of the German Constitution. Calls for the establishment of Islamic theology departments at universities are also increasing. In response, the

[3]See the empirical study of Andreas Feige and Werner Tscheetzsch: Christlicher Religionsunterricht im religionsneutralen Staat? Stuttgart 2005.

first chair for Islamic Religious Education was established at the University of Münster in 2004. Many argue that incorporating Islamic religious education in public schools would provide an alternative to religious education in the mosques, where some fear that Islamic fundamentalism is being taught.

## Aims and Standards of Religious Education: Comparing Germany and England

Public religious education sponsored or run by the state can play a valuable societal role. A comparison between religious education in Germany and England can show this. Religious education is voluntary in Germany and compulsory in England. Both countries have distinct philosophical approaches to the notion of religion and to ›teaching‹ versus ›teaching about‹ religion. In the end, however, these differences reveal to us that whether there is division or cooperation between the state and religious authorities, the stated aims of religious education are strikingly similar, and these distinct and separate paths of religious education end at the same destination: to foster inter-religious understanding.

### *Voluntary vs. Compulsory Religious Education*

In Germany, where religious education classes are voluntary, both the churches and the state emphasize that religious competence is indispensable for creating and maintaining a peaceful, pluralistic society. Education should enable pupils to participate in the modern world, and the ability to interact with a plurality of religions and worldviews is a necessary component of this view. In keeping with that spirit, the preface of the new curriculum for religious education in Berlin states: »Today, an enlightened dealing with one's own religion as well as the religion of others is important in order to make living together in a multicultural society possible. This is why religious literacy is one of the fundamental aims of religious education.«[4]

Standards for German students taking (Christian) religious education classes during their school career are designed to promote religious literacy. At various stages in their educational careers, the curriculum is designed to ensure that students grasp a number of different religiously based concepts. By the end of second grade, for example, students are expected to express their own ideas and images of God. By the end of fourth grade, students learn that there are different, even contradictory images of God and that Jesus was a Jew and comes from the Jewish tradition. At the end of sixth grade, students should be able to interpret the plurality of images of God as an expression of a plurality

[4]Grundsätze und Rahmenlehrplan. Entwurf. Evangelischer Religionsunterricht in Berlin und Brandenburg, Berlin 2006, p 2. (Translation by the author.)

of religious experiences. Eighth-grade graduates are expected to be able to express their understanding of God, to relate religion to the human life cycle, to accept different religious positions, and to understand the historical character of the biblical tradition. After completing tenth grade, students are expected to grasp the relationship between fundamental texts of the New Testament and the teachings of the churches, to understand the relevance of Christian liberty in opposition to totalitarianism, to discuss ethical issues by taking biblical advice into consideration, and to know the arguments of the critique of religion and to reflect on the correlation between faith and doubt.

When German standards are compared to the standards of religious education in England, no major differences can be discerned. At level 1, students in England

> use some religious words and phrases to recognize and name features of religious life and practice ... Pupils talk about their own experiences and feelings, what they find interesting or puzzling and what is of value and concern to themselves and others.

At level 5, pupils

> explain how religious sources are used to provide answers to ultimate questions and ethical issues, recognising diversity in forms of religious, spiritual and moral expression, within and between religions.

At the highest level

> pupils use a complex religious, moral and philosophical vocabulary to provide a consistent and detailed analysis of religions and beliefs. They evaluate in depth the importance of religious diversity in a pluralistic society. They clearly recognise the extent to which the impact of religion and belief on different communities and societies has changed over time. They provide a detailed analysis of how religious, spiritual and moral sources are interpreted in different ways, evaluating the principal methods by which religion and spirituality are studied ... They give independent, well-informed and highly reasonable insights into their own and others' perspectives on religious and spiritual issues, providing well-substantiated and balanced conclusions.[5]

It is interesting to note that religious education both in Germany, which is voluntary and taught in cooperation with the churches, and in England, where it is compulsory[6] and state-run, is designed to foster inter-religious understanding and is designed to strengthen students' ability to change perspectives and to reflect on their own and others' beliefs. While religious education in Germany begins with the religion that children were taught at home and then gradually expands their knowledge about other religions, in England, religious education focuses on comparing religions from the very beginning and ends when

[5] Level descriptions for religious education. Online at: `http://www.betterreligiouseducation.org.uk`.

[6] Parents can exempt their children from religious education classes, though.

the student is supposedly able »to synthesize« the various forms of religious expression.

*›Teaching Religion‹ vs. ›Teaching about Religion‹*

Comparing the content and aims of religious education in Germany and England, no significant difference between the German philosophy of ›teaching religion‹ and the English philosophy of ›teaching about religion‹ can be found. Differences do arise, however, when questions such as »Who attends religious education?«, »Where did religious education teachers acquire their knowledge about religion and how do they define their role,« and »Which notion of religion is used,« are asked.

Religious education in England is compulsory, while in Germany, students and their parents have the right to choose between Protestant or Catholic religious education and an ethics course. It is interesting to note that in the eastern states of Germany, about one third of the students who voluntarily attend religious education are not baptized. Their parents are of the opinion that it might be useful to learn about the history of religion and the impact of religion on culture and society, lessons they themselves were not taught under the socialist East German school system. Some parents argue that they send their child to religious education classes because they expect them to become ›decent‹ people. While this may seem a better argument for sending the child to an ethics class, religious education is percieved to do a better job of developing good habits, virtues, and values.

Religious education teachers in Germany usually teach two subjects. At the university they studied theology and another subject. High school teachers have to learn Latin and Greek and are trained in biblical literature, history of religions, systematic theology, and religious studies as well as in didactics of religion. A teacher who wants to teach Protestant religious education has to belong to a Protestant church, a Catholic teacher to the Catholic Church. In England, courses in religious education can be attended by students »who have a good honours degree in Religious Studies or Theology. However we are keen to hear from graduates in other subjects, such as Philosophy and Anthropology, where the degree has included some opportunity to examine issues related to religious beliefs.«[7] Also, graduates in Sociology or Social Studies may be considered »if they are able to provide evidence of relevant study within the context of world religions.« The religious education program at the University of Warwick invites graduates who are interested in »the diversity of religious and cultural experience in the modern world,« in »universal questions about the nature and meaning of life,« and »in contemporary spiritual, ethical and political issues.« The program is open »for graduates of all faiths or none.«

[7] Online at: `http://www.warwick.ac.uk/fac/soc/wie/itt/pgce/secondary/re`.

Although the aims of German and English religious education are similar, the ways in which they fulfill this aim are different indeed. While German religious education teachers gain a considerable familiarity with the religion they teach, religious education teachers in England may or may not have a theological background. Their interest in religion can be a purely sociological or philosophical one. While parents and students in Germany get a clear picture of the religious background and the professional training of their teachers, a teacher of religious education in England can even be an atheist. While the English religious education teacher is more or less a mediator between diverse religious traditions, the German religious education teacher is expected to identify with the religion he teaches. The German religious education teacher serves as a role model: he or she is a religious person who is able to cope with religious diversity but teaches about religion from an insider's perspective. The English religious education teacher, in contrast, looks at different religious traditions from the outside, and, in the worst cases, from above.

From the perspective of parents and their children, the German system is the more liberal one because they have the right to choose what religious tradition they will learn about, and they know the religious and theological background of the teacher. For Germans, it would seem strange for a teacher with a strong interest in ancient Germanic religion and mythology and a political right-wing orientation to teach a Jewish child about the religious meaning of the Holocaust, or for an anti-clerical socialist to explain the meaning and practice of confession to a Catholic child. It seems less than useful for a superficially informed teacher to try to instruct students on a matter as complex as religion. Every theologian knows how difficult it is to understand the nature of one's own religious culture, how much time it takes to grasp even a small part of that tradition. How can someone who does not know how religion »feels,« what the practices and doctrines of a religious tradition mean for daily life, teach about religion? How can something which is strange to the teacher be meaningfully conveyed to students?

## *The Notion of Religion*

The core differences between the German and the English systems lie in the notion of religion. The phenomenological approach presupposes that despite the diversity of religious teachings, practices, and forms, a common set of functions performed by religion can be identified. All religions raise questions about identity and belonging, meaning, purpose, truth, values, and commitments. While pupils learn about the different teachings, practices, and forms, they implicitly learn to raise questions about meaning, purpose, truth, values, and commitment. The differences between the world religions, then, are just the external form taken by a common essence. This, however, is a very Protestant approach to religion.

The German approach takes the differences between religions more seriously. Just as it is impossible to eat ›fruit,‹ but only *an* apple, *a* banana, or *a* strawberry, no one can practice ›religion‹ as such, but only one specific religion at a time. Even the best religious studies department cannot provide a point of view that describes all of the world's religions objectively, because the study of religion is automatically situated in a particular religious-cultural tradition. Therefore, the starting point for the scientific study of religion is a thorough reflection upon one's own religious tradition in order to discover its similarities to and differences from other religious cultures. Reflection on one's own ›situatedness‹ in a religious culture seems to be a more promising avenue for religious understanding than a merely superficial overview of religion.

From this perspective, the difference between ›teaching about religion‹ and ›teaching religion‹ shrinks to a minimum. The teacher who teaches about religion, as well as the teacher who teaches religion, has a distinct perspective on his topic. In other words, both types of teachers have integrated religious material into their own worldview or religion. All human beings rely on certainties about the origin, condition, and purpose of life that cannot be proven, but which are necessary for making choices and decisions. Whether connected to the idea of a deity or not, these certainties are the basis upon which judgments are made about the certainties expressed by others. A teacher teaching ›about‹ religion cannot avoid this reality; rather, teaching about religion means employing a civic religious approach, while teaching religion employs a denominational approach. Teaching about religion actually is teaching religion, but from a civic religious perspective.

The appeal of the concept of teaching about religion comes from the idea that public schools must be religiously neutral, as neutral as the state. This, however, begs the question of whether a distinction should be made between ›a public school‹ and ›a state school.‹ While the state must remain religiously neutral, religion cannot be excluded from the public sphere. A current debate in Germany concerns school development and how schools can be better integrated into their communities. Better integration with the community may mean being more interested in the religious life of the neighborhood in which a school is located. Schools should develop a profile in inter-religious communication by offering courses in the Protestant, Catholic, Jewish, and Islamic religions. As school subjects these courses are not designed to proselytize, but to give useful information about a religion and its way of relating to other religions.

## Current Challenges for Religious Education in Germany

While similar religious education structures are established in most German states—Bayern, Baden-Württemberg, Hessen, Rheinland-Pfalz, Nordrhein-Westfalen, Niedersachsen, Schleswig-Holstein, Mecklenburg-Vorpommern, Sachsen-Anhalt, Sachsen, and Thüringen—Berlin and Brandenburg follow different models. When Berlin was conquered by the Soviets in 1945, Marshal Zhukov, the Soviet commander-in-chief, ruled that religious education should be excluded from public schools. Surprisingly, the Protestant church of Berlin-Brandenburg welcomed this decision. Otto Dibelius, the Evangelical Bishop of Berlin and Brandenburg, was of the opinion that the church should become independent of the state. Since the church suffered oppression under the Nazis, he felt it should gain new autonomy and organize religious education on its own. After the division of Berlin, politicians in the West offered state cooperation with the Berlin churches on the grounds of Article 7:3, but the Protestant Church refused. The small minority of Catholics sent their children to private Catholic schools anyway. Recently, however, the Protestant Church changed its mind and asked the Berlin Senate to again establish religious education in Berlin, but the majority of Social Democrats and Socialists did not approve the proposal. Instead, a compulsory subject called ›ethics‹ was instated. The difference between Berlin's ethics course and those in other states is the compulsory character of the subject in Berlin. Religious education in Berlin is not under supervision by the state, and all religious communities have the right to use the school classrooms for such instruction.

The state of Brandenburg also refused to adopt the West German model, introducing instead a new subject called »Lebensgestaltung-Ethik-Religionskunde (LER).« The course was intended to be compulsory, but after several lawsuits were filed against the compulsory nature of the course, the state of Brandenburg decided instead to exempt children taking religious education class from the LER course. One of the reasons Brandenburg decided not to establish the West German model was the fact that only a minority of children belonged to one of the Christian churches, and religious education would have reached only that minority. Even highly committed Christians opted for LER because they wanted their children to learn about world religions and value orientation.

As a result of the refusal by Berlin and Brandenburg to establish religious education in public schools, the number of church-run private schools increased considerably. Thirty such schools exist in Berlin and Brandenburg, serving more than 5,000 students and receiving about three times as many applications for enrollment than they can accommodate. Many parents do not trust the public school system anymore. Unfortunately, this undermines one of the achievements of German public schools, namely, a social as well as religious plurality in the school community—children of different backgrounds learned to live together through their school experiences. The increase in attendance at private schools necessarily decreases the social and religious plurality in public schools and thereby, perhaps, also decreases the ability of future generations to understand and live comfortably with those of other nationalities and faiths.

With about three million Muslims now living in Germany, comprising almost four percent of the German population, the multicultural experience and understanding children have in public schools may be more important than ever. While politicians in Berlin and Brandenburg would like to provide ethics and LER instruction to children from Christian, Jewish, Muslim, atheistic, and agnostic backgrounds, the German Muslim population voices a strong desire for Islamic religious education according to Article 7:3 of the Constitution. In Berlin, the Green Party has argued that ethics courses should »relativize religion« in order to promote tolerance. Muslims, on the other hand, have argued that a religiously neutral state may not attempt to influence children in religious matters. Most German states are willing to establish Islamic religious education along the same lines as Protestant and Catholic religious education.

However, defining ›the principles of Islam‹ in the same way that the principles of Protestantism and Catholicism have long been defined remains a problem. The lack of a religious authority representing all Muslims in Germany means that the state does not have a partner with which to develop an Islamic religious education curriculum. As a first-step attempt toward creating such a partnership, many states have established committees where the most influential German Islamic associations can try to work out a commonly agreed-upon curriculum. Another next step should be the establishment of more chairs for Islamic education at German universities. It is in the best interests of the German states for the training of Islamic religious education teachers to take place in Germany. While in the past Muslim children have received religious education within the framework of ›muttersprachlichen Unterricht‹—instruction in their mother tongue, i.e. Turkish or Arabic—this meant that students were being taught about Islam from a predominantly non-German perspective. With a growing Muslim population, Germany must focus on the creation of an Islamic religious education curriculum that puts Islam into the context of German society, giving the religion and its followers an identifiable position within the public sphere and acknowledging that the practice of Islam in Germany occurs against the background of religious tolerance and the civil values that have shaped European nations.

With the successful implementation of Islamic religious education, the German system and German society can prove their ability to handle religious plurality. Unfortunately, a considerable number of Germans would like to exclude Muslim culture from the German social landscape. For example, when the German Supreme Court ruled that a Muslim teacher has the right to wear a headscarf in the classroom and that school authorities may not violate that personal and religious right, several individual German states ruled that wearing a headscarf is a political statement identifying an individual with radical Islamism and the acceptance of the violation of women's rights. Consequently, Germany may one day find itself in the paradoxical situation that a Muslim teacher teaching Islamic religious education is not allowed to wear a headscarf while doing so. Given this situation, there is a growing danger that religion will be used as a means of social exclusion. Theologians and religious historians must be called upon to remind the public that, ultimately, both Christianity and Islam can be viewed as Jewish ›heresies,‹ that is to say, both Christianity and Islam are off-shoots of the older Jewish tradition and the three religions therefore have common roots. Ensuring cooperation between different social and religious groups and fostering the integration of these groups into a sustainable, healthy society means stressing those commonalities more than the differences that are currently at the center of the debate about religious education in Germany.

## Conclusion

German religious education, with its ties to an era when secular powers determined the religious traditions of their populations, seems anachronistic in an age where the accepted paradigm is one of separation of church and state and a multi-faith approach in religious education. One of the problems with this perception lies with term »separation of church and state,« which too often is defined as the exclusion of religion from public life. This is a false interpretation. Religion has a claim on the public sphere that cannot be suppressed, as countless historical and even contemporary examples teach us.

There is, then, a role for the state in questions of religion. It is here where the German case for religious education merits serious consideration. As in civic education courses, where pupils learn to deal with their civil liberties responsibly, they also have to learn how to use their religious freedom responsibly. This education should not be totally delegated to the families and the denominations. The German system of religious education taught not in churches but in public schools is designed to create ›civilized religions‹ through education.

# How Jews Became Americans or How Religion Became a Racial and Ethnic Category—A Model for Germany?

JEFFREY M. PECK

As a traditional *Einwanderungsland*, the United States, unlike Germany, has an abundance of minorities, many of them defined in religious terms. In fact, aside from the white, Anglo-Saxon Protestants (know rather disparagingly as WASPS and usually Episcopalians) and the Germans (who were, of course, primarily Mennonite/Lutheran and Catholic), it could be said that almost everyone in the United States is a minority of some kind. Indeed, Germans, at least non-Jewish ones along with America's English forebears, as white Christians, contributed substantially to this historically dominant religious, racial, and ethnic makeup of the United States. The 21st century, however, is challenging this hegemony, as Latinos, Hispanics, and Asians of multiple religions immigrate to the United States and abundantly produce new progeny. In short, America as white and Christian is no longer to be taken for granted, and Germany has not yet learned this lesson about itself.

Even with the dominance of white Christians in the United States, however, diversity of all sorts that allows citizens to be religiously, ethnically, and racially different and simultaneously American characterizes the nation's ethos. Protestants and all their denominations, especially Evangelicals (who importantly call themselves »Christians«), Catholics (the largest religious minority), Jews, Muslims, Mormons, Christian Scientists, Jehovah's Witnesses, Buddhists, and Hindus constitute among others the religious spectrum of the country that prided itself, as the Constitution states, on freedom of worship (and the freedom to be ›American‹) institutionalized in the separation of church and state.

Intertwined with religious categories in the United States, are, of course, the very deeply embedded identifications of ethnicity and race. The attention to these richly connotative terms is necessary because their inflections of religious identity further complicate and differentiate how one identifies as a Protestant (African-American Methodist), a Catholic (Pole or Irish), an Arab Muslim, or a German or Eastern European Jew. They also provide in the German context the most challenging and, I think, the most interesting questions about how

Americans identify themselves with religious institutions or faith traditions. Consequently, the term ›minority‹ alone, or even ›religious minority‹, is not very helpful aside from providing numbers, since it does not account for the complex multiple identities that most Americans occupy in what is coming to be called a ›post-ethnic America.‹ The post-modernist urge as well that situates variable third identities in what is known as ›multiple subject positions‹ finds a fertile ground within the United States, whether this theoretical terminology is used or not.

Analogous to the changing popular culinary terminology describing America's heterogeneity religiously, ethnically, and racially as a ›melting pot‹ to the more appropriate category of a ›mosaic‹, ›salad‹, or even ›stew‹, American scholars, and not only postmodern ones, consequently now approach the issue of minorities in more differentiated ways that reflect, at least in an ethnic vocabulary, the language of hyphenated identities: Afro-American, Italian-American, Irish-American and, of course, Jewish-American. The self-identity of the latter, as much an ethnicity as a religion, and sometimes even a ›race‹, today (at approximately 6 million) makes up about 2% of the American population, is the subject of this essay. While categories such as Catholic Americans, Protestant Americans, or Christian Science Americans are used little or at least not with a hyphen, Jewish-Americans, (and increasingly after 9/11) Muslim-Americans, precisely because of how these religious traditions are affected by other forces, are granted this special status. In short, religion is only one of many factors in contemporary Jewish identity in America. And the more religion merges with ethnicity, the more the hyphen seems to signify difference.

As a scholar of transatlantic German-American relations, especially Jewish life, I want to break the conventional binary positions of studying American Jews or German Jews in isolation. I want to develop a comparative point of view on Jewish lives in the two countries, which admittedly have very different immigration histories and very different relationships to their Jewish and other minority populations. Nevertheless, I think there is something to be learned in Germany for talking about minorities in general and religious minorities in particular, when in my case, an American Jew who has just written a book on *Being Jewish in the New Germany*, turns his attention to Jewish minority identities in his own country.[1] While models of assimilation and/or integration cannot be merely transferred from one historical context to the other—in this case Jews becoming ›Americans‹ to Jews becoming ›Germans‹, I think that this juxtaposition may provide some insights—as such intercultural perspectives often do—to both the German and American sides about how minorities like the Jews became Americans and the role of religious minorities in American

[1]See J.M. Peck, Being Jewish in the New Germany, New Brunswick 2006. I quote liberally in this article and especially in the later discussion of Zafer Şenoçak from my book, 3.

life. In addition, an essay in a volume produced from a transatlantic conference on religion and politics, cannot ignore the new Jewish minority in Germany. They, who are primarily immigrants from the former Soviet Union and ironically now the third largest and fastest growing Jewish community in Europe, need to be seen in their relationship to the major German religious and ethnic minority, the Turks, and to the dominant German Christian population.

But let us begin with some important facts about American Jews. The majority of America's Jewish population came to the United States in two large waves, as reports Benny Kraut in a fascinating article entitled appropriately *Jewish Survival in Protestant America.*[2] He notes that between 1825 and 1880, 150,000 to 175,000 European Jews, three quarters of German national or cultural background arrived swelling the small American Jewish population of 4,000 in 1825 to 250,000 by 1880. The second wave was even larger—between 1880 and 1920 (when my own grandparents arrived) more than 2.1 million primarily from Russia and Russian Poland, one third of all Eastern European Jewry—a large part of which would later perish at the hands of the Nazis—brought the Jewish population of the United States to 3.5 million or 3% of the American population. It was a larger percentage then than now.

But my interest here is not in demographics, as foundational as this empirical data is, but rather the way that Jews in America from these major immigrations forward were transformed from being Jewish to being American, at least to be Jewish-Americans in a dominant Protestant America. And this question requires addressing inter-group, ethnic and racial relations and identities. Jews observed the Catholics, the other large religious immigrant minority in their midst, often in adjacent neighborhoods, or even among themselves. They saw how they built community and identity through educational, ethnic, religious and political associations, and even more importantly, drew color lines between themselves and African-Americans (called ›Negroes‹ or ›coloreds‹ at the time). Similarly, Turks in Germany today are drawing conclusions about their place in German society from what Jews in Germany have recently accomplished. They understand that while ›becoming German‹ is more than citizenship and may not be easy or even possible, the Jewish population has made strides worth emulating. These are advances that American Jews discovered in their own indigenous ways over the course of 50 years and made them a ›model minority‹, that, in fact, brought them into close relations with Blacks in the 1960s, a solidarity that has deteriorated dramatically since then. And I will return to the Turks and the Jews in Germany as I proceed to make my case about Jewish Americans and other minorities.

---

[2]B. Kraut, Jewish Survival in Protestant America, in: J. Sarna (ed.), Minority Faiths and the Protestant American Mainstream, Chicago 1998, 15-60.

My approach to Jews in American life may follow an unusual and unfamiliar trajectory for a German audience or for that matter for Americans unschooled in the recent American historical, anthropological, and cultural studies' research on identity, race, nationality, ethnicity that coalesces around what is called, ›critical race theory‹ broadly, and specifically the notion of ›whiteness.‹ Recent studies such as Eric Goldstein's *Race and the Construction of Jewish Identity in America,* 1875-1945, Karen Brodkin's, *How Jews Became White Folk. What That Says about Race in America*, Matthew Jacobsen's *Whiteness of a Different Color. European Immigrants and the Alchemy of Race*, and David Roediger's *The Wages of Whiteness. Race and the Making of the American Working Class* are some of the prominent examples. And while this volume focuses on religion and politics, the former definition of a Jew is overshadowed by these other dimensions of Jewishness whose relationship to each other are precisely unclear enough to make the issue of Jewish identity quite complicated, especially when it comes to Jewish identity formation in a country like America. In fact, in Germany and in German scholarship on the Jews, religion, ethnicity, and especially race (problematic in Germany since the term cannot be translated as *Rasse*) are understood in radically different ways than I am presenting here. Thus, it is important to understand that this difference in marking boundaries and proposing new definitions among these three prescient categories is precisely part of the problem and difference in comparing minorities in the two countries. The intellectual territory and discourse of ›being Jewish‹, rather than perhaps, being a Jew, is defined in Germany (as I learned in writing my book) and the United States in as many ways as the categories used to define it.

To discuss Jews in America, as with any minority, is to establish their relationship to a dominant population which in this case was white and predominantly Protestant. But rather than different religious practices which became more invisible with the growth of the Jewish Reform Movement (transplanted from Germany) that mimicked many Protestant styles of worship (sexes sitting together, use of English, organs and choirs, etc.), ethnicity and its relationship to race, stand out more prominently as categories of difference for the Jews. They were occupied with issues of self-definition in their new country, unlike what they experienced before their immigration where being Jewish, in the words of historian Eric Goldstein, »was an all-encompassing identity that marked them off from their non-Jewish neighbors«, especially in the shtetls (closed communities of Eastern Europe). In fact, Jewishness in America had to view other commitments and loyalties and, as a result, had to be compartmentalized. Yet, according to Goldstein, this was difficult since »no single term available in the Western World—race, nation, religion—seemed to account for all of the ways Jews continued to understand themselves.« Elaborating distinctions was primarily defined along color lines, a distinction that Germany obviously did not have, at least until Nazi racial ideology turned Jews into an ›other‹ that was essentially non-white. [Goldstein continues],

> definitions of Jewishness that did emerge—imperfect and contradictory as they may have been—were shaped decisively by the demands of the national cultures and prevailing patterns of group life in the countries where they were produced (...). The fact that Jews did not fit neatly into the categories of ›black‹ and ›white‹, however, posed a particular challenge for American Jews as they faced the question of self-definition (...). Thus, despite the fluidity of racial categorization during the immigrant period, the overarching power of [these two categories] in American culture gave Jews an opportunity to be counted as racial insiders, [in other words, as whites] in a way that remained impossible in countries such as England, France, and Germany.[3]

While ingredients were added to the ›melting pot‹, that changed in the course of the twentieth century from Europeans/Jewish immigration to massive Asian populations who become their own ›model minority‹, especially in the West, America continued to pride itself on its diverse populations. Finally in the 1960s and 1970s, the United States initiated a discourse of multiculturalism that has had less success in Germany. Jews had an anomalous position in this post 1960s multicultural world, especially post-Civil Rights legislation (1964-65) because they were torn between their traditionally liberal positions that made them want, on the one hand, to identify with oppressed African American's struggle to achieve equality and, on the other hand, to celebrate their acceptance and integration into white middle-class American society. In addition, their economic success and integration into mainstream American life seemed to exclude them from being included in the dominant multicultural discourses that became so prominent in universities. The question remained however: how white were they to be? Or in other words, where did they belong in the typical minority tug of war with dominant cultures: between assimilation/accommodation, on the one side, and resistance in order to preserve individuality and tradition on the other. While race or specifically color marked African-Americans as an ›other‹ whose integration was limited (who also, one should not forget, came involuntarily to America), Jews occupied an indeterminate and vacillating position, beholden to political, historical and cultural developments. They still remained a diaspora population in their host nation.

In order to focus this broad theoretical discussion about the transition of religious categories on ethnicity and race, I want to look more closely at just one particular institutional example that resonates in Germany, especially Berlin

[3] E.L. Goldstein, Introductory Essay. Fitting In and Standing Out. The Paradoxes of Jewish Identity in the American World of ›Difference‹, in: M.L. Raphael (ed.), ›Jewishness‹ and the World of ›Difference‹ in the United States, Williamsburg/PA 2001, 2-3.

today, where interest in studying and talking about Jews is growing.[4] I will address the institutionalization of Jewish Studies in the American university since it is a template for the anomalous position of Jews in America post-60s as a whole. Again we will see how religion plays a minor role in Jews' self-understanding, except perhaps for Orthodox Jews, and its perception by the public. As the title of an important volume called *Jews and Multiculturalism* suggests, Jews are both ›insiders‹ and ›outsiders‹ simultaneously.[5] In the 1960s and especially in the 1970s precisely because of the repercussions of the Civil Rights Act, American universities, as in Germany, a hotbed for revolution both political and educational, began to accommodate its curricula to changes external to the university, in this case to the rise of consciousness and identity of minority groups who felt their languages, cultures, and political interests were not represented in academia: Afro-American studies, Women's Studies, Chicano Studies, Asian American Studies, Gay and lesbian studies, and of course Jewish Studies programs emerged and flourished in an atmosphere of intellectual and cultural transformation. In Germany, much of this territory is occupied by American Studies. Resources flowed to these new programs: faculty were hired, students matriculated with large scholarships, and publications proliferated.

But just as outside the university, individual groups vied for resources, attention, and recognition, within the institution tensions grew among these groups as well as with the dominant more conservative powers that wanted to preserve traditional disciplines, historical canons, and from the perspective of these minority groups, white male power. The elimination of Shakespeare or Jonson from the required reading of an English department in favor of a Black African or unknown female author could create animosity and political battles akin at least in its intensity to a battle for military power. It was consequently, not surprising that these skirmishes led to what was called the ›Culture Wars‹ in the United States.

Amidst this turmoil, Jewish Studies, as the Jews in America, held a conflicted position. Indeed, Jewish Studies programs or departments flourish at literally hundreds of American universities and colleges, from large state universities to small private colleges, from prestigious Ivy League institutions to little known schools in small towns in Middle America. They are promoted and supported by university administrators and faculty (not all of them Jewish),

[4] For example, the Humboldt University in Berlin is now housing the new Leo Baeck Summer University in Jewish Studies (LBSU), an international Jewish Studies program in English that will focus on postwar and contemporary issues concerning Jewish life in Germany. www.lbsu.de.

[5] D. Biale/M. Galchinsky/S. Heschel, Insider/Outsider. American Jews and Multiculturalism, Berkeley 1998. In my opinion, this is the most important text for understanding this complex relationship and potentially its application to Germany.

as well as initiated or built by strategically thinking fund raisers or wealthy Jewish donors who want to leave a lasting legacy at a university or in their community. While religious Jewish organizations such as the campus Hillel Foundation groups spread its crusade for drawing young Jewish students primarily through religious and social events across America without any furor or even notice, the place of Jewish Studies in the multicultural map of ›ethnic studies‹ was much more contentious, proving again that ›being Jewish‹ was far more than a religious affiliation, and a far more emotional topic. Again, as an interdisciplinary program, with historians, literary critics, sociologists, theologians, philosophers, and others, Jewish Studies was no different than other such curricular newborns. But just as Jews were defined in multiple ways: as a religion, ethnicity and even race, Jewish Studies could be a stepchild in the collection of minority disciplines whose place in the university was to educate and fortify those that were oppressed, even in the American melting pot that guaranteed all minorities their rights. In short, Jews were seen as winners, not losers.

Indeed, one had to ask if the Jews were underprivileged, oppressed, or disadvantaged in post-1960s America? Of course, there was a legacy and history of anti-semitism and prejudice from their immigration to America, not to speak of their long history of persecution and flight, as well as death and destruction in Europe which even prompted Michael Lerner, the editor of the prominent progressive Jewish magazine TIKKUN to declare, »Jews are not white.« But for the American academy, like for Americans in general, the Jews were now a successful people with almost no inhibitions or limitations on their success. Quotas which once had existed at the finest Ivy League universities and restrictions to clubs or job were negligible or non-existent. Jewish Studies emerged at the same time as ethnic studies programs, but precisely for opposite reasons. Jewish Studies represented the Jews' acceptance into American society, not their rejection. Finally, in 2000, even a Democratic Vice-Presidential candidate was a Jew, and an Orthodox one at that! Had the Jews succeeded in becoming ›white‹ and accepted into the mainstream of society since color was the dividing line rather than religion? If so, while Jewish Studies could flourish anywhere on campus, why was there so much resistance to their inclusion in the multicultural curricula? In short, where did they belong?

In the introduction to the collection on multiculturalism I mention above, the editors, all prominent Jewish Studies' scholars, make a decisive claim as they differentiate mere ›cultural pluralism‹ as an American ethos represented in the early twentieth century during the highpoints of immigration to multiculturalism in the last thirty years. First, they repeat the claim I have made here about the struggle »to achieve a multicultural society in the contemporary nation state« namely, »What can and should be the role of religious, ethnic, and cultural groups in a state whose theory of citizenship is based on individuals rather than collectivities?« »How are the identities of such groups to be defined and understood in a world that has undermined all traditional identities, in which terms like *religion, ethnicity* and *culture* are constantly being torn apart and refashioned?«[6] Like Germany, where a dominant collective identity exists—white and Christian—and one in recent times recast in the questionable notion of *Leitkultur*, the United States before the 1960s could accommodate, what the editors call, »privately held ethnic identities as long as groups publicly affirmed the Anglo-Saxon character of America. But multiculturalism challenges the priority of this monolithic identity in American history, highlighting racial as well as ethnic diversity and claiming public resources on behalf of these groups.«[7] The same is slowly happening in Germany, yet the country has resisted recognizing this obvious situation.

Jews' own »double consciousness« (to use a term from the early Black activist W.E.B. DuBois) was being played out on these campuses who were making commitments to multiculturalism but were having difficulty placing Jewish Studies within this curriculum. Jews were viewed as white and part of the mainstream in America. But what about Jews in Germany and Turks as well who have even been called the »new Jews« by some observers? Are the categories discerning minorities or religious minorities applicable to the German situation?

Certainly, this discussion also prompts questioning whether these categories in Germany are not also changing based on the influx of Jews from the former Soviet Union, non-Jewish Russians and other immigrants. Even more to the point, since Turks in Germany (officially guestworkers/ *Gastarbeiter* and not immigrants) have a very different migration history than Jews to Germany, especially in comparison to the Russian Jews, can one even make legitimate comparisons? As is obvious, the Jewish relationship to Germany is fraught with persecution and genocide that does not distinguish the massive move of Turks to Germany to work from the 1960s onward. The term *Gastarbeiter* connoted a very specific legal and economic relationship to Germany that later came to characterize a social, cultural, and religious position as well. While in the minds of some people, Jews and Turks are both ›Orientals‹, and historical literature bears out the ›darkness‹ of Jews, simple comparisons do not adequately account for linking the two groups, at least not today.

The Jews in Germany, of course, according to the official *Jüdische Gemeinde,* are defined as a *Glaubensgemeinschaft* and predominantly Orthodox or Liberal. In fact, the difficulty in defining the mass of Jews from the former Soviet Union who have swelled the Jewish Community and actually saved it from extinction

[6] Op. cit., 1.

[7] Op. cit., 3.

confound the German and Jewish authorities because many if not most are not Halakichly Jewish, that means that they do not have a Jewish mother or gone through Orthodox conversion. Since the Soviet Union categorized ›Jewish‹ by paternal as well as maternal lineage, as one of many Soviet nationalities (or national minorities) within its borders on the famous fifth line of the passport, many Jews who came to Germany are recognized as Jews by the German government politically, and not by the Jewish community religiously. Many of the problems that have emerged with this immigration have been caused by these differing definitions of religious versus ethnic Jewishness as well as ethnic differences among the Jewish community itself, in this case ›German‹ versus ›Russian.‹

However, the Jewish Community remains firm in its definition of what is a Jew, although hundreds of Jewish immigrants are not able to join the Community. Some find outlets elsewhere such as the growing Reform Movement that is returning to Germany from the United States, in Chabad Lubavitch, or in the very secular *Jüdischer Kulturverein* established in the former GDR. Others simply reject the official community and, as one informant told me, continue to identify as a Jew without any religious trappings or affiliation. Like many, if not most of American Jews who do not officially belong to a synagogue, they continue being Jewish ethnically or culturally. Halakach definitions or synagogue affiliation are obviously not the only way to identify as a Jew, being Jewish is not only a religious affiliation as the new situation of Jewish life after immigration bluntly reveals.

If the question of Jewish identity still plagues Israel, the Jewish homeland itself, the problem will not be solved in Germany. However, I do think that the unique situation of a newly complicated German Jewish identity spawned from a particular immigration can raise some new perspectives about how one defines the Jewish minority. As these new Jews make a home, have children, and become Germans through citizenship, there undoubtedly will be a new hyphenated German Jewish identity, unlike the one that existed in such rich traditions and forms before the war and largely destroyed by the Holocaust. These ›new German Jews‹ will be hybrid, maintaining Russian heritage and combining it with Jewish, German and European elements. This new German Jew that will evolve in a few generations may resemble much more Jewish Americans: more secular, non-religious, and distinctively cosmopolitan, the final category particularly applicable to Jews in New York, Los Angeles, and other large urban areas. It remains to be seen, however, how the official Community will accommodate this newly constituted Jew and whether there will be an institutional home for them.

But in Germany, it is necessary perhaps for other categories to change as well in order to accommodate the hybrid, fluid, and multiple identities that characterize these new Jews and all minority identities in the United States. Especially as Germany recognizes that it is, in fact, an immigration country, perhaps it is worthwhile to rethink some of the defining categories that set off ›minorities‹ from the white Christian dominant population and contribute to linking Jews and Turks in some people's imagination, but now with a different inflection. As we know, Germany has been resistant to such changes. For a long time, for example, the only official ›minorities‹ in Germany were the Danes in Schleswig-Holstein and the Sorbs in the former East Germany. But once the term *Ausländer* has been disavowed (since most of the so-called *Ausländer* are actually *Inländer*, live in Germany or were born there) the term looses its valence as an adequate category of meaning. The term *Nicht-Deutsche*, while more neutral and less pejorative, continues to reify and instantiate binary positions of German and other that does not reflect hybridization of ethnic, religious, or even racial positions.

Perhaps it would be helpful to revisit the categories ›ethnicity‹ and even ›race‹ and ascribe some new associations or definitions to them. This discursive and semantic shift could not only break down categories of ›otherness‹ that bring prejudice and disenfranchisement, but also create more space, at least discursively, for creating more flexible identities for Jews, Turks, and other minority groups. Especially in Germany, Jews and Turks' categorization as religious minorities does not capture the most important considerations for their integration into German life, nor does it do justice to who they actually are. Clearly the notion of ›race‹, left out of the debate, has been tainted by the pernicious policies of the Third Reich, and the term ethnicity, defined only as *Ethnie*, has a narrower anthropological meaning in German than in English. In the Nazi period, secular Jews were separated from their fellow citizens with whom they identified ›ethnically‹ as Germans and Nazism changed the vocabulary of distinction catastrophically from religion to race. While in the postwar period it is understandable then why religious definitions seemed safer from ideological manipulation, perhaps it is now time in Germany to bring race and ethnicity back into the discussion with religion. Today, as Jewish religious and ethnic diversity grows, these notions account much better for the status of minorities—how they experience their everyday life—than religion alone, often defined merely by church attendance. In other words, these categories need to be released from their historically tainted moorings.

Unfortunately, few people in Germany speak about Jews and Turks in the ways that I have here. Most recently, the work of Gökçe Yurdakul, a Turkish Canadian sociologist and her collaborator Y. Michal Bodemann is shedding new light on the ways that the Turkish community draws on the experience of the Jewish Community in Germany for new political strategies.[8] Before her, stemming from a tradition where minorities of various kinds seek political solidarities, such as the Jews and Blacks in the 1960s and 1970s, and later Blacks and Latinos, American scholars of Germany and a few German Turks themselves have drawn attention to these two groups' potential relationship to each other. Zafer Senoçak, as one of the latter, speaks directly to this issue in his 1995 interview for the Berlin daily Der Tagesspiegel published in his collection as, »May one compare Jews and Turks, Mr. Senoçak?«[9] In fact, Senoçak often addresses minority issues dealing with home, belonging, and community. In Senoçak's terms a comparison is appropriate. But for Senoçak, as Leslie Adelson, his translator and editor, points out, comparisons should not be »ready made prototypes of sociological comparison«, but rather the »imaginative project of *Berührungsgeschichte*, among Germans, Turks and Jews.«[10] Adelson comments on how Senoçak confirms that these groups must come to terms with the implications of their interaction with each other's histories for their own pasts, presents, and futures. Senoçak, a Turk living in Germany, must come to terms with a »vexed German history.«[11] When he questions,

> Doesn't immigrating to Germany also mean immigrating to, entering into, the arena of Germany's recent past? (...) Even the bitter experiences that led to the [near] annihilation of the Jewish minority must be reflected upon in the conception of a multicultural Europe.[12]

Occupying the same temporal and historical space and confronting differential cultural norms and values means that Turks coincide with the traumas of German Jewish history, as well contemporary battles over identity and integration in a new Europe. While critical of Germany, at least in 1995, Senoçak is optimistic, albeit guarded,

> There is hope, in the fact that, fifty years after the nearly complete annihilation of the Jews in Germany, there are once more citizens of

[8]Cf. J.M. Peck, Jews and Turks. Discourses of the ›Other‹, in: Id., Being Jewish in the New Germany, op. cit. (n. 1); and more recently, the work of G. Yurdakul/M. Bodemann, We Don't Want to Be the Jews of Tomorrow. Jews and Turks in Germany after 9/11, in: German Politics and Society 24/2 (2006), 44-67. Reprint: M. Laskier (ed.), Bridging the Worlds of Judaism and Islam, Florida. G. Yurdakul, State, Political Parties and Immigrant Elites. Turkish Immigrant Associations in Berlin, in: Journal of Ethnic and Migration Studies 32/3 (2006), 435-453; M. Bodemann/G. Yurdakul, Geborgte Narrative. Wie sich türkische Einwanderer an den Juden in Deutschland orientieren [Borrowed Narrative: How Turkish Immigrants Orient Themselves After Jews in Germany], in: Soziale Welt 56 (2005), 441-452. English version: M. Bodemann (ed.), German Jewry in the European Context, London. (forthcoming)

[9]Z. Senoçak, Atlas of a Tropical Germany. Essays on Politics and Culture 1990-1998, translated and edited by L. Adelson, Lincoln 2001, 53-57.

[10]Loc. cit.

[11]Loc. cit.

[12]Op. cit, 6.

> Jewish faith there. That there can be something like a Turk who is Muslim, but also a German citizen. The hope that people of Italian, Greek, Turkish, and Arab descent can communicate with each other in German in Germany and are citizens, from my perspective, is still a utopia.[13]

Now almost a decade later, the German immigration law has changed and a third and even fourth generation of Turk resides in Germany. There are 2.3 million Turks in Germany, 28% of the 7.3 million foreigners. Only a small number have become citizens. In 1999, there were approximately 298,000 Turks with German citizenship and 41,000 in Berlin alone. It remains to be seen in the future how Jews and Turks may work together, be it in political lobbying against discrimination or through multicultural events that demonstrate that there are different ways to be German. Today in the context of September 11 and the Middle East conflicts that might pit Jews against Muslim Turks in Germany, it is gratifying that the Turkish community supported the Jewish community during the Jürgen Möllemann debate on anti-semitism as well as in 2004 after the Istanbul synagogue bombing. They continue to reach out to the Jews just as Ignatz Bubis and Paul Spiegel, both presidents of the Jewish Community, appeared at Turkish rallies against discrimination. Increasingly, prominent conservative Jews such as Michael Wolffsohn are calling for more collaboration,

> Germany's Jews need now an important strategic partner who stands outside of party lines. They would find such a partner in the German Turkish community. As we are, they are a minority (substantially larger than us). They are pro-Western, market oriented, and reject Islamism, precisely because they are Muslims.[14]

However, as the violent response to the Danish cartoons of the prophet Mohammed in 2006 reminded us, Senoçak's optimism may have to be tempered by the realities of a factionalized Muslim population in Europe who are not as sensitive or interested in European Jews, much less Israelis and their policies. As the growing European Union also struggles with Turkish ascension, each country must examine not only its attitudes towards Muslims, but also its own historical treatment of all minorities. Each will also have to find ways today to integrate disparate groups of immigrants, minorities, and other subjugated communities in their double national and European identities. This integration will have to recognize the »discourse of the other« in the Turkish German Senoçak's terms,

> Integration is not achieved when the differences of others are used to consolidate one's own image of the world. For real integration one must

[13] Op. cit., 56-57.

[14] M. Wolffsohn, Allein auf weiter Flur. Nach der Bundestagwahl. Juden fühlen sich von keiner Partei vertreten, in: JÜDISCHE ALLGEMEINE WOCHENZEITUNG, 25. September 2002.

> cultivate, in encounters with others, a sense for multiplicity and contradiction. In the process one would have to analyze sources of knowledge beyond preconceived opinions and identities. Disparate factors would have to be deciphered as a precondition for an encounter.[15]

These encounters, like the Turkish Jewish in Germany, will force these countries and their minorities to disentangle their individual histories from the dominant national narratives that in many cases are still being written and revised. We have seen Afro- and Native Americans, as Jews before them, demand to be recognized as part of the national chronicle. Although these stories become increasingly complex and often contradictory, this difficult process will produce more open societies that understand themselves as composed of ›others‹ who offer alternative versions of national and ethnic identities. We can only hope that there will be space enough for multiple stories to be told.

What I have tried to do here, at least structurally and discursively, is to draw attention to the ways that categories such as minority, religion, ethnicity, and race need to be unpacked for their historical and ideological underpinnings. To be sure, the German situation around minorities does not resemble the American for reasons that we know. However, it is necessary to address the terms of discussion, the categories of definition used in both debates, and to recognize at least how particular definitions determine not only the outcome, but also the process. As Americans, now governed under the second Bush administration (even after the Republican Congressional defeat of 2006) come to terms with their own confusion about categories and their relationships such as the separation of church and state, they too can benefit from hearing European perspectives on these debates and the ways they frame them. In the United States today, the invocation of religion, belief, and moral values, even by Democrats, figures prominently in public discourse in ways that seem strange to many Americans who prefer the strict separation of Church and State. In his new book *Divided by God. America's Church-State Problem—And What We Should Do About It*, Noah Feldman argues that

> the United States has always been home to striking religious diversity (...). At the same time we strive to be a nation with a common identity and a common project. Religious division threatens this unity.[16]

Ironically, while America may have done better with recognizing ethnic and racial minorities, the Bush policies threaten to destroy the cherished freedom of religious diversity guaranteed in our Constitution. Increasingly, being a Christian, and a particular kind of Christian at that, rather than a Catholic, a Jew, or a Muslim weighs more heavily in one's favor when it comes to making

---

[15] Z. Senoçak, op. cit. (n. 9), 93.

[16] N. Feldman, Divided by God. America's Church-State Problem—And What We Should Do About It, New York 2005, 8.

claims about politics, religion, ethnicity, or race. In America, the danger is that religion may become the divisive factor of the future. In Germany, it is ethnicity and race that need to be addressed more seriously. Clearly, both countries have something to learn from the other in a transatlantic dialogue that needs to remain open on both sides.

# Christlich-jüdischer Dialog sechzig Jahre nach der Shoah

DAGMAR PRUIN

## 1. Einleitung und Standortbestimmung

Im Zusammenhang unserer Thematik »Jüdisches Leben in Deutschland« werde ich Ihnen im Folgenden Themen und Einsichten aus dem christlich-jüdischen Dialog in Deutschland vorstellen.

Die Wahl dieses Zuganges eröffnet Chancen und begrenzt gleichermaßen. Ich spreche über das Judentum in Deutschland aus einer ganz bestimmten Perspektive. Ich spreche gerade *nicht* über Juden und *Deutsche*—sondern über den Dialog zwischen Juden und *Christen*. Es stellt ein Wesensmerkmal des Judentums dar, dass sich Religion und Nation nicht voneinander trennen lassen. Die Gegenüberstellung von Juden und Deutschen kann—wie es Rolf Schieder betont hat—*zivilreligiös* durchaus angemessen sein.[1] Jeffrey M. Peck insistiert aus seiner Perspektive, dass sich Jüdinnen und Juden in Deutschland nicht primär unter die Kategorie der Religion, als vielmehr unter die der Ethnizität subsumieren sollten.[2] Mein *theologisch* orientierter Zugang ist ein anderer, wobei hier nicht allein—wenn auch vorrangig—die Disziplin, sondern auch die Nationalität die Begründung für die Wahl des Blickes darstellt. Angesichts der deutschen Geschichte bin ich zurückhaltend mit Blick auf eine Gegenüberstellung von Juden und Deutschen und in diesem Zusammenhang erscheint auch der Begriff der Ethnizität weitaus komplizierter als im US-amerikanischen Kontext. Gleichzeitig aber—und dieser Problematik bin ich mir bewusst—reduziere ich mit meinem Zugang das Judentum auf seine religiöse Dimension, obwohl sich die Mehrheit der heute in Deutschland lebenden Jüdinnen und Juden als säkular versteht.[3] Daher bin ich froh, dass der interdisziplinäre Charakter unseres Projektes eine Kombination verschiedener Perspektiven ermöglicht.

Zum Abschluss meines Beitrages werde ich Ihnen einige Überlegungen zum *interreligiösen Dialog* überhaupt mit einer besonderen Perspektive auf den Is-

---

[1] Vgl. R. Schieder, Wieviel Religion verträgt Deutschland?, Frankfurt/M. 2001, 143ff.

[2] Vgl. den voranstehenden Aufsatz: J.M. Peck, How Jews Became Americans or How Religon Became a Racial and Ethnic Category—A Model for Germany? und ders., Being Jewish in the New Germany, New Brunswick u.a. 2006.

[3] Im November 2006 haben die jüdischen Gemeinden in Deutschland rund 108.000 Mitglieder, davon sind mehr als zwei Drittel nach 1989 aus der ehemaligen Sowjetunion eingewandert. Vgl. das SPIEGEL-Interview »Öffnung zur Gegenwart« mit Salomon Korn im SPIEGEL-Spezial »Weltmacht Religion. Wie der Glaube Politik und Gesellschaft beeinflusst«, 22. November 2006, 92-95.

lam vorstellen. Die Forderung nach einem solchen ist angesichts der heutigen politischen Lage in aller Munde, gleichzeitig bleibt aber im öffentlichen Diskurs oft mehr als unscharf, was tatsächlich darunter zu verstehen ist. »Akzeptanz« und »Offenheit«—um nur zwei der beliebtesten Schlagworte aufzugreifen—sind zwar Grundbedingungen für das interreligiöse Gespräch, aber darin kann es sich nicht erschöpfen.

## 2. Aspekte der Wahrnehmung von Juden durch Christen

»Dem christlich-jüdischen Gespräch kann man sich als Christ relativ leicht entziehen, dem christlich-jüdischen Verhältnis nicht.«[4] Der christliche Glaube muss sich zum Judentum positionieren, denn diese Verhältnisbestimmung, wie sie auch immer aussehen mag, ist ein untrennbarer Topos christlicher Theologie. Die größere Hälfte ihrer Heiligen Schrift, das Alte Testament bzw. die Hebräische Bibel, bindet das Christentum mit dem Judentum zusammen, der kleinere Teil, das *Neue Testament*, läßt die Wege auseinander gehen und bezieht sich doch dabei ständig auf die jüdische Lebenswelt. »Der Glaube Jesu einigt uns (...), aber der Glaube an Jesus trennt uns«—in diesem Ausspruch des jüdischen Theologen Schalom Ben-Chorin sind die Verhältnisse in aller Kürze auf den Punkt gebracht.[5]

Überblickt man die christliche, d. h. in diesem Fall die *abendländische* Kirchengeschichte, stellt das Gefühl der Überlegenheit gegenüber dem Judentum eine der Grundlinien der christlichen Theologie dar. So wird das Judentum weit verbreitet als eine Vorläuferreligion zum Christentum verstanden. Die Christenheit als das ›wahre Israel‹ ersetzt im Neuen Bund Israel als Partner Gottes.[6] Das Alte Testament wird herabgewürdigt und verkörpert als das ›Gesetz‹ angeblich einen vom ›Evangelium‹ überwundenen Gottesbegriff und Heilsweg. Damit wird die jüdische Gemeinschaft zu einer Größe der Vergangenheit.[7]

---

[4] P. von der Osten-Sacken, Zum gegenwärtigen Stand des jüdisch-christlichen Dialogs und seinen Perspektiven, in: R. Kampling/M. Weinrich (Hg.), Dabru Emet—Redet Wahrheit. Eine jüdische Herausforderung zum Dialog mit den Christen, Gütersloh 2003, 206-218, hier 206.

[5] Sch. Ben-Chorin, Bruder Jesus. Der Nazarener in jüdischer Sicht, München 1974, 12 (Hervorhebung D.P.).

[6] Vgl. zu diesem so genannten Substitutionsmodell und anderen Verhältnisbestimmungen der Kirche gegenüber dem Judentum D. Ritschl, Die nie verheilende Wunde. Kirche/Israel—Christen/Juden, in: ders., Theorie und Konkretion in der Ökumenischen Theologie. Kann es eine Hermeneutik des Vertrauens inmitten differierender semiotischer Systeme geben?, Münster 2003, 71-76.

[7] Vgl. dazu von der Osten-Sacken, Zum gegenwärtigen Stand (Anm. 4), 206.

Darüber hinaus war praktischer christlicher Antijudaismus eine mögliche und tatsächliche Begleiterscheinung christlicher Theologie.[8] Theologische Überlegungen, die das Judentum nicht nur abwerten, sondern Israel als Gottesmörder an den Pranger stellten, finden sich bereits im 2. nachchristlichen Jahrhundert.[9] Biblische Verse wie das Wort aus der Passionsgeschichte des Matthäus in 27, 25—»Sein Blut komme über uns und unsere Kinder«—boten die Grundlage für die These einer Kollektivschuld aller Juden am Tod Jesu Christi.[10]

Die Anknüpfungspunkte für diesen Antijudaismus finden sich—wie dieser Zusammenhang beispielhaft zeigt—bereits im Neuen Testament, also in den Schriften, die einen Teil der christlichen Heiligen Schrift bilden und das macht die Sachlage so problematisch.[11] Denn die Schilderung des Heilsgeschehens von Tod und Auferstehung Jesu Christi und das Bild, das von den Juden hier gezeichnet wird, werden unter gewissen Bedingungen von Religion und Politik im Römischen Reich an der Schwelle zum 2. nachchristlichen Jahrhundert dargeboten.

Ein genauerer Blick auf die jahrzehntelange Entstehungsgeschichte des Neuen Testaments kann hier weiterhelfen. Die Briefe des Paulus entstanden in der Mitte des 1. nachchristlichen Jahrhunderts, die Evangelien erst einige Jahrzehnte später. So wurde das Markusevangelium erst um die Zeit der Tempelzerstörung durch die Römer im Jahre 70 n. Chr. geschrieben, das Evangelium des Johannes erst ein halbes Jahrhundert später. Vergleicht man nun die Passionsdarstellungen der Evangelien unter chronologischen Gesichtspunkten, so ist eine steigende Feindseligkeit den Juden gegenüber unverkennbar. Die Erklärung hierfür liegt in den Zeitumständen ihrer Entstehung begründet, denn es lagern sich hier zwei unterschiedliche geschichtliche Ebenen übereinander. In der ersten Ebene, den Jerusalemer Ereignissen um den Tod Jesu von Nazareth, spiegelt sich die zweite Ebene—der Konflikt zwischen Juden und Christen zur

[8] Terminologisch unterscheide ich zwischen einem religiös argumentierenden Antijudaismus und einem rassistisch, biologisch, ökonomisch oder sozial argumentierenden Antisemitismus.

[9] Der Vorwurf des Gottesmordes wird zuerst ca. 180 n.Chr. durch den Bischof Melito von Sardes in einer poetisch strukturierten Predigt über das Passah formuliert. »Der die Erde aufhing, ist aufgehängt worden; Der die Himmel festmachte, ist festgemacht worden; Der das All festigte, ist am Holze befestigt worden. Der Herr—ist geschmäht worden; Der Gott—ist getötet worden; Der König Israels—ist beseitigt worden von Israels Hand. O des unerhörten Mordes! O des unerhörten Unrechts!«, zitiert nach Melito von Sardes, Vom Passa. Die älteste christliche Osterpredigt. Übersetzt, eingeleitet und kommentiert von J. Blank, Sophia, Quellen östlicher Theologie Bd. 3, hg.v. Julius Tyciak und Wilhelm Nyssen, Freiburg i.Br. 1963, 127f.

[10] So bereits im 2. nachchristlichen Jahrhundert bei Tertullian, adv. Jud 8,18; 10,9 (CCL 2,1363; 1377).

[11] Vgl. hierzu W. Kraus, Neues Testament und christlich-jüdisches Gespräch, in: Lernen auf Zukunft hin. Einsichten des christlich-jüdischen Gesprächs—25 Jahre Studium in Israel. Im Auftrag des Arbeitskreises von »Studium in Israel e.V.« hg.v. K. Kriener und B. Schröder in Verbindung mit E.M. Dörrfuß, Neukirchen-Vluyn 2004, 72-84.

Zeit der Evangelisten und der Beginn der Christenverfolgungen durch den römischen Staat. Auf dem Hintergrund der Trennung der Kirche von der Synagoge und in dem Bemühen darzustellen, dass Pilatus, der Römer, an Jesus *keine* Schuld fand (vgl. etwa Joh 18, 38), entstanden die späteren Darstellungen.

Werden diese Entstehungshintergründe jedoch nicht aufgedeckt, so besteht die Gefahr, dass das verzeichnete Bild der Juden im Neuen Testament den Blick auf das Judentum prägt—vor allem dort, wo—wie in Deutschland, anders als in den USA—kaum Begegnung mit dem lebendigen Judentum stattfindet. Diese Gefahr ist insbesondere auch dann gegeben, wenn in stärker fundamentalistischen Kreisen, wie sie nun wiederum in den USA weit verbreitet sind, die oben vorgestellten Ebenen per se nicht unterschieden werden, da dieses nur mit den Mitteln der hier nahezu immer abgelehnten historisch-kritischen Bibelwissenschaft zu leisten ist.[12] Mel Gibsons Film »The Passion of Christ«gehört in die Linie dieser problematischen Rezeption des Neuen Testaments, insofern dort eine harmonisierende Fassung der Passionsgeschichten des Neuen Testaments, die noch über den geschilderten Charakter der Evangelien hinausgeht, als historisches Geschehen ausgegeben wird.

## 3. Christlich-jüdischer Dialog in den evangelischen Kirchen in Deutschland nach der Shoah—Theologie nach Auschwitz

Mit meinem nächsten Punkt nehme ich einen Perspektivenwechsel vor. Ich werde weder die Kirchengeschichte durch die Jahrhunderte verfolgen, noch die Ereignisse im Dritten Reich fokussieren. Mit einigen Ausnahmen, die trotz allem nicht vergessen werden dürfen, begegnet eine Geschichte von Schuldverstrickung auf christlicher Seite.

Stattdessen richte ich meinen Blick auf den protestantisch/christlich-jüdischen Dialog *nach* der Shoah. Betrachtet wird also eine Zeit, in der Kreise protestantischer Christinnen und Christen zu erkennen und formulieren begannen, zu welchen Konsequenzen nicht allein der säkulare Antisemitismus, sondern auch der religiöse Antijudaismus geführt hatte.

Der christlich-jüdische Dialog ist ein weites Feld. Christen setzen sich aus ganz unterschiedlichen und nicht immer unproblematischen Gründen mit dem Judentum auseinander oder für Israel ein.[13] So geht die nachhaltige Unter-

[12]»Fundamentalismus« ist in der amerikanischen Geschichte zunächst als Glaube an die Irrtumslosigkeit der Schrift in Ablehnung der historisch-kritischen Bibelwissenschaft definiert worden. Der Begriff ist aus der 1910 ins Leben gerufenen Schriftenreihe »The Fundamentals« entlehnt. Vgl. R.C. Neville, Religion, Fundamentalismus und die Politik des Weißen Hauses, in: St. Alkir/H. Deuser/G. Linde (Hg.), Religiöser Fundamentalismus. Analysen und Kritiken, Tübingen 2005, 63-79, bes. 66ff.

[13]Stellvertretend gebe ich hier die Argumentation des einflussreichen Fernsehpredigers und Gründers des Christian Broadcasting Network Pat Robertson wieder, der sich in der Diskus-

stützung der »Religious Right« in den USA für Israel oft—wenn auch nicht einschließlich—einher mit einer zutiefst antijüdischen Theologie.

Es gibt nicht *das* Christentum oder *das* Judentum und entsprechend auch nicht den *einen* Dialog, sondern vielmehr Themen, die das Verhältnis von Christen und Juden betreffen, und Menschen, die sich mit diesen Themen beschäftigen. Es ist der Dialog derer, die sprechen, und nicht derer, die nicht sprechen wollen oder nicht zu Wort kommen. Dass auf der Seite der evangelischen Kirchen nahezu alle Landeskirchen bzw. deren Synoden Verlautbarungen zu diesem Thema abgegeben haben, darf nicht darüber hinwegtäuschen, dass sich viele Mitglieder dieser Kirchen nicht darin wieder finden. Jedes Konsens-Ergebnis ist nur begrenzt repräsentativ. Dies gilt verstärkter noch auf jüdischer Seite, wo es vereinzelte jüdische Gesprächspartner waren, die den Dialog stützten und trugen, aber viele sich aus unterschiedlichen Gründen gerade nicht am Dialog beteiligten. Von da auf Judentum und evangelische Kirche in ihrer Gesamtheit zu schließen, wäre völlig verfehlt. Gleichwohl erachte ich den Dialog aus meiner—christlichen—Perspektive als ermutigenden Anfang—wenn auch noch längst nicht alle Ziele eingelöst sind.

Daher sollte der hier verwendete Singular nicht als Hinweis auf eine monolithische Struktur verstanden werden. Gleichwohl sind im protestantisch/christlich-jüdischen Dialog Linien zu erkennen, die ich im Folgenden nachzeichnen werde.[14] Dabei geht es mir nicht allein aber vor allem um die Auswirkungen des Dialogs mit dem Judentum auf das Selbstverständnis der christlichen Kirchen, denn das ist die Perspektive über die ich angemessen sprechen kann.

Beleuchtet man die Geschichte dieses Dialogs, so sind vier verschiedene Phasen zu erkennen.[15] Die ersten drei schildere ich als abgeschlossen, die vierte Phase stellt die Gegenwart dar und prägt nicht zuletzt die Perspektive, aus der ich die früheren Verhältnisse darlege. Hier ist jedoch die Ebene der Gleich-

---

sion um den Friedensfahrplan für den Nahen Osten, der so genannten Road Map, 2003, für Jerusalem als ungeteilte jüdische Hauptstadt einsetzt. Wer hier anders agiere, lege sich—so Roberts—mit der Macht und dem Wort Gottes an. Erst wenn die Juden nach Zion zurückkehrten und den Tempel wieder errichteten, sei der Grundstein für das zweite Kommen Christi gelegt. Das bedeutet dann jedoch gleichzeitig für die Juden wie für die anderen Ungläubigen den Tod. Vgl. dazu H. Finemann/T. Lipper, A Very Mixed Marriage, Newsweek June 2, 2003. In Deutschland gibt es ebenfalls starke evangelikale Kreise, die in eine ähnliche Richtung argumentieren. Sie sind jedoch hier nur eine kleine Minderheit, während die Evangelikalen in den Vereinigten Staaten eine auch politisch einflussreiche größere Gruppe darstellen.

[14]Für den christlich-jüdischen Dialog der katholischen Kirche in Deutschland vgl. D. Mensink, Christlich-jüdischer Dialog und katholische Kirche in Deutschland, in: Lernen auf Zukunft hin (Anm. 11), 155-165.

[15]Vgl. zu den ersten drei Phasen B. Petersen, Theologie nach Auschwitz? Jüdische und christliche Versuche einer Antwort. Mit einem Vorwort von O.H. Pesch, VIKJ Bd. 24, Berlin 1996, 32ff. Petersen stützt sich dabei auf die Überlegungen Rolf Rendtorffs und Eberhard Bethges.

zeitigkeit des Ungleichzeitigen zu beachten. Ich fasse den akademischen Dialog in den Blick, der in ganz bestimmten Kreisen geführt wurde. Geht es darum, die Ergebnisse des Dialogs einer größeren Öffentlichkeit zu vermitteln oder in breiteren Kreisen der Kirche umzusetzen, kann sich die Sachlage ganz anders darstellen.

1. Die *Nachkriegsphase* war geprägt von moralischer Betroffenheit, wie sie beispielsweise der Rat der EKD 1945 im Stuttgarter Schuldbekenntnis gegenüber Vertretern des Ökumenischen Rates der Kirchen formulierte.[16] Gleichzeitig jedoch wird in diesem Dokument wohl symptomatisch für die Verhältnisse der damaligen Zeit weder explizit eine Mitschuld der Kirchen an den Verbrechen des Nationalsozialismus benannt, noch werden die Verbrechen am jüdischen Volk ausdrücklich erwähnt. Die Möglichkeit, dass die christliche Theologie des Judentums zu überprüfen sei, lag zu dieser Zeit wohl außerhalb des Blickfeldes. Fünf Jahre später zeigte die Synode der Evangelischen Kirche in Deutschland in ihrem »Wort zur Judenfrage« erste Ansätze eines neuen theologischen Nachdenkens über das Verhältnis der Kirche zum Judentum, indem betont wird, »dass Gottes Verheißung über dem von ihm erwählten Volk Israel auch nach der Kreuzigung Jesu Christi in Kraft geblieben ist«[17]. Dieses Dokument benennt eine passive Schuld der Kirchen an der Shoah.[18]

1948 wurden auf Initiative der amerikanischen Besatzungsmacht in Deutschland im Kontext der *reeducation* verschiedene Standorte der »Gesellschaft für Christlich-Jüdische Zusammenarbeit« in Leben gerufen und 1949 auch deren Koordinierungsrat in Bad Nauheim.[19] Aber von einem tatsächlichen Dialog

[16]»Durch uns ist unendliches Leid über viele Länder und Völker gebracht worden (...). Wohl haben wir lange Jahre hindurch im Namen Jesu Christi gegen den Geist gekämpft, der im nationalsozialistischen Gewaltregiment seinen furchtbaren Ausdruck gefunden hat; aber wir klagen uns an, daß wir nicht mutiger bekannt, nicht treuer gebetet, nicht fröhlicher geglaubt und nicht brennender geliebt haben.« Das Dokument ist abgedruckt in R. Rendtorff/H.H. Henrix (Hg.), Die Kirchen und das Judentum. Dokumente von 1945-1985, Paderborn/München 1987, 528-529, hier 528.

[17]Das Dokument findet sich bei Rendtorff/Henrix, Die Kirchen und das Judentum (Anm. 16), 548f. hier 549.

[18]»Wir sprechen es aus, dass wir durch Unterlassen und Schweigen vor dem Gott der Barmherzigkeit mitschuldig geworden sind an dem Frevel, der durch Menschen unseres Volkes an den Juden begangen worden ist.« Vgl. Rendtorff/Henrix, Die Kirchen und das Judentum (Anm. 16), 549.

[19]Bei aller Schuldgeschichte und Schuldverstrickung auf christlicher Seite musste in den Gesellschaften für Christlich-Jüdische Zusammenarbeit (GCJZ) nicht vollständig neu begonnen werden. Es waren auch Menschen beteiligt, die sich in Deutschland bereits vor 1933 bemüht hatten, eine andere Praxis und Theologie mit dem Judentum zu leben und die in der Zeit des Nationalsozialismus an der Seite von Juden standen. Vgl. dazu M. Stöhr, Notwendigkeiten und Schwierigkeiten einer Christlich-jüdischen Zusammenarbeit, in: C. Münz/R.W. Sirsch (Hg.): »Wenn nicht ich, wer? Wenn nicht jetzt, wann?«. Zur gesellschaftspolitischen Bedeutung des Deutschen Koordinierungsrates der Gesellschaften für Christlich-Jüdische Zusammenarbeit, Forum Christen und Juden Bd. 5, Münster 2004, 30-106.

lässt sich zu dieser Zeit nicht sprechen. Die wenigen jüdischen Menschen, die in Deutschland zu diesem Zeitpunkt lebten, hatten mit anderen Schwierigkeiten zu kämpfen!

2. Dieses änderte sich seit den *sechziger Jahren.* Auf dem evangelischen Kirchentag in Berlin 1961 wurde die Arbeitsgemeinschaft »Christen und Juden« begründet und in den Akademien erste Versuche christlich-jüdischer Begegnung begründet. Kennzeichen dieses Dialoges war eine große personelle Kontinuität. Ohne diese Beständigkeit auf beiden Seiten wäre die notwendige Vertrauensbildung kaum möglich gewesen. Interreligiöser Dialog bedeutet zunächst einmal das Hören aufeinander. Die Gespräche waren nicht einfach und konnten es auch gar nicht sein, umso dankbarer war man auf christlicher Seite dafür, dass es in jener konkreten historischen Situation jüdische Gesprächsteilnehmer gab, die sich der Situation aussetzten.

Gleichzeitig aber waren diese Gespräche von einer eindrücklichen Asymmetrie auf unterschiedlichen Ebenen geprägt: Wenige jüdische Gesprächspartner saßen einem ganzen Saal voll Christinnen und Christen gegenüber, die sich damit auseinander setzen mussten, dass die eigene Theologie in Schuld an dem Schicksal der jüdischen Gegenüber verstrickt war. Die Kommunikationsvoraussetzungen waren völlig ungleich—das Verhältnis von Mehrheit und Minderheit in der konkreten Begegnung spiegelte und spiegelt die Verhältnisse in Deutschland überhaupt wider. Darüber hinaus ist auch das theologische Interesse asymmetrisch. Wie bereits angedeutet, muss sich das Christentum in theologischer Perspektive mit dem Judentum auseinandersetzen, um seine Identität zu verstehen. Dieses gilt umgekehrt nicht in der gleichen Weise—die Auseinandersetzung mit dem Christentum gehört nicht in das Zentrum der jüdischen Theologie. »Das Judentum muss sich nicht mit dem Christentum auseinandersetzen, um sich selbst und seine Identität zu begreifen.«[20]

Eine asymmetrische Struktur—wenn auch in modifizierter Form—prägt den Dialog bis heute.

3. Nachdem sich der jüdisch-christliche Dialog auf den Kirchentagen und in den Akademien an den Rändern bewegt hatte, begann in den *achtziger und neunziger Jahren* des letzten Jahrhunderts eine dritte Phase. Sie ist gekennzeichnet durch die Verabschiedung synodaler Verlautbarungen. Den Anfang und Grundstein legte die Synode der Evangelischen Kirche im Rheinland, eine der größten Landeskirchen in Deutschland, mit dem Synodalbeschluss zur Erneuerung des Verhältnisses von Christen und Juden vom 11. Januar 1980;

[20] M. Stöhr, Das Bekenntnis zu dem einen Gott in der Vielfalt der Gottesbilder bei Juden, Christen und Muslimen. Beobachtungen im christlich-jüdischen und im christlich-islamischen Dialog—Fragen und Thesen, in: R. Weth (Hg.), Das Bekenntnis zu dem einen Gott? Christen und Muslime zwischen Mission und Dialog, Neukirchen-Vluyn 2000, 90-97, hier 91.

»Nicht du trägst die Wurzel, sondern die Wurzel trägt dich«.[21] Viele Erklärungen anderer Landeskirchen sind ihr gefolgt und haben einzelne Aussagen leicht modifiziert. Die Grundlinien blieben jedoch dieselben. Da hier nicht der Platz für eine umfassende Analyse aller Topoi sein kann, konzentriere ich mich auf den Ausgangspunkt der Erklärung und werde anschließend einige weitere neuralgische Punkte aufzeigen.[22]

Der Text bestimmt seinen Ausgangspunkt nach den einleitenden Worten unter 1. in 2.1. mit der Shoah.[23]

> In Übereinstimmung mit dem ›Wort an die Gemeinden zum Gespräch zwischen Christen und Juden‹ der Landessynode der Evangelischen Kirche im Rheinland vom 12. Januar 1978 stellt sich die Landessynode der geschichtlichen Notwendigkeit, ein neues Verhältnis der Kirche zum jüdischen Volk zu gewinnen. 2. Vier Gründe veranlassen die Kirche dazu: (1.) Die Erkenntnis christlicher Mitverantwortung und Schuld an dem Holocaust, der Verfemung, Verfolgung und Ermordung der Juden im Dritten Reich.

---

[21]Der gesamte Text des Synodalbeschlusses findet sich bei: K. Kriener/J.M. Schmidt (Hg.), Gottes Treue—Hoffnung von Christen und Juden. Die Auseinandersetzung um die Ergänzung des Grundartikels der Kirchenordnung der Evangelischen Kirche im Rheinland, Neukirchen-Vluyn 1998, 24-41.

[22]So würde etwa die Diskussion des Unterpunktes 1.3., in dem die Errichtung des Staates Israel ein »Zeichen der Treue Gottes gegenüber seinem Volk« genannt wird, eine ganz eigene Darstellung im Horizont der Verhältnisbestimmung von Religion und Politik erfordern. Vgl. dazu M. Bongardt, Christen können den Anspruch des jüdischen Volkes auf das Land Israel respektieren, in: Kampling/Weinrich (Hg.), Dabru Emet—Redet Wahrheit (Anm. 4), 94-102. Interessanterweise sind die Erklärungen im US-amerikanischen Kontext mit Blick auf den Staat Israel oft weitaus zurückhaltender als die deutschen. Möglicherweise hängt dies mit der einseitigen Unterstützung Israels in den evangelikalen Kreisen zusammen.

[23]Bewusst wird hier der Begriff Shoah (neuhebräisch für ›Katastrophe‹oder ›Untergang‹, vgl. auch bereits alttestamentlich beispielsweise Hiob 30,3) und nicht Holocaust gewählt. Der Begriff ›Holocaust‹ steht seit der gleichnamigen US-amerikanischen Fernsehserie aus dem Jahre 1978 für die millionenfache Ermordung von Jüdinnen und Juden und anderer Opfergruppen in Europa. Theologisch ist diese Bezeichnung jedoch nicht unproblematisch. Der Begriff leitet sich von dem griechischen Wort *holocautōma*—die Übersetzung der Septuaginta für den hebräischen Begriff ʿola. Mit diesem Wort werden im Alten Testament Ganzopfer, die verbrannt werden, bezeichnet (vgl. L. Koehler/W. Baumgartner, Hebräisches und aramäisches Lexikon zum Alten Testament Bd. 3, 786), so etwa Lev 16,5. Die Bezeichnung ›Holocaust‹ stellt damit die Auslöschung jüdischen Lebens in einen religiösen Kontext und lässt die Assoziation einer Opferung oder Selbstopferung zu. Aufgenommen wird die Perspektive des jüdischen Opfers u.a. in der Deutung von J. Teitelbaum, dem ehemaligen Rabbiner aus Satmar, der in der Shoah das Strafgericht für den Zionismus sieht. Diese Deutung stellt jedoch eine schmale und wenig rezipierte Nebenlinie innerhalb der jüdischen theologischen Deutungen des Holocaust dar. Um die religiösen Konnotationen des »Opfers« bewusst zu vermeiden, hat sich in den beiden letzten Jahrzehnten vor allem in theologischen Kreisen eingebürgert, wie auch im Judentum verbreitet, den Begriff ›Shoah‹ zu verwenden. Vgl. zu den Deutungen innerhalb des Judentums aus einer christlich-deutschen Perspektive das instruktive Buch von Chr. Münz, Der Welt ein Gedächtnis geben. Geschichtstheologisches Denken im Judentum nach Auschwitz, Gütersloh 1996.

Damit korrespondierend heißt es unter 4.1.:

> Wir bekennen betroffen die Mitverantwortung und Schuld der Christenheit in Deutschland am Holocaust.[24]

Die Frage von Verantwortung und Schuld der Christen kam damit auf die Tagesordnung. Die Erkenntnis, dass der christliche Antijudaismus mitverantwortlich war für den Mord an sechs Millionen Jüdinnen und Juden, führt zu einer Überprüfung der Theologie. Ein geschichtliches Ereignis wird zum Ausgangspunkt einer neuen und veränderten Rede von Gott.

Lassen Sie mich die theologischen Hintergründe der Rede von Gott nach Auschwitz kurz erläutern. Seit den sechziger Jahren hatten sich vor allem in Nordamerika, aber auch in Israel jüdische Theologen theologisch mit der Shoah auseinandergesetzt.[25] Mit der industriellen Ermordung von sechs Millionen Jüdinnen und Juden gerieten auch die Säulen jüdischer Theologie ins Wanken. Nach Auschwitz angemessen von einem Gott zu reden, der nach jüdischem Verständnis immer auch ein Gott der Geschichte war, stellte den jüdischen Glauben vor eine Zerreißprobe. Auschwitz bedeutet einen Bruch, im Leben wie im Glaubensleben, des jüdischen Volkes.

Jüdische Theologen setzten sich zuerst tastend mit dieser Thematik auseinander. Richard L. Rubenstein vertrat in seinem 1966 erschienenen Buch »After Auschwitz« eine radikale »Gott ist tot«-Theologie.[26] Emil Fackenheim lehnt in seinem 1970 erschienenen Buch »God's Presence in History« ebenfalls jede religiöse Deutung der Shoah ab, aber hält an Gottes Gegenwart auch in Auschwitz fest.[27] Eliezer Berkovits stellt in seinem 1973 veröffentlichten Buch »Faith after the Holocaust« die Frage, wie ein gerechter Gott die Shoah zulassen konnte, und findet die Antwort darin, dass das Böse nicht die Bestrafung der Sünden ist, wohl aber der angesichts des menschlichen Leidens unerklärbare Rückzug Gottes in sich selbst.[28] Diese wenigen Sätze können die Tiefe der theologischen Fragen nur unzureichend wiedergeben, aber doch die Wunde verdeutlichen, welche die Shoah im jüdischen Glaubensleben geschlagen hat.

In Auseinandersetzung mit der amerikanisch-jüdischen ›Holocaust-Theologie‹ versuchte man auch auf deutsch-christlicher Seite Ansätze einer ›Theologie

---

[24] Vgl. Rendtorff/Henrix, Die Kirchen und das Judentum (Anm. 16), 594.

[25] Der Begriff »Theologie nach Auschwitz« ist ein Sammelbegriff, der »eher eine thematische Orientierung als eine methodische und inhaltliche Einheitlichkeit anzeigt«, so B. Krondorfer, Abschied von (familien-)biographischer Unschuld im Land der Täter. Zur Positionierung theologischer Diskurse nach der Shoah, in: K. von Kellenbach/B. Krondorfer/N. Reck, Von Gott reden im Land der Täter. Theologische Stimmen in der dritten Generation seit der Shoah, Darmstadt 2001, 11-28, hier 11.

[26] R.L. Rubenstein, After Ausschwitz. Radical Theology and Contemporary Judaism, Indianapolis 1966.

[27] E. Fackenheim, God's Presence in History. Jewish Affirmations and Philosophical Reflections, New York 1970.

[28] E. Berkovits, Faith After the Holocaust, New York 1973.

nach Auschwitz‹ zu formulieren. In einer nicht immer unproblematischen Art und Weise gelangte dabei in den gleichwohl verdienstvollen Arbeiten der neuen Politischen Theologie von Dorothee Sölle, Jürgen Moltmann und Johann Baptist Metz die Theodizeefrage ins Zentrum.[29] Die Frage: »Wo war Gott in Auschwitz?« musste aufgenommen, ausgehalten und eigenständig formuliert werden. Darüber hinaus sind Aporien wie die folgenden in den Blick zu nehmen, wie Dorothea von Tippelskirch formuliert:

> Die Erkenntnis von einer doppelten Unmöglichkeit tut not: Wir können von Gott in Auschwitz nicht sprechen. Und: Wir können von ihm nicht schweigen. Wir können nur anerkennen, daß fortan zu den Bedingungen der ›Möglichkeit‹ weiterer Rede von Gott das Berührt-Werden als ein Modus der Beziehung zum Anderen gehört. Konkret: Unter die Bedingungen der Möglichkeit weiterer Rede von Gott ist seither die Teilnahme an Entsetzen und Trauer der Überlebenden, das Mitleiden mit Israel zu rechnen.[30]

Gleichzeitig konnten die Erben der Täter bei der Theodizeefrage nicht stehen bleiben. So mussten deutsche christliche Theologen weitergehend fragen »...und wo waren wir in dieser Zeit?« Welche Linien christlicher Theologie führen zu einer Mitschuld an der Shoah? Welche Aussagen über das Judentum müssen neu durchdacht werden, und inwieweit kann und muss christliche Theologie neu formuliert werden? In diesem Zusammenhang sind die Namen von Friedrich-Wilhelm Marquardt, Martin Stöhr, Peter von der Osten-Sacken und Berthold Klappert zu nennen. Leitfrage für Aussagen über das jüdische Volk wurde die programmatische Arbeitsthese des jüdischen Theologen Irving Greenberg, dass keine theologische Aussage gemacht werden darf, die angesichts der in den Flammen sterbenden Kinder nicht glaubwürdig ist.[31] Die Auseinandersetzung mit Auschwitz wird zum Wendepunkt der Theologie, ein »Datum der Theologiegeschichte«, das eine »geduldige, aber umfassende Sichtung der gesamten Tradition der Kirche« erfordert.[32]

---

[29] Vgl. dazu S.K. Pinnock, Die Theologie der zweiten Generation nach Auschwitz. Eine kritische Analyse, in: von Kellenbach/Krondorfer/Reck, Von Gott reden im Land der Täter (Anm. 25), 95-109.

[30] D.C. von Tippelskirch, Nach Vernichtung und Umarmung—Zeit für die Auslegung?, in: C. Kurth/P. Schmid (Hg.), Das christlich-jüdische Gespräch. Standortbestimmungen, Judentum und Christentum Bd. 3, Stuttgart u.a. 2000, 147-161, hier 148.

[31] I. Greenberg, Augenblicke des Glaubens, in: M. Brocke/H. Jochum (Hg.), Wolkensäule und Feuerschein. Jüdische Theologie des Holocaust, München 1982, 136-177, vgl. bes. 136. Vgl. dazu auch die kritische Entgegnung durch M. Wyschogrod, Gott—ein Gott der Erlösung?, in: Brocke/Jochum, a.a.O., 178-194.

[32] K. Haacker, Der Holocaust als Datum der Theologiegeschichte, in: E. Brocke/J. Seim (Hg.), Gottes Augapfel. Beiträge zur Erneuerung des Verhältnisses von Christen und Juden, Neukirchen $^{2}$1988, 137-145. Kritiker der Erklärung setzten hier an und sahen in dieser Rede von Auschwitz einen Kategorienfehler. Auschwitz sei kein Wendepunkt der Theologie, sondern »Konkretion des Bösen, von dem wir als Christen immer schon wissen«—so

Diese Rede von Auschwitz sperrt sich gegen die Beliebigkeit, die sich im öffentlichen Diskurs weit verbreitet in Deutschland findet. Oft steht die Rede »nach Auschwitz« in der Gefahr, nahezu ins Mystische und Unbestimmte abzugleiten, indem die Konturen des Leides völlig verschwinden. Die Redeweise und Begründungszusammenhänge »das kann man nach Auschwitz nicht mehr sagen ...« müssen stets genau daraufhin befragt werden, ob es dabei wirklich um eine Auseinandersetzung mit diesem Datum und eine kritische Sichtung geht—oder lediglich um eine bloße Legitimierung eigener Positionen, die nicht in einem tatsächlichen Begründungszusammenhang mit den Ereignissen im Dritten Reich steht.

Als nächstes möchte ich auf den Punkt 4.4. der Erklärung der Evangelischen Kirche im Rheinland hinweisen: »Wir glauben an die bleibende Erwählung des jüdischen Volkes als Gottes Volk und erkennen, daß die Kirche durch Jesus Christus in den Bund Gottes mit seinem Volk hineingenommen ist.« An dieser Stelle findet die entscheidende Abkehr von in Jahrhunderten eingefahrenen Gleisen in der christlichen Theologie statt. Der Bund zwischen Gott und Israel wird nicht als aufgehoben, sondern als ungekündigt bekannt. Statt das Judentum zu beerben, versteht sich die Kirche als Tochterreligion.[33] Das Judentum wird als lebendige Religion und gerade nicht mehr als vergangene Größe wahrgenommen. Die Erwählung des jüdischen Volkes bleibt bestehen.

Fragt man nach der theologischen Begründung dieser Umkehr, so ist auf 2.2. hinzuweisen. Nach dem oben genannten Verweis auf die Shoah heißt es hier, dass »neue biblische Einsichten über die bleibende heilsgeschichtliche Bedeutung Israels (z.B. Röm. 9-11) ... im Zusammenhang mit dem Kirchenkampf gewonnen worden« seien.

Es war bereits von Auschwitz als Wendepunkt gesprochen worden. Dass es sich um einen solchen handelt, hat konkreten Einfluss auf die Auslegung der Heiligen Schrift. So formuliert der Neutestamentler Wolfgang Kraus:

der Neutestamentler G. Strecker (Votum auf der Landessynode der Evangelisch-lutherischen Landeskirche Hannovers am 8.5.1992 zum Aktenstück Nr. 36A.). Vgl. zur Diskussion um den Beitrag G. Streckers P. von der Osten Sacken, Katechismus und Siddur. Aufbrüche mit Martin Luther und den Lehrern Israels, 2. überarbeitete und erweiterte Aufl., VIKJ Bd. 15, Berlin 1994, 345ff.

[33] Die Sicht, dass sich das Christentum als Tochterreligion vom Judentum als Mutterreligion gelöst hat, ist weit verbreitet und m.E. auch richtig, vgl. dazu etwa G. Theißen, Die Religion der ersten Christen. Eine Theorie des Urchristentums, Gütersloh 2000. Anders etwa A.F. Segal (Rebecca's Children. Judaism and Christianity in the Roman World, Cambridge/MA 1986), der beide Religionen als Zwillinge versteht, die zur gleichen Zeit entstanden. Er nimmt eine größere Differenz zwischen dem rabbinischen Judentum und dem Judentum des 2. Tempels an und begründet von daher seine Entscheidung.

> Kennzeichen von Wendepunkten ist es, dass die Art und Weise, wie die religiöse Überlieferung gelesen, verstanden und weiter tradiert wird, vor und nach einem solchen Wendepunkt fundamental differieren.[34]

Eine neue und intensivere Beschäftigung mit dem Apostel Paulus, insbesondere mit seinem Brief an die Römer und hier besonders mit den Kapiteln 9-11, aus denen auch die programmatische Überschrift der Erklärung stammt, bot die Grundlage für eine Theologie, welche die bleibende Erwählung Israels betonte. Diese Rückbindung an die Schrift war von fundamentaler Bedeutung, denn in letzter Konsequenz ermöglichte sie allein eine tatsächliche Neuformulierung der Theologie.

Gleichzeitig rief diese Interpretation jedoch auch Widerspruch hervor. Denn die Argumentationslinie des Paulus, die in den genannten Kapiteln des Römerbriefes hervortritt, formuliert eindeutig die bleibende Erwählung Israels, sie steht aber gleichzeitig in Spannung zu anderen Aussagen in den paulinischen Briefen, vgl. etwa 1 Thess 2, 14-16 mit Röm 11, 25-29 oder Gal 4, 21-31 und Röm 11, 28-32.[35] Lässt sich m. E. nicht bezweifeln, dass die genannten Kapitel aus dem Römerbrief in das Zentrum der paulinischen Theologie gehören, so bleibt das Faktum der anderen Aussagen bestehen. Exegetische Eindeutigkeit ist in diesem Zusammenhang ein Wunschgedanke.

Die Konsequenz dieser neuen Theologie wird in 4.6. formuliert—dem vielleicht wichtigsten Satz der Erklärung: »Wir glauben, daß Juden und Christen je in ihrer Berufung Zeugen Gottes vor der Welt und voreinander sind: darum sind wir überzeugt, daß die Kirche ihr Zeugnis dem jüdischen Volk gegenüber nicht wie ihre Mission an der Völkerwelt wahrnehmen kann.« Die Kirche, zu deren Grundlagen das missionarische Selbstverständnis gehört, verzichtet gegenüber Israel auf jegliche Mission—und das grundlegend. Es geht nicht allein darum, dass deutsche Christen aufgrund der jüngsten Vergangenheit nicht mehr unter Juden missionieren, es geht um ein grundsätzliches Absehen von der Mission gegenüber Israel.[36]

Konsequent finden sich dazu in 4.8. die Sätze: »Indem wir umkehren, beginnen wir zu entdecken, was Christen und Juden gemeinsam bekennen: Wir bekennen beide Gott als den Schöpfer des Himmels und der Erde und wissen, daß wir als von demselben Gott durch den aaronitischen Segen Ausgezeichnete im Alltag der Welt leben.« Die Erklärung endet und zielt auf das Bekenntnis zu demselben Gott.

Der Großteil der evangelischen Landeskirchen in Deutschland ist vor allem im Verlauf der 80er und zu Beginn 90er Jahre ebenfalls mit Synodalbeschlüssen

[34]Kraus, Neues Testament und christlich-jüdisches Gespräch (Anm. 11), 73.

[35]Vgl. dazu Kraus, Neues Testament und christlich-jüdisches Gespräch (Anm. 11), 74ff.

[36]Auch dieser Punkt hat zu heftigsten Diskussionen geführt, vgl. dazu von der Osten-Sacken, Katechismus und Siddur (Anm. 32), 343ff.

an die Öffentlichkeit getreten.[37] So kann diese dritte Phase als *konfessorische Phase* bezeichnet werden.[38] Der jüdisch-christliche Dialog hält Einzug in das kirchliche Establishment.

4. Und wo stehen wir heute? Versucht man für die vierte Phase eine passende Überschrift zu finden, so sollte diese vielleicht »Entflechtung statt Umarmung« lauten. Gleichzeitig aber—und das gilt es nicht zu verschweigen—ist die Gegenwart auch von einer Art Rückschritt geprägt.

Den Begriff der Entflechtung (disentanglement) hatte bereits Mitte der 80er Jahre Krister Stendahl—zunächst Neutestamentler in Harvard und späterer schwedischer Landesbischof—in die Diskussion eingebracht:

> So sehe ich, wenn ich an die nächste Generation denke, die Notwendigkeit für ein weitergefaßtes Programm, das weniger festgelegt ist durch unser wechselseitiges Verflochtensein und das hungrig danach ist, den anderen in seiner Ganzheit kennenzulernen. In gewissem Sinne könnte die Gründung des Staates Israel, durch die die jüdische Präsenz zu einer Nation unter Nationen wurde, auf lange Sicht zu dieser Entflechtung kräftig beitragen, so dass wir Christen die Juden in ihrer Ganzheit und Unverwechselbarkeit sehen lernen und nicht nur an unserer Vorgeschichte mit einer bestimmten Kontinuität denken, die im jüdisch-christlichen Dialog positiv bewertet wird. Nur wenn wir unverwechselbar und frei sind in unserem jeweiligen Anderssein, kann die Freundschaft wachsen und sich vertiefen zur Bereicherung der gegenseitigen Beziehungen.[39]

Das Judentum in seiner Ganzheit wahrzunehmen, bedeutet, auch das wahrzunehmen, was Judentum und Christentum trennt und unterscheidet. Es geht gerade nicht um eine Vereinnahmung, eine Umarmung der Juden durch die Christen, die ersteren aufgrund der Suche der letzteren nach dem Verbindenden vielleicht auch manches Mal die Luft zum Atmen genommen haben mag.[40]

Gleichzeitig ist es aber auch die Aufgabe der Christen, die trennenden Fragen ihrerseits zu benennen—beispielhaft seien hier die Fragen der Christologie und Trinität hervorgehoben. Die Differenz zwischen den beiden Religionen muss

[37] Die Dokumente finden sich bei Rendtorff/Henrix (Hg.): Die Kirchen und das Judentum (Anm. 16) und H.H. Henrix/W. Kraus (Hg.): Die Kirchen und das Judentum Bd.II. Dokumente von 1986-2000, Gütersloh/Paderborn 2001. Vgl. als instruierende Übersicht H.-J. Barkenings, Zur christlichen Neupositionierung im Verhältnis und im Verhalten der Christen zu den Juden in Kirchenordnungen und Kirchenverfassungen nach 1980, in: Bilanz und Perspektiven des christlich-jüdischen Dialogs, epd-Dokumentationen Nr. 9/10, Frankfurt/M. 2005, 45-60.

[38] Vgl. Petersen, Theologie nach Auschwitz? (Anm. 15), 37.

[39] K. Stendahl, Die nächste Generation in den christlich-jüdischen Beziehungen, Kirche und Israel 1 (1986), 11-15, hier 15. Vgl. dazu auch P. von der Osten-Sacken, »Das Geheimnis des anderen«. Versuch einer Orientierung im christlich-jüdischen Verhältnis, in: Lernen auf Zukunft hin (Anm. 11), 7-23.

[40] Vgl. dazu R. Seligman, Klezmer, Klemperer und Harmoniesucht, in: Im Gespräch. 50 Jahre Gesellschaft für Christlich-Jüdische Zusammenarbeit in Berlin e.V., Berlin 1999, 29-33.

nicht aufgehoben werden, und die Rede von dem einen Gott kann als eine unterschiedliche in eschatologischer Perspektive ausgehalten werden. Aber dieser zweite Schritt war und ist erst möglich nach dem ersten, denn es brauchte den gesicherten Boden der Erfahrung im Dialog, um dann die jeweils eigene Identität auch deutlicher aussprechen zu können.

Ich habe die verschiedenen Phasen des Dialogs aufgezeigt. In diesem Zusammenhang ist auch die Ungleichzeitigkeit des Gleichzeitigen zu beachten. Menschen, die eher am Anfang ihrer Beschäftigung mit der Thematik stehen, wollen manchmal nicht von den Unterschieden hören. Das kann die Konsequenz haben, dass Menschen, die im Dialog schon lange engagiert sind, Anfängern nahezu als ›rückständig‹ erscheinen. Darüber hinaus ist zu beachten, dass nahezu identische theologische Aussagen je nachdem von wem und zu welchem Zeitpunkt sie getroffen werden, völlig unterschiedliche Implikationen beinhalten. Wer zuerst das Gemeinsame aber dann auch das Trennende betont, macht eine ganz andere Aussage als jemand, der mit derselben Aussage allein das Trennende unterstreicht!

In diese gegenwärtige Phase gehört auch die in jüdischen Kreisen kontrovers diskutierte, von 300 jüdischen Gelehrten und Rabbinern vor allem aus Nordamerika, aber auch aus Israel und Europa unterzeichnete Erklärung *Dabru Emet* aus dem Jahre 2000, die zunächst in der NEW YORK TIMES und der Baltimore Sun veröffentlichet wurde und einen Meilenstein innerhalb des jüdisch-christlichen Gesprächs darstellt.[41] Zwar ist auch dieses Dokument nur begrenzt repräsentativ, aber es anerkennt auf das Nachdrücklichste die Bemühungen auf christlicher Seite und ist Vertrauenswerbung und Vertrauenskundgabe zugleich. Es ist kein abschließendes Dokument, sondern markiert den Beginn einer Diskussion primär unter Juden und Jüdinnen selbst, inwieweit eine neue und veränderte Sicht auf das Christentum festgestellt werden kann und muss. Sie formuliert darüber hinaus, dass die Frage nach der Identitätsbildung im Dialog gerade nicht nur eine christliche Aufgabe sei, sondern ebenso von Jüdinnen und Juden wahrgenommen werden sollte.

> In den vergangenen Jahren hat sich ein dramatischer und beispielloser Wandel in den christlich-jüdischen Beziehungen vollzogen. Während des fast zwei Jahrtausende anhaltenden jüdischen Exils haben Christen das Judentum zumeist als eine gescheiterte Religion oder bestenfalls als eine Vorläuferreligion charakterisiert, die dem Christentum den Weg bereitete und in ihm zur Erfüllung gekommen sei. In den Jahrzehnten seit dem Holocaust hat sich die Christenheit jedoch dramatisch verändert. Eine wachsende Zahl kirchlicher Gremien, unter ihnen sowohl römisch-katholische als auch protestantische, haben in öffentlichen Stellungnahmen ihre Reue

[41] Vgl. zu der Erklärung und ihrer Diskussion T. Frymer-Kensky/D. Nowak/P. Ochs/D.F. Sandmel/M.A. Signer (eds.), Christianity in Jewish Terms, Boulder/CO/Oxford 2000. Nach einer kurzen Einführung werden acht Thesen vorgestellt und erläutert.

> über die christlichen Misshandlungen von Judentum und Juden ausgedrückt. Diese Stellungnahmen haben zudem erklärt, dass christliche Lehre und Predigt reformiert werden können und müssen, um den unverändert gültigen Bund Gottes mit dem jüdischen Volk anzuerkennen und den Beitrag des Judentums zur Weltkultur und zum christlichen Glauben selbst zu würdigen.[42]

Man wird diese Erklärung nicht einfach als *die* jüdische Antwort auf die hier vorgestellten christlichen Erklärungen lesen können. Letztere stammen aus dem deutschen Kontext, *Dabru Emet* aus dem amerikanischen.[43] Gleichzeitig aber verliefen die Dialoge keineswegs unabhängig voneinander, und es waren gerade auch christliche deutsche Dialogpartner, die der amerikanischen Erklärung wichtige Impulse gaben.[44]

Zugleich wäre es jedoch verfehlt, aufgrund der hier geschilderten Beobachtungen darauf zu schließen, dass auf allen Ebenen von Theologie und Kirche tatsächlich Fortschritte zu verzeichnen seien, denn auch der oben erwähnte Rückschritt gehört in das Panorama der gegenwärtigen Situation. Das Thema des christlich-jüdischen Dialogs ist in den Kirchen und Universitäten längst nicht mehr so präsent wie in den Jahrzehnten zuvor und in manchen Augenblicken erscheint es nahezu wie zu den Akten gelegt und gerade nicht im kirchlichen Bewusstsein verankert. Dieses zeigte sich nachdrücklich bei einem Blick in die Verlautbarung der EKD »Christlicher Glaube und nichtchristliche Religionen«.[45] In diesem Dokument werden die Neuanfänge der Kirchen und die vorangegangenen kirchlichen Verlautbahrungen zum jüdisch-christlichen Gespräch nicht erwähnt. Die Stellungnahme der EKD, die eigentlich das Gespräch mit den nichtchristlichen Religionen fördern sollte, führt selbst kein Gespräch mit den bisher stattgefundenen Dialogarbeiten im eigenen Raum.[46]

[42] Deutsche Übersetzung in: Kampling/Weinrich (Hg.), Dabru Emet—Redet Wahrheit, (Anm. 4), 9.

[43] Vgl. zur Diskussion der Erklärung in Deutschland Kampling/Weinrich (Hg.), Dabru emet—Redet Wahrheit (Anm. 4).

[44] Vgl. dazu M.A. Signer, Ein jüdischer Blick auf Dabru Emet, in: Kampling/Weinrich (Hg.), Dabru Emet—redet Wahrheit (Anm. 4), 15-30, bes. 19f.

[45] »Christlicher Glaube und nichtchristliche Religionen«. Theologische Leitlinien. Ein Beitrag der Kammer für Theologie der Evangelischen Kirche in Deutschland, hg. vom Kirchenamt der EKD, Hannover 2003 (EKD-Texte 77).

[46] Vgl. dazu F. Piper, Ermüdungserscheinungen oder Krise in der christlich-jüdischen Zusammenarbeit—eine Problemanzeige aus christlicher Sicht, in: Der christlich-jüdische Dialog auf dem Prüfstand, epd-Dokumentation Nr. 12, Frankfurt/M. 2004, 11-17, bes. 14f.

## 4. Jüdisch-christlicher Dialog und interreligiöser Dialog

In einem letzten Punkt möchte ich einige Überlegungen vorstellen, welche Erkenntnisse sich aus dem jüdisch-christlichen Dialog für andere interreligiöse Dialoge in Deutschland gewinnen lassen.[47]

Die Frage liegt auf der Hand und kann doch erstaunen. Der christlich-jüdische Dialog in Deutschland hat lange Zeit agiert, ohne sich die Frage zu stellen, ob er ein Teil eines größeren Dialogs der Religionen sei. Mag dies manch einer heute als Schwäche empfinden, so ist es auf zweifache Art und Weise begründet: *historisch* durch die Positionierung nach der Shoah und *theologisch* durch die besondere Beziehung von Judentum und Christentum.

Mit Blick auf die Konsequenzen für den interreligiösen Dialog möchte ich zunächst allgemein formulieren: Der jüdisch-christliche Dialog ist meiner Meinung nach eine Erfahrung, dass interreligiöser Dialog selbst unter schwierigen Bedingungen gelingen kann.[48] Dazu braucht es jedoch zum einen Zeit, zum anderen personelle Kontinuität, das heißt Gruppen, die sich über einen längeren Zeitraum treffen. Gelegentliche Veranstaltungen mit einem wechselnden Publikum reichen nicht aus. Nicht allein ist Vertrauensbildung ein wichtiges Element, vielmehr hat der Dialog verschiedene Phasen, die durchlaufen werden können und müssen.[49] Hier ist die Ungleichzeitigkeit des Gleichzeitigen zu beachten. Asymmetrien müssen beachtet und reflektiert werden—und sollten, wenn möglich, auf der Ebene der Kommunikationstruktur vermieden werden.

Doch wie verhält es sich nun mit dem Dialog mit anderen Religionen, in Deutschland bzw. Europa konkret mit dem Dialog mit dem Islam? So wird verbreitet gefordert, angesichts der Fortschritte, die im jüdisch-christlichen Dialog erzielt worden sind, das Gespräch um diesen Partner zu erweitern.[50] Ignaz Bubis plädierte dafür, bei der jährlichen »Woche der Brüderlichkeit« der Gesellschaften für Christlich-Jüdische Zusammenarbeit auch die Muslime zu inte-

[47] Ich beschränke mich hier bewusst auf meinen eigenen Kontext, denn die Überschneidungen von Politik und Religion bewirken, dass sich in anderen Ländern Europas und erst recht in den USA die Situation völlig anders darstellt.

[48] Doch noch einmal sei hier betont: Ich spreche aus einer christlichen Perspektive und mit Blick auf die Selbstreflexion christlicher Theologie. Für andere Dialogteilnehmer kann sich dieses anders darstellen. Vgl. etwa die in vielen Punkten berechtigte Kritik von H.G. Brandt, Ist der Dialog wirklich schon ein Dialog, in: Bilanzen und Perspektiven des christlich-jüdischen Dialogs, epd-Dokumentation 9/10, Frankfurt/M. 2005, 88-90.

[49] Vgl. zum Dialog zwischen Christentum und Islam L. Kaulig, Ebenen des christlich-islamischen Dialogs. Beobachtungen und Analysen zu den Wegen einer Begegnung, Christentum und Islam im Dialog Bd. 3, Münster 2004, und: J. Sperber, Christians and Muslims. The Dialogue Activities of the World Council of Churches and Their Theological Foundation, Theologische Bibliothek Töpelmann, Berlin u.a. 2000.

[50] So beschäftigt sich der ICCJ—die Dachorganisation von weltweit 38 nationalen christlich-jüdischen Dialogvereinigungen—zunehmend mit dem abrahamitischen Dialog und hat hier ein eigenes Forum eingerichtet.

grieren. Er wies darauf hin, dass Pauschalverdächtigungen, Sündenbockdenken und rechtsextremes Gedankengut Juden wie Muslime zu Opfern machten. Gerade die Juden—so Bubis—wüssten, was es heißt, unter Verallgemeinerungen leben zu müssen. Aber gegenseitige Solidarität in gesellschaftlichen Fragen ist noch kein interreligiöser Dialog. Hier handelt es sich um politische und gesellschaftliche Fragen. Diese beeinflussen den Dialog nachhaltig, gleichzeitig aber gilt es die Unterschiede zu beachten,[51] denn sie sind symptomatisch für die derzeitige Situation: Der Dialog mit dem Islam gelangte seit dem 11. September 2001 vorrangig aus *politischen* und *nicht* aus *theologischen* Gründen so nachhaltig auf die Tagesordnung—und das mit Blick sowohl auf die Verhältnisse im Westen als auch im Nahen Osten.[52]

Asymmetrien, wie wir sie bereits vorher gestreift haben, gilt es auch mit Blick auf den so genannten ›abrahamitischen Trialog‹ zu beachten—ein Begriff, der hier aus praktischen Gründen verwendet werden soll, obwohl er mehr als problematisch ist.

Wenn wir von solch einem ›Trialog‹ in der Bundesrepublik sprechen, so herrscht eine deutliche Ungleichheit in politischer und sozialer Hinsicht. Der größere Teil der Muslime, die in Deutschland leben, hat nicht einmal die deutsche Staatsangehörigkeit und damit wenig Rechte und kaum Möglichkeiten zu einem sozialen Aufstieg. Als »Körperschaften öffentlichen Rechts« haben die Gemeinden von Kirchen und Synagogen in Deutschland andere Rechte als die Moscheen—und dies ist nicht allein der anderen Organisationsstruktur des Islams[53] geschuldet. Bis auf wenige Ausnahmen findet muslimischer Religionsunterricht in unseren Schulen (noch) nicht statt,[54] und in einigen Bundesländern kann eine muslimische Frau mit Kopftuch nicht unterrichten, wohl aber eine Nonne im Habit.[55] Diese Ungleichheiten sind unübersehbar, und es wird die Aufgabe der Kirchen sein, hier zu prüfen, wann—aber auch unter welchen Bedingungen—sie an der Seite der Moscheen für die religiösen Rechte der Muslime einzustehen haben und welche Rolle sie bei der Integration der Muslime

[51] Darüber hinaus bin ich skeptisch, ob sich Antijudaismus und ›Islamphobie‹ so einfach parallelisieren lassen, wie es in der heutigen Zeit insbesondere im Bereich der Deutschen Linken sehr leicht geschieht.

[52] Betrachtet man hingegen die Geschichte des christlich-islamischen Dialogs insgesamt, so ist die obengenannte Differenzierung weniger zutreffend.

[53] Zum Islam in Deutschland vgl. A.Th. Khoury/P. Heine/J. Oebbecke, Handbuch Recht und Kultur des Islams in der deutschen Gesellschaft. Probleme im Alltag. Hintergründe. Antworten, Gütersloh 2000.

[54] Vgl. dazu U. Baumann (Hg.), Islamischer Religionsunterricht. Grundlagen, Begründungen, Berichte, Projekte, Dokumentationen, Frankfurt/M. 2001.

[55] Vgl. zur Kopftuchdebatte R. Schieder, Der Streit um das Kopftuch in diskursanayltischer Perspektive, Zeitschrift für Evangelische Ethik 49 (2005), 9-21.

spielen können.[56] Und nicht zuletzt gilt es auch für die Kirchen, ihre *gesellschaftspolitische* Rolle wahr und ernst zu nehmen und der Dämonisierung, aber auch Romantisierung der islamischen Religion entgegenzutreten.

Auf der *theologischen* Ebene wird die Auseinandersetzung mit dem Islam für das Christentum nie so im Zentrum der Theologie stehen, wie die Auseinandersetzung mit dem Judentum—auch das eine Asymmetrie. Wie die hebräische Bibel nichts vom Christentum weiß, so weiß das Neue Testament nichts vom Islam, entsteht diese Religion doch erst Jahrhunderte später. Aber gerade die Gesprächsbereitschaft von Jüdinnen und Juden den jüngeren Geschwistern gegenüber, die die Christinnen und Christen erfahren durften, ruft diese in die Pflicht zum Dialog mit dem Islam—auch und gerade um ihrer selbst willen. Auch gegenüber dem Islam hat sich die Kirche stets als einzig wahre Erbin der abrahamitischen Verheißung erklärt—dieser Vergangenheit und ihrer Konsequenzen gilt es sich zu stellen und im Dialog mit dem Islam das eigene Selbstverständnis zu reflektieren. Gleichzeitig aber handelt es sich jedoch in vielen Punkten um eine theologisch *andere* Verhältnisbestimmung als gegenüber dem Judentum. So wird auch die Frage der Mission in einer ganz anderen Art und Weise diskutiert werden müssen. Sowohl Christentum als auch Islam verstehen sich als Religionen, zu deren Aufgaben die Mission gehört. Mit Blick auf das Judentum haben—wenn auch nicht unbestritten—viele Kirchen Position bezogen. Mit Blick auf den Islam wird diese Frage noch einmal ganz neu und anders diskutiert werden müssen.[57] Und auch innerhalb des Islams steht man hier erst am Beginn einer Diskussion.[58]

Kann man nun umgekehrt formulieren, es gäbe in theologischer Perspektive eine ähnliche Asymmetrie zwischen Islam und Judentum/Christentum wie zwischen dem Christentum und dem Islam? Hier wird man einerseits vorsichtig sein müssen, aber sich gleichzeitig vor Konturierungen nicht scheuen dürfen. Der Islam teilt nicht mit den anderen beiden Religionen einen Teil der Heiligen Schrift, und die Definition seiner Identität hängt nicht in dem Maße von der Bestimmung seines Verhältnisses zu den anderen beiden Religionen ab, wie es sich mit Blick auf die Bestimmung des Christentums gegenüber dem Judentum

[56] Vgl. dazu V. Meißner, Die Integration von Muslimen in Deutschland—Herausforderungen für die Institution Kirche, in: H. Schmid/A. Renz/J. Sperber (Hg.), Herausforderung Islam. Anfragen an das christliche Selbstverständnis. Theologisches Forum Christentum—Islam. 2. durchges. Auflage, Stuttgart 2005, 135-148.

[57] Vgl. dazu die von islamischer Seite in der Presse z.T. heftig kritisierte Handreichung des Rates der EKD »Klarheit und gute Nachbarschaft. Christen und Muslime in Deutschland«, Hannover 2006.

[58] Bereits 1976 formulierten Vertreter des Ökumenischen Rates der Kirchen und des Muslimischen Weltkongresses in Chabésy/Schweiz gemeinsam, dass »Muslime und Christen das uneingeschränkte Recht haben müssen, zu überzeugen und überzeugt zu werden und ihren Glauben zu leben, sowie ihr religiöses Leben so zu ordnen, daß es mit ihren jeweiligen religiösen Pflichten und Prinzipien übereinstimmt«.

darstellt. Gleichzeitig schöpft der Koran jedoch sehr wohl aus den biblischen Traditionen und es gibt—um es vereinfacht auszudrücken—viele Bezugnahmen auf Mose und Jesus im Koran.[59] Hier ist es ist die Aufgabe muslimischer Theologen zu prüfen, inwieweit diesbezüglich Resourcen und Chancen für ein besseres Verständnis des Verhältnisses der Religionen zueinander zu entdecken sind. Diese Betrachtung der Schrift, die von nachhaltiger Bedeutung für den Dialog zwischen den Buchreligionen ist, kann nur von muslimischer Seite vorgenommen werden.

Aufgrund der Vielzahl der unterschiedlichen Asymmetrien und angesichts der Aktualität der Geschichte und der Sprengkraft der Verhältnisse im Nahen Osten auch für den Dialog im Westen, bin ich zurückhaltend mit Blick auf eine zu rasche Konzentration auf den ›abrahamitischen Trialog‹. Es gilt vielmehr von Fall zu Fall konkret zu prüfen, ob die Zeit am jeweiligen Ort dafür tatsächlich da ist oder ob die Gefahr besteht, dann in eine nebulöse multikulturelle Unbestimmtheit abzugleiten. Und sicherlich kann es nicht darum gehen, einem vielleicht an manchen Orten scheinbar ermüdeten jüdisch-christlichen Dialog durch einen weiteren Gesprächspartner neuen Zunder zu geben. Den Ermüdungserscheinungen gilt es *anders* zu begegnen!

An vielen Orten wird es sinnvoll sein, zunächst kleinere Schritte zu gehen und neben dem christlich-jüdischen zunächst auch den christlich-islamischen und jüdisch-islamischen Dialog zu intensivieren, wie es bereits auch hier und da geschieht. So können die einzelnen Beziehungen in ihren unterschiedlichen Facetten ausgelotet werden, bevor damit begonnen werden kann, das Gesamtbild zu zeichnen. Vor diesem Hintergrund plädiere ich für einen Dialog der kleinen Schritte. So mag gewährleistet werden, dass der Boden des interreligiösen Gesprächs tatsächlich fester wird, statt unter zu großer Belastung zu brechen.

[59] Vgl. zur Einführung A. Renz/St. Leimgruber, Christen und Muslime. Was sie verbindet—was sie unterscheidet, Krugzell $^{2}$2005, 103-162.

# Die zivilreligiöse Funktion des Amtes des Bundespräsidenten der Bundesrepublik Deutschland am Beispiel der Weihe der Dresdner Frauenkirche

Rolf Schieder

Die Verwendung religiöser Semantik durch die Präsidenten der Vereinigten Staaten von Amerika hat eine lange Tradition. Wenn George W. Bush die Politik Amerikas in einen heilsgeschichtlichen Kontext stellt, so verdankt sich das nicht seiner Sympathie für die so genannte religiöse Rechte. Die Überzeugung, dass Amerika eine besondere Rolle in Gottes Heilsplan zu spielen habe, äußerten alle Präsidenten ganz unabhängig von ihrer Konfessionszugehörigkeit. Am Grabmal des katholischen Präsidenten John F. Kennedy auf dem Arlington-Friedhof in Washington steht zu lesen, dass »God's work must truly be our own«. Die USA sind ein Werkzeug Gottes—mehr oder weniger stark konturiert findet diese Überzeugung in Ansprachen aller Präsidenten der USA ihren Ausdruck.

Demgegenüber zeichnete sich das Bundespräsidentenamt in der alten Bundesrepublik gerade dadurch aus, dass sie alle religiösen Anspielungen peinlich zu vermeiden suchte. Theodor Heuss, der erste Präsident der Bundesrepublik Deutschland, hätte am liebsten auf die Erwähnung Gottes in der Präambel des Grundgesetzes verzichtet, um den Atheisten im Lande keinen Stein des Anstoßes zu geben. Schließlich konnten sich auch die Sozialisten auf die Formel der »Verantwortung vor Gott« verständigen und so finden sich im Grundgesetz der Bundesrepublik einige wenige religiöse Bezüge: einmal in der Präambel, und dann in der Vereidigungsformel für die Regierung. Hier wird von den Amtsträgern erwartet, dass sie ihren Amtseid mit der Formel »So wahr mir Gott helfe!« beschließen. Freilich wird das Recht eingeräumt, auf diese Formel zu verzichten.

Bemerkenswert ist, dass gerade die Präsidenten, die eine starke religiöse Bindung hatten, ihre Reden von allen religiösen Formeln freizuhalten suchten. Bundespräsident Heinemann vermied nicht nur religiöse Semantik, er hielt selbst Begriffe wie »Vaterlandsliebe« für höchst problematisch: er liebe seine Frau, nicht aber sein Vaterland. Hier zeigt sich ein Erbe des Kirchenkampfes im Dritten Reich. Der überbordenden religiösen Aufladung des faschistischen

Staates stellten die christlich geprägten Politiker im Nachkriegsdeutschland eine bewusst sachliche, pragmatische, semantisch geradezu dürre Rhetorik entgegen. Der Staat hatte eine begrenzte Funktion zu erfüllen, er war für die vorletzten Dinge des Lebens da und sollte sich tunlichst nicht mit einer Sprache schmücken, die die letzten Dinge des Lebens betraf. Dafür waren die Religionsgemeinschaften da. Die bewusste Zurückhaltung des Staates in religiösen Dingen führte zu einer intensiven Partnerschaft des Staates mit dem Kirchen. Es herrschte sozusagen eine Art Arbeitsteilung: Einerseits verzichteten Staat und Kirchen auf Einmischung in den Bereich des je anderen, gleichzeitig aber unterstützte der Staat die Kirchen auf vielfältige Weise, während die Kirchen bei der Bildung mündiger und kritischer, zugleich aber loyaler und sozialer Staatsbürger eine wichtige Rolle übernahmen.

Die explizite Verwendung religiöser Semantik in den Ansprachen von Bundeskanzlern und Bundespräsidenten taucht erst mit der Wiedervereinigung Deutschlands auf. In der Rede von Bundespräsident Richard von Weizsäcker zum Tag der Deutschen Einheit am 3. Oktober 1990 heißt es bereits im vierten Satz seiner Rede: »Für unsere Aufgaben sind wir uns der Verantwortung vor Gott und den Menschen bewusst.« Weizsäcker spielt damit auf die Präambel des Grundgesetzes an. Dort heißt es, dass sich das deutsche Volk in seiner »Verantwortung vor Gott und den Menschen« ein Grundgesetz gegeben habe. Mit dieser Formel geht das Grundgesetz nur unwesentlich über die französische Menschenrechtserklärung hinaus, die von der Präsenz eines »suprême-être« spricht. Der grundlegende Unterschied zwischen der Formulierung des Parlamentarischen Rates aus dem Jahre 1949 und der Rede des Bundespräsidenten im Jahre 1990 besteht darin, dass die Erwähnung Gottes dem Akt der Gesetzgebung zwar eine religiöse Aura verleiht, dass damit aber keine Verpflichtung für die Zukunft eingegangen wird. Eben dieser Zukunftsaspekt wird aber von Weizsäcker betont: Die künftigen Aufgaben sollen in der Verantwortung vor Gott und den Menschen erledigt werden.

Bedeutsam an der Rede des Bundespräsidenten zum Tag der Deutschen Einheit ist ferner, dass er die Zukunft an die »Last der Geschichte« bindet. Die Erinnerung an die Vernichtung der jüdischen Bürgerinnen und Bürger ist zum integralen Bestandteil der Erinnerungskultur der Deutschen geworden. Gerade am Tag der Deutschen Einheit betonte der Bundespräsident die gemeinsame Verantwortung der ehemals beiden deutschen Staaten für die deutsche Geschichte zwischen 1933 und 1945. Das schrecklichste aller Verbrechen, der ›Holocaust‹, verpflichtet zur Versöhnung. Dass ein deutscher Bundespräsident den Anglizismus ›Holocaust‹ verwendet, sei nur am Rande erwähnt. Hätte er sich über den Begriff wirklich kundig gemacht, hätte er ihn wahrscheinlich vermieden. Der Begriff hat seine Wurzeln im Buch Lev 16, 5. Dort ist die Rede von *holocautōma*, dem Brandopfer, das am großen Versöhnungstag Gott dargc bracht werden soll. Die Verwendung des Begriffs ›Holocaust‹ spielt also ganz bewusst mit einer Deutung der Vernichtung der Juden in Europa als Sühnopfer. Eigentlich müsste es sich für Nicht-Juden, zumal aber für Deutsche, von selbst verbieten, diesen Begriff, über den sinnvoll nur von Juden mit Juden gestritten werden kann, zu verwenden.

Einen weitaus weniger befangenen Umgang mit religiöser Semantik zeigte Bundespräsident Horst Köhler. Seine erste Rede schloss er mit den Worten: »Gott segne unser Land.« Die Reaktionen auf diese für deutsche Ohren ungewohnte Formulierung waren aber offenbar so, dass der Bundespräsident auf diese Formulierung künftig verzichtete. Sowohl Konfessionslose als auch Christen, die die Trennung von Politik und Religion im Interesse der Religionsfreiheit für wichtig halten, nahmen an diesem Segenswunsch Anstoß. Keine Kritik, sondern ausschließlich Lob erntete der Bundespräsident dagegen für seine Rede bei der Einweihung der Frauenkirche in Dresden am Reformationstag des Jahres 2005, obwohl die zivilreligiöse Rolle, die der Bundespräsident hier übernahm, weit über den harmlosen Segenswunsch hinausging, der beispielsweise den amerikanischen Präsidenten so ganz selbstverständlich von den Lippen geht.

## Die zivilreligiöse Funktion des Katholizismus und des Protestantismus in Deutschland

Es gehört zu den Besonderheiten der deutschen zivilreligiösen Kultur, dass sie auf die selbständige Verwendung religiöser Semantik und religiöser Rituale durch politische Amtsinhaber ausgesprochen allergisch reagiert, dass sie es aber mit Wohlwollen hinnimmt, wenn diese für die Traditionen der beiden großen Konfessionen, die die Geschichte Deutschlands geprägt haben, eintreten. Dabei eignet sich der Katholizismus aufgrund seiner eigenen politischen Verfasstheit weitaus weniger zur zivilreligiösen Funktionalisierung als der Protestantismus. Während die Protestanten in Deutschland seit der Reformation in so genannten ›Landeskirchen‹ organisiert sind und insofern in das nationale Ganze vollständig integriert sind, ist das Oberhaupt der katholischen Kirche ein selbständiges Völkerrechtssubjekt und die katholische Kirche eine global agierende Institution. Gleichwohl hat die Wahl eines Deutschen zum Papst durchaus kollektive nationale Gefühle ausgelöst. Die BILD-Zeitung brachte die Gefühlslage auf den Punkt: »Wir sind Papst« titelte sie nach der Wahl von Kardinal Ratzinger zum Oberhaupt der katholischen Kirche. Das war natürlich in mehrfacher Hinsicht falsch. Das Papstamt ist das letzte absolutistische Monarchenamt auf diesem Globus—insofern ist das Pronomen »wir« mehr als unpassend. Bedeutsam ist der Versuch, Katholizismus und deutsches Nationalgefühl miteinander zu versöhnen.

Der Wunsch, den Katholizismus auch für nationale Zwecke zu funktionalisieren, ist nicht neu, aber immer konfliktreich. Die Geschichte der Fertigstellung des Kölner Doms kann dafür als symptomatisches Beispiel gelten. Im Jahre 1914 rief der katholische Intellektuelle Joseph Görres zur baulichen Vollendung des Kölner Doms auf, um so ein »Symbol des neuen Reiches, das wir bauen wollen« zu errichten.[1] Als ein »Dom der deutschen Freiheit« sollte er die geistig-geistliche Festung des frommen Deutschlands gegen ein atheistisch-revolutionäres Frankreich sein. Mit den Geldern des protestantischen preußischen Königs wurde der Dom 1880 fertiggestellt. Die Einweihungsfeierlichkeiten fanden wegen des Kulturkampfes ohne Beteiligung des katholischen Klerus statt. Der protestantische Kaiser dagegen war anwesend. Für ihn war der Kölner Dom in erster Linie kein Bauwerk, das den katholischen Christen als Ort des sonntäglichen Ritus diente, sondern »die Wacht am Rhein«—ein Bauwerk also, das die Grenze zwischen Deutschland und Frankreich markieren sollte.

Obwohl also diesseits und jenseits des Rheins katholische Christen lebten und ihren Glauben praktizierten, hatte das protestantische Deutschland keine Probleme damit, den Kölner Dom—jenseits seiner Funktion als Versammlungsstätte katholischer Christen—als zivilreligiöses Heiligtum anzunehmen. Auf protestantischer Seite gehören zu den herausragenden zivilreligiösen Kirchen zweifellos der Berliner Dom, mehr noch aber die Dresdner Frauenkirche.

## Die protestantische Dresdner Frauenkirche als zivilreligiöses Symbol

Am Reformationstag des Jahres 2005 wurde die wieder aufgebaute Dresdner Frauenkirche geweiht. Die öffentliche Aufmerksamkeit war enorm. Im Festgottesdienst waren neben den deutschen Ehrengästen Horst Köhler, Gerhard Schröder, Angela Merkel, auch der Herzog von Kent und die Botschafter der Vereinigten Staaten, Großbritanniens und Frankreichs anwesend. Tausende von Bürgern Dresdens und Touristen aus aller Welt verfolgten den auf dem Neumarkt übertragenen Gottesdienst. 2,86 Mill. Zuschauer sahen den Gottesdienst im ZDF, 1,02 Mill. im MDR.[2] Mit einem Marktanteil von 23,7% war die Weihe der Dresdner Frauenkirche die erfolgreichste Gottesdienstübertragung in der Geschichte des ZDF.[3] Die Presse bediente sich religiöser Bilder und Semantiken, um zu beschreiben, was dort passierte: die BBC sprach von »Dresden's miracle«, von Auferstehung war die Rede, mehrsinniger noch von der Auferstehung »aus Ruinen«.

---

[1]Die Ereignisse und Aussagen zur Geschichte des Dombaus zu Köln dokumentiert M.-L. von Plessen, Marianne und Germania (1789-1889), Berlin 1996.

[2]Der Festakt ist dokumentiert auf der DVD des ZDF »Frauenkirche Dresden«.

[3]Nach Auskunft des ZDF (Ingo Witt am 7.12.2005).

Zwei Drittel der 131 Millionen Euro der reinen Baukosten kamen allein aus Einzelspenden von Privatleuten zusammen. In einer von Dirk Fischer durchgeführten und von Gerald Kretzschmar und Michael Häder ausgewerteten Studie[4] zur Typisierung der Spender für die Frauenkirche ließ sich ein Cluster der »wohlhabenden Regionalspender« mittleren Alters ausmachen. Diese Gruppe zeichnet sich dadurch aus, dass sie zum größten Teil konfessionell nicht gebunden ist, dass sie über überdurchschnittliche Bildungsabschlüsse und Gehälter verfügt und in Dresden und Umgebung lebt. Damit reiht sich die Dresdner Frauenkirche in eine Kirchbaubewegung im Osten Deutschlands ein, die von kleinen Dorfkirchen eben bis hin zur Dresdner Frauenkirche reicht. In allen diesen Kirchbaufördervereinen besteht die Mehrzahl der Mitglieder und Spender aus Konfessionslosen.[5] Die Faszination von der Bedeutung und der Ausstrahlung der Frauenkirche als Bau- und Kulturdenkmal prägte in dieser Gruppe die Spendenmotivation.

Der Wiederaufbau ging von einer Dresdner Bürgerinitiative im Jahr 1990 aus, die sich mit einem »Ruf aus Dresden« an die Öffentlichkeit wandte und ein weltweites Echo auslöste. Widerstand kam aus Kreisen der Landeskirche. Dort befürchtete man nicht nur, dass die wieder aufgebaute Kirche anschließend leer stehen würde, man wollte auch die symbolische Bedeutung der Ruine—die ›Wunde‹ der Stadt als Erinnerung an Krieg und Zerstörung—erhalten wissen. Denn bereits die Ruine der Frauenkirche war symbolisch aufgeladen. Als Zeichen der Zerstörung erinnerten die Überreste der Frauenkirche, deren Beseitigung wiederum durch Bürgerengagement verhindert werden konnte, an den so genannten Feuersturm, in dem im Februar 1945 mehr als 35000 Menschen durch britische Fliegerbomben starben und die Stadt fast vollständig zerstört wurde.[6] Als Mahnmal von Krieg und Zerstörung wurde die mit Unkraut überwucherte Ruine der symbolische Ort für die ostdeutsche Friedensbewegung, die sich dort seit 1982 zu Mahnwachen versammelte.

Die Befürworter des Wiederaufbaus nahmen das Symbol der ›Wunde‹ auf, wendeten es aber durch die Metapher ›Heilung der Wunde‹ so, dass gerade die wieder aufgebaute Kirche ein Zeichen der Versöhnung sei. Nicht eine rückwärtsgewandte Restauration sollte das Ziel des Wiederaufbaus sein. Vielmehr

---

[4] M. Häder/G. Kretzschmar, Die ›Religion‹ der Dresdner Frauenkirche. Empirische Befunde zur Bindung an ein schillerndes Phänomen, in: International Journal of Practical Theology 9 (2005), 4-24. Vgl. auch M. Häder/G. Kretzschmar, Mit welcher Zukunft darf die Dresdner Frauenkirche rechnen?, in: Pastoraltheologie 94 (2005), 330–340.

[5] Vgl. R. Schieder, Dorfkirchen als Orte der Identifikation. Kirchbaufördervereine in praktisch-theologischer Perspektive, in: Pastoraltheologie 95 (2006), 410-453.

[6] Zur medialen Thematisierung trug hier auch der ZDF-Zweiteiler »Dresden« vom 5. und 6. März 2006 bei. In diesem Spielfilm, einem »Antikriegs- und Liebesfilm«, versprechen sich die Dresdner Krankenschwester Anna und der britische Bomberpilot Robert ihre Liebe auf der Kuppel der Frauenkirche.

ging es darum, den Wiederaufbau zu einem Sinnbild für Tod und Zerstörung überwindendes Versöhnungshandeln zu machen. Die Beteiligung der ehemaligen Kriegsgegner am Wiederaufbau durch zeichenhafte Gaben und Gesten unterstrich den Friedenswillen aller Beteiligten. Die Frauenkirche integriert gerade diese ambivalente Struktur von Zerstörung und Wiederaufbau, Ruine und Prachtbau, Krieg und Frieden, aus der sie ihre symbolische Dichte bezieht. Dass man sich für einen so genannten ›archäologischen Aufbau‹ entschieden hat, das heißt, dass man die in dem Ruinenschutt enthaltenen Steine und weiteren Bauelemente in den Neubau sichtbar hineingebaut hat, stärkt das integrative Moment.[7]

## Die Weihe der Frauenkirche als zivilreligiöses Ritual

Die evangelisch-lutherische Landeskirche von Sachsen legte den Termin der Weihe der Kirche auf ein denkwürdiges Datum. Sie fand am Reformationstag statt. Damit schien der konfessionelle Charakter des Ereignisses noch unterstrichen zu werden. Da vor der Frauenkirche ein großes Lutherdenkmal steht, war die Wahl dieses Tages aber durchaus plausibel. Auch der Einzug der kirchlichen Würdenträger in ihren schwarzen Talaren war als durch und durch konfessionelle Feier gestaltet. Lediglich der Titel des Gottesdienstes »Friede sei mit Euch« erinnerte an die symbolische Rolle, die die weltweite Öffentlichkeit diesem Kirchbau gab.

Allerdings sorgten die Fernsehkameras dafür, das Besondere dieses Kirchenraums zur Geltung zu bringen. In dieser Kirche bildet die Gemeinde den Mittelpunkt. Sie versammelt sich unter der riesigen Kuppel und hat so symbolisch unmittelbaren Zugang zu Gott. Die Bankreihen der Zuhörer bilden eine Kreuzform. Kameraeinstellungen aus der Kuppel und von unten gaben den Blick frei auf das Kreuz der Bankreihen und den geöffneten Himmel der Kuppel. Der Altar ist zurückgezogen platziert, und über ihm thront die gewaltige Orgel. Die protestantische Zurücknahme des Rituellen, die Betonung der Gemeinde und der Musik finden in der Architektur dieser Bürgerkirche sinnfälligen Ausdruck. Die Kanzel ragt wie ein (Lauf-) Steg in den Kirchenraum hinein. Und wie ein Laufsteg ist sie nur wenig erhöht. Die Gemeinde kann ihren Prediger genau beobachten. Ihm steht nur ein kleines Lesepult zur Verfügung, das den Prediger eigentümlich ungeschützt wirken lässt. Von hier aus kann entweder ein Funke der Begeisterung überspringen—oder aber die Leere der Worte unmittelbar gespürt werden.

[7] Wesentliche Anregungen zu diesem Kapitel verdanke ich B. Weyel, Predigt und Öffentlichkeit. Die Weihe der Dresdner Frauenkirche, in: International Journal of Practical Theology 10 (2006), 168-177.

Der Bischof der sächsischen Landeskirche betrat als erster die Kanzel. Er gab sich wenig Mühe, die Feststimmung der Gemeinde und der Millionen Spender und Zuschauer in Worte zu fassen. Zwar begann er seine Ansprache mit den Worten: »Unsere Herzen sind bewegt von Dankbarkeit und Freude. Obwohl wir seit Jahren auf ihn gewartet haben, staunen wir, dass dieser Tag möglich wurde.« Er fuhr dann aber fort: »Vor 271 Jahren, als die neu erbaute Frauenkirche geweiht wurde, wird es nicht anders gewesen sein. ›Ist jemand nur hierher gekommen, etwas Neues zu sehen und zu hören, wie den neuen Dingen der eitlen Welt Brauch ist‹, fragte damals Superintendent Löscher[8] in seiner Predigt, vermutlich mit strengem Unterton, und erklärte der Gemeinde, dass es gerade an einem solchen Tag darauf ankommt, das Evangelium aufmerksam zu hören. Da hatte er Recht und so wollen wir uns dem Gleichnis vom Senfkorn zuwenden.« Es folgte dann eine Textauslegung des sonntäglichen Predigttextes mit nur wenigen Bezügen auf den Anlass.

Zu einem zivilreligiösen Ritual wurde dieser Gottesdienst dadurch, dass direkt im Anschluss an die lutherische Segenshandlung Bundespräsident Horst Köhler die Kanzel betrat. Hatte der Bischof eher leidend gewirkt, so zeigte der Bundespräsident ein strahlendes Lächeln. Er schien die Nähe der Gemeinde zu genießen. Seine Ansprache begann so:

> ›Suchet der Stadt Bestes.‹ Diese Aufforderung des Propheten Jeremia steht auf einer der Glocken der Frauenkirche. Meine sehr verehrten Damen und Herren, der Kirchbau, dessen Einweihung wir heute feiern, zählt zu dem Besten, was freie Bürger leisten können. Dieser wunderbare Bau ist mehr als ein Gebäude. Er steht für das Gute, das uns eint. Die Dresdner Frauenkirche, die schon kurz nach ihrer Fertigstellung 1743 als der schönste Kirchbau des Protestantismus beschrieben wurde, war nach dem Zweiten Weltkrieg vor allem eine schmerzliche Erinnerung und eine Wunde, ihre Ruine ein Mahnmal gegen Zerstörung und blinde Gewalt. Doch mit dem Herbst 1989 wurde die Vision, die sich mancher Dresdner durch die Zeit der DDR hindurch bewahrt hatte, dann zum konkreten Projekt. Dazu brauchte es mehr als die tausende Kubikmeter Sandstein, die in über einem Jahrzehnt zusammengefügt wurden. Es brauchte mehr als die weit über 100 Millionen Euro, die der Bau gekostet hat. Nötig waren vor allem die Tatkraft, die Zuversicht und der unermüdliche Einsatz von Menschen in Dresden und weit darüber hinaus.

Hatten sich die Pfarrer bemüht, dem Gottesdienst ein konfessionelles Gepräge zu geben, so stellt der Bundespräsident die Feier konsequent in einen zivilreligiösen Rahmen. Dieser Kirchbau zeige, was »freie Bürger« leisten könnten. »Er steht für das Gute, das uns eint«. Das ist eine bemerkenswerte Formulierung in einem Land, das Jahrhunderte lang unter der konfessionellen Spaltung gelitten hatte. Nun soll ausgerechnet eine lutherische Kirche ein Symbol der deutschen Einheit sein! Dem Bundespräsidenten gelingt diese ›Entkirchlichung‹ durch die

[8] Valentin Ernst Löscher (1673-1749) war seit 1709 Oberkonsistorialrat und Superintendent in Dresden.

Erinnerung an die jüngste Geschichte Dresdens. Erst die Wiedervereinigung Deutschlands rückte den Wiederaufbau in den Bereich des Möglichen. Und es waren in der Tat einige Bürger Dresdens, die sich gegen den Widerstand der Kirche für den Wiederaufbau einsetzten.

Diese Geschichte des Wiederaufbaus nimmt der Bundespräsident auf, wenn er fortfährt:

> Hatte nicht Ostdeutschland Straßen, Dächer und Fabriken nötiger als einen teuren Kirchbau? Aber eine Gruppe von Bürgerinnen und Bürgern sagte: Dresden braucht mehr! Und spätestens heute erkennen wir: Diese Bürger hatten Recht! Menschen leben vom Brot, aber eben nicht vom Brot allein. Das Jahr 1989 hat gerade uns Deutschen gezeigt: Freiheit braucht man wie die Luft zum Atmen.

Wieder nimmt der Bundespräsident ein biblisches Zitat (»Der Mensch lebt nicht vom Brot allein ...«) auf, wendet es aber wiederum bürgerschaftlich. Die Opposition lautet nicht »Brot vs. Wort Gottes«, sondern »Brot vs. Freiheit«. Die Erinnerung an das Jahr 1989 und die Einweihung der Frauenkirche verknüpft der Bundespräsident so:

> Aber der Drang nach Freiheit, nach Meinungsfreiheit, nach Demokratie lässt sich nicht dauerhaft unterdrücken und wegschließen. Es kam der Herbst 1989, es kam die Wiedervereinigung und mit ihr auch die Vision vom Wiedererstehen der Frauenkirche. Damals haben 14 Dresdner den entscheidenden Anfang gemacht. Sie schlossen sich bereits Ende November 1989 in einer Bürgerinitiative für den Wiederaufbau der Frauenkirche zusammen. Für sie war klar: Eine Stadt ist mehr als eine Ansammlung von Gebäuden. Eine Stadt lebt von der Tatkraft und der Haltung ihrer Bürger—Menschen, die der Stadt Bestes suchen.

Die Frauenkirche ist ein Symbol der Freiheit, ein Symbol der Wiedervereinigung und ein Symbol bürgerschaftlichen Engagements:

> Der Wiederaufbau der Frauenkirche ist in einzigartiger Weise Ausdruck des Guten, das in einer Bürgergesellschaft und ihren Bürgern steckt und das darauf wartet, geweckt zu werden. Und die Frauenkirche hat diese Kräfte nicht zum ersten Mal geweckt. Schon ihr Bau im Jahre 1726 wurde nicht von oben verordnet, sondern von den Dresdnern selber beschlossen: So war es nicht der sächsische Kurfürst, sondern der Rat der Stadt Dresden, der die Errichtung der Kirche durchsetzte.

Es folgt dann ein langer Redeabschnitt, in dem der Bundespräsident den unzähligen Spendern dankt.

> Stellvertretend für sie alle möchte ich nur einige nennen: Die Dresdner Taxigenossenschaft erklärte sich über mehrere Jahre bereit, für jede über die Funkzentrale vermittelte Fahrt einen Pfennig für den Wiederaufbau zur Verfügung zu stellen. (...) Britische Handwerker haben ihr Können in die Anfertigung des goldenen Turmkreuzes eingebracht. Werner Jahn, der als politischer Häftling über vier Jahre in der berüchtigten DDR-Haftanstalt Waldheim einsaß, hat seine Haftentschädigung für den Wiederaufbau gespendet. Und was kann uns mehr Hoffnung machen als die Anwesenheit

einer Abordnung der polnischen Stadt Gostyn bei diesem Festakt? Zwölf ihrer Söhne wurden als Widerstandskämpfer 1942 nicht weit von hier, im ehemaligen Gebäude des Landgerichtshofs am Münchner Platz, von den Nazis hingerichtet. Und ausgerechnet in dieser Stadt sammelte Marian Sobkowiak, ein überlebendes Mitglied der Widerstandsgruppe, mit anderen Bürgern für die Frauenkirche und ließ eine der Flammenvasen auf dem Turm dieser Kirche von einem polnischen Steinmetz anfertigen. Was kann uns mehr Hoffnung machen?

Damit ist ein weiteres Thema angeschlagen: die Versöhnung zwischen den ehemaligen Kriegsgegnern in Europa:

Wer Schülern heute erklären will, was der Ausdruck ›Europa als Friedenswerk‹ bedeutet, dem empfehle ich eine Klassenfahrt nach Dresden und Coventry. Den Partnerstädten ist es über Jahrzehnte gelungen, Deutsche und Engländer aus zwei Orten zusammenzubringen, die durch ihre Geschichte immer miteinander verbunden sein werden. Und der *Dresden Trust* hat diese Stadt und den Wiederaufbau der Frauenkirche vielen Menschen in Großbritannien nahe gebracht. Wer konnte sich dies nach den verheerenden Bombardements damals vorstellen? Frieden ist ein Geschenk, für das man aber immer wieder arbeiten muss, und manchmal grenzt das, was Versöhnung bewirken kann, an ein Wunder. Die Dresdner Frauenkirche kann uns Kraft geben, uns gemeinsam und grenzenlos noch stärker für Frieden und Versöhnung einzusetzen.

Ein Kirchenbau als Kraftquelle für politische Friedens- und Versöhnungsarbeit. Damit wagt sich ein Bundespräsident, in dessen Land ein Drittel Konfessionslose leben, sehr weit. Da er aber das Deutungsspektrum dieses Kirchbaus sehr weit auslegt, muss man auch als Konfessionsloser nicht unbedingt Anstoß daran nehmen. Denn man kann einfach die menschliche Kraftanstrengung beim Bau der Kirche bewundern. Darauf verweist der Bundespräsident dann auch ausdrücklich:

Wir bewundern die Handwerker und Planer aus Dresden und Sachsen. Die Glocken wurden in Bad Friedrichshall in Baden-Württemberg gegossen, das Holz für die Emporen im Chor ist im Schwarzwald geschlagen und in Chemnitz gebogen. So zeigt die Frauenkirche ganz praktisch, was uns als Deutsche eint und was wir zustande bringen können, wenn wir gut zusammenarbeiten.

Gegen Ende seiner Ansprache folgen—wie es auch bei Predigten der Fall ist—Ermahnungen, die in die Form von Wünschen gepackt sind:

Ich wünsche jedem von uns ein Stück von dem Mut, von der Begeisterung und von der Zuversicht, die die Einweihung dieser Kirche möglich gemacht haben. Ich wünsche der Stadt Dresden und all ihren Bewohnern und Freunden, dass sie beim Blick auf die Frauenkirche an das denken mögen, was uns eint: Als freie Bürger der Stadt Bestes zu erstreben. Und ich wünsche unserem Land, dass die Dresdner Frauenkirche uns stets daran erinnern möge, was wir an Gutem zustande bringen können, wenn wir einig sind. Noch einmal wird der Vers aus dem Propheten Jeremia zitiert: ›Suchet der Stadt Bestes!‹

Aber auch für das persönliche Leben soll die Kirche »Mut«, »Begeisterung« und »Zuversicht« schenken.

Hatte der Bundespräsident zu Beginn seiner Ansprache in die Vergangenheit geblickt, so wagt er zum Schluss einen Blick in die Zukunft:

> Wir Deutsche schreiben gemeinsam mit unseren Freunden und Partnern in aller Welt an einem neuen Kapitel unserer Geschichte. Das alles zeigt, wofür die Frauenkirche steht—für die Kraft der Versöhnung und für das, was uns eint. Wenn wir diese Erkenntnis dauerhaft beherzigen, dann können wir gewiss sein: Dieses Kapitel, das wir gemeinsam jetzt schreiben, es wird ein gutes Kapitel.

Der Bau der Dresdner Frauenkirche symbolisiert also auch ein neues Kapitel in der Geschichte Deutschlands, ein Kapitel der europäischen Einigung auf der Grundlage von Versöhnungsbereitschaft und Friedenswillen. Die Kirche wird so in die Sicht der Deutschen auf ihre eigene Geschichte eingeschrieben—als ein Symbol der Einheit und der Zuversicht.

## Zusammenfassung

Der Präsident der Bundesrepublik Deutschland besitzt keine operative, sondern lediglich eine repräsentative Macht. Während die Bundeskanzlerin die Richtlinien der Tagespolitik bestimmt, kann der Bundespräsident lediglich durch seine Reden Einfluss nehmen. In diesen Reden ist es seine Aufgabe, die kollektiven Gewissheiten vom Fundament der gegenwärtigen Verfassung und der Bestimmung des Volkes zum Ausdruck zu bringen. Es ist ganz bezeichnend für die Arbeitsteilung zwischen dem Präsidenten und der Kanzlerin, dass der Präsident jährlich eine Ansprache am Weihnachtsfest hält, während die Kanzlerin die Neujahrsansprache hält. Darin bilanziert die Kanzlerin, legt Rechenschaft über das Geleistete ab und blickt planend voraus, der Präsident dagegen ruft zur Besinnung auf, öffnet den Blick für die weiteren Horizonte und die elementaren Grundlagen eines Gemeinwesens.

Und es ist auch bezeichnend, dass der Bundespräsident die Rede zum Volkstrauertag hält. Wenn Bürgerinnen und Bürger ihr Leben für das Gemeinwesen opfern mussten, dann gehört es zur Rolle des Präsidenten, den Hinterbliebenen und dem Volk zu erklären, warum dieses Opfer notwendig war. In den vergangenen Jahrzehnten haben nur wenige deutsche Soldaten ihr Leben verloren. Sollte allerdings der so genannte ›Krieg gegen den Terror‹ zu keinem guten Ende kommen und sollten auch deutsche Soldaten in Afghanistan oder in Afrika ihr Leben verlieren, dann wird die deutsche Öffentlichkeit nach der Legitimation dieser Opfer fragen und dann wird es die Aufgabe des Bundespräsidenten sein, die politischen Entscheidungen, die dazu geführt haben, in einen Zusammenhang zu stellen, der vor den religiösen und moralischen Überzeugungen der Bürgerinnen und Bürger Bestand haben kann.

Da der deutsche Präsident aber—anders als der amerikanische—nicht die Möglichkeit hat, die Nation selbst in einen heilsgeschichtlichen Rahmen zu stellen, werden auch in Zukunft die großen repräsentativen Kirchengebäude in Deutschland dazu genutzt werden, das Gemeinwesen—in Freud wie in Leid[9]—daran zu erinnern, wie sein religiös-weltanschauliches Fundament beschaffen ist.

[9]Vgl. R. Schieder, Gottesdienste in politisch-diakonischer Verantwortung, in: Zeitschrift der gemeinsamen Arbeitsstelle für gottesdienstliche Frage der EKD 19 (2005), 13-23.

# The Importance of Religious Affiliations among Political Elites A comparison of Germany and the United States

NILS OLE OERMANN

## 1. Introduction[1]

> America makes no sense without a deeply held faith—and I do not care what it is. – Dwight D. Eisenhower

The link between religion and politics is an increasingly debated topic on both sides of the Atlantic, especially after 9/11, leading the *Financial Times* Washington Bureau Chief, James Harding, to publish a full-page article titled »Preaching to the converted« on January 4/5 2003.

Harding argues that George W. Bush and his White House staff have woven faith into his presidency to a point where critics (including Harding) fear that the wall between church and state is being straddled to dangerous effect. He asserts that through the increase in the frequency of White House Bible Studies, through George W. Bush's declaration of Jesus Christ as »the most important political philosopher in his life«, through his working with »a fundamentalist Christian« chief speechwriter[2] and advisors such as the Pentecostal Christian John Ashcroft as his fomer Attorney General, the President seems to infest the White House and America with the views of an exclusive Christian circle enforced on society as a whole. Most US-Presidents have professed their faith to some extent, from Jimmy Carter's teaching of Bible Studies to Billy Graham's role as an evangelical Teiresias to several presidents. However, the current Bush administration is a more extreme case, Harding argues, especially since the fight against an »axis of evil« has increasingly been motivated and shaped by G. W. Bush's religious views. Harding concludes that by mixing politics with religious motivations, Bush is softening the vital separation between church and state.

Having described the relationship between religion and government in the US, the journalist goes on to present a comparison with Europe as the second pillar of his argument: Bush's moral clarity unnerves people in Europe, an essentially post-religious continent in which people who treat the political podium

[1] I would like to thank Prof. Samuel P. Huntington who supervised the research for this paper and Prof. Jim Guth for his helpful comments.

[2] James Harding refers to Michael Gerson.

as a pulpit are viewed with suspicion or distaste. Only 20% of Europeans say they attend weekly religious services, as opposed to 50% of Americans who claim to do so. It is this faith gap, Harding argues, that has quietly begun to aggravate the US-European relationship and appears to be sending the New and the Old Worlds and their political elites on starkly different paths.[3]

This article aims to test Harding's assertions about religious differences between American and European political elites. Are his transatlantic observations correct? To whom does he refer when he talks about »people in Europe«? It is certainly true that America is and has been more religious than Europe—85% of Americans tell pollsters that they identify with a religious faith, making the United States one of the most religious countries in the world.[4] But does the fact that most European countries show low rates of church attendance imply that European political elites are mirroring this more secular trend? Do European voters prefer to vote for politicians who are less religious?

This article does not aim to give a legal analysis of the relation between religion and state, but rather attempts a theological evaluation and socio-political analysis of developments in terms of religious affiliations among political elites in two leading Western democracies. Is religious affiliation becoming less important in Germany and Europe, while the importance of religion increases in the US? Has the thickness of the Jeffersonian wall between church and states increased or decreased? How do the religious affiliations of political elites mirror and affect national identities? Political discussions about assumed Western values on the one hand and Islamic militant threats on the other are a vivid illustration of how virulent this question about the link between politics and religion currently is.

## 2. The importance of religion for national identity

Huntington provides a clear answer to the question of why one should study religious affiliations of politicians and societies in general. In his book *The Clash of Cultures and the Remaking of World Order* he suggests that in order to understand a society or particular civilization, one must understand what defines it in terms of »blood, language, religion, way of life«.[5] Huntington points out that values, beliefs or societal institutions can only be fully understood if one recognizes their roots. The latter often rest, directly or indirectly, in religion, shaping the political elites of a society as well as the general population. Those

[3]Cf. J. Harding, Preaching to the Converted, in: Financial Times. International Edition on 4/5 January 2003, FT Weekend, 1.

[4]Cf. Harding, op. cit. (n. 3), 1.

[5]S.P. Huntington, The Clash of Cultures and the Remaking of World Order, New York 1996, 42.

elites are elected to make political decisions which are likely to be influenced by the respective values, upbringing, education and religious affiliations of those who choose them. This can be seen in R. Putnam's analysis of the differences between Mezzogiorno and Northern Italy in terms of existing »civil societies« in those places or in Max Weber's differentiation between a Protestant/Calvinist and a Catholic work ethic in order to explain economic differences in Protestant and Catholic communities related to their economic performance; these are sociological approaches which perceive religious affiliations as a key characteristic and building block of civil societies.[6]

It therefore seems promising to analyze the way in which political elites affiliate themselves with certain religious confessions and how those affiliations reflect the national identities of the populations which elect them. Is there a correlation between religious affiliation and elite selection and do political elites mirror certain religious trends within their societies or vice versa? Germany and the United States will be considered here as two states within the Western hemisphere with comparable democratic structures but with both significant differences in their societal and cultural traditions, which make a comparison particularly interesting.

What is it that makes the German or American religious landscape particular? Have German reunification or the emancipation of American minorities in the 1960s have had an impact on the religious affiliations of political elites? Is it important for American national identity that John F. Kennedy was Catholic, Richard Nixon Quaker and Jimmy Carter a Southern Baptist? Is it coincidental that the majority of German Federal Presidents tend to be rather active Protestants? In other words: are statistical data about religious affiliations of political elites random, or are certain patterns emerging which reveal something about the societies and the identities of their citizens? This paper will conclude by considering statistical data on religious affiliations of political elites in the US and Germany in order to identify certain characteristic patterns within political systems and to explain the religious roots that shape national identities.

[6] Cf. R.C. Putnam, Bowling Alone. The Collapse and Revival of American Community, New York 2000; M. Weber, Die protestantische Ethik und der Geist des Kapitalismus, in: Gesammelte Aufsätze zur Religionssoziologie, Band I, Tübingen 1963, 17-206, here 23; D. Käsler, Max Weber. Eine Einführung in Leben, Werk und Wirkung, Frankfurt/New York 1995, 101-103; H.J. Hohm, Politik als Beruf, Opladen 1987, 170-177; E. Wolf, Rechtstheologische Studien, Frankfurt/M. 1972, 11.

## 3. Religious affiliations and national identity in the US and Germany

Harding's article could give the impression that he is reporting a completely new phenomenon about an American President frequently referring to God and religion in regards to political decision-making. However, this observation is anything but new: Alexis de Tocqueville wrote about the Americans in a way which links religious and political zeal:

> On my arrival in the United States the religious aspect of the country was the first thing that struck my attention (...).[7] Religion in America takes no direct part in the government of society, but it must be regarded as the first of their political institutions; for it does not impart a taste for freedom, it facilitates the use of it. (...) I do not know whether all Americans have a sincere faith in their religion—for who can search the human heart?—but I am certain that they hold it to be indispensable to the maintenance of republican institutions. This opinion is not particular to a class of citizens or to a party, but it belongs to the whole nation and to every rank of society. (...) The Americans combine the notions of Christianity and of liberty so intimately in their minds that it is impossible to make them conceive the one without the other (...). Thus religious zeal is perpetually warmed in the United States by the fires of patriotism. These men do not act exclusively from a consideration of a future life; eternity is only one motive of their devotion to the cause. If you converse with these missionaries of Christian civilization, you will be surprised to hear them speak so often of the goods of this world (...).[8]

One may disagree with Tocqueville's observations, but in terms of identifying a trend he is certainly correct: America is an exceptionally religious country. Describing its Puritan roots, Huntington suggests aligning Christianity with other American values such as liberty, democracy and pluralism, asking whether an America without its Protestant core would still be America.[9] Religion plays a key role when one tries to reflect about national identity in the US in comparison to Europe.

In both Germany and the US, church and state are clearly separated, but for reasons which are historically very different. In many European countries, church and state were separated mainly to emancipate and protect the state from the influence of the churches and to prevent religiously motivated wars as a result of the Westphalian Peace. In America, it was the other way round: many Puritans left Europe because they were being persecuted for their faith and thus felt the need to protect their churches and religious believes from the influence of the state. In the 19th and 20th century, confessional boundaries tended to be less important in the United States, as a nation of immigrants,

[7] A. de Tocqueville, Democracy in America, Volume I, New York 1976, 308.

[8] A. de Tocqueville, op. cit. (n. 7), 305-306.

[9] Cf. S.P. Huntington, American Politics and the Promise of Disharmony, Cambridge/MA 1981, 229.

than they were in Europe. And Dwight D. Eisenhower went so far to assert: »America makes no sense without a deeply held faith—and I do not care what it is!«[10]

Today, the United States may not be a »multicultural« nation in the deconstructionist sense of the term which can be critically assessed by analyzing Gutman's or Appiah's interpretation.[11] However, America is certainly a diverse nation, not only in ethnic, but also in religious terms. Based on the 1992 National American Election Study Wald identifies 27% of Americans as Evangelical Protestant, 21% as »Mainline Protestant«, 9% as Black Protestant, 25% as Catholic, 2% as Jewish and 16% as secular.[12]

Germany has a very different religious landscape, which is dominated by a high rate of nominal church membership and an almost excatly 50: 50 split between Roman Catholics and Protestants, the latter being predominantly Lutheran. In the West, more than 75% of the population is at least nominally Protestant or Roman Catholic, while only around 20% of East Germans are Protestant and just over 3% Catholic. At the same time, over 3, 5 million Muslims live in Germany, mainly as a result of Turkish immigration within the last 40 years. However, the majority of them do not hold German passports, which would allow them to vote in national elections. While their societal presence is increasing, Muslims currently have little influence in terms of building societal elites.

There is a regional split between Protestants and Catholics in Germany: The South-East (Bavaria) is predominantly Catholic, while the North is predominantly Protestant. The number of evangelical/born-again Christians is also small in comparison to the US, so with its Protestant and Catholic churches, Germany can be described as rather homogenous in religious terms. This also has a noticeable effect on German politics, as can be observed in voting patterns at general elections.

[10] R.H. Nelson, Economics as Religion. From Samuelson to Chicago and Beyond, Pennsylvania State University Press, University Park/PA 2001, 301.

[11] Cf. Ch. Taylor et al., Multiculturalism. Examining the Politics of Recognition, Princeton 1994.

[12] Cf. K.D. Wald, Religion and Politics in the United States, 3rd edition, Congressional Quarterly, Washington DC 1997, 173.

## 4. The religious affiliations in the German *Bundestag* before and after German reunification

*Before reunification (until 1990)*

While the East German Socialist Party (SED), which became the PDS after 1990[13], declared atheism an integral part of its socialist doctrine, West Germany's politicians have always tended to be either Protestant or Catholic along historically rather impermeable denominational lines: the Christian Democrats (CDU) are traditionally strong in the predominantly Catholic German South with more Catholic MPs, while the Social Democrats (SPD) have tended to be more Protestant with most of their voters in the North and West of the Federal Republic. To assess the impact of religion within political elites, the religious affiliations of West German MPs are compared for the years 1953 and 1983.

Among the 509 MPs in the 2nd West German *Bundestag* of 1953 there were 173 Catholics, 153 Protestants, 1 Jewish, 1 self-declared Atheist and 179 MPs either not declaring their religious affiliation or without religious confession (Figure 1).[14]

**Figure 1: 2nd West German *Bundestag* of 1953**

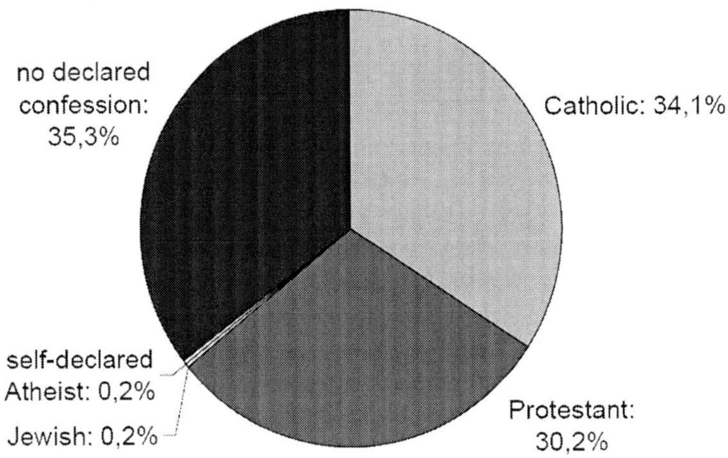


The large majority of MPs who did not comment on their religion were Social Democrats (SPD) or Liberals (FDP) while nearly all Conservatives (CDU) declared their religious affiliation.

[13]The PDS is the successor party if the SED after 1990 and stands for Partei des Demokratischen Sozialismus, Party of Democratic Socialism, now called Die Linke.

[14]Based on the CVS of all MPS, published in: Amtliches Handbuch des Deutschen Bundestages, 2. Wahlperiode, Darmstadt 1954. Reflecting the West German population at that time (over 80%) the majority of these Social Democratic and Liberal MPS were likely to be nominal church members, but did not list their religious affiliation in the Bundestag handbook as faith was regarded a personal affair.

Among the 518 MPs in the 9th West German *Bundestag* of 1983 the picture was rather similar while the number of MPs who declared there religious affiliation was higher than in 1953: 191 Catholic MPs, 171 Protestant MPs, 1 self-declared Atheist, 155 MPs either not declaring their religious affiliation or without religious confession (Figure 2).[15]

**Figure 2: 9th West German *Bundestag* of 1983**

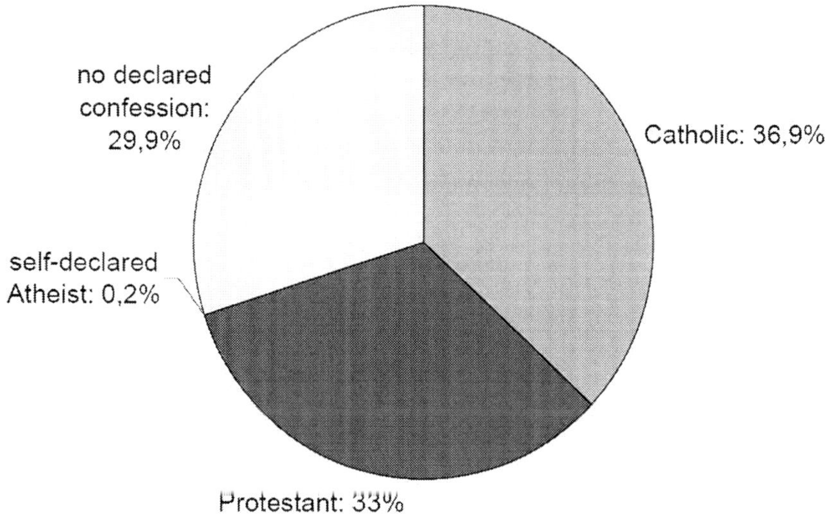


In terms of formal education, B. Badura makes the interesting observation that the tertiary educational level of Protestant West German MPs in the 1970s and 1980s was higher than the education level of their Catholic colleagues.[16] While the general population of West Germany was becoming more secularized in the 1970s and 1980s, German MPs remained an integral part of an establishment in which schools and last but not least churches remained a socially important and respected aspect. With Gustav Heinemann, Richard von Weizsäcker, Roman Herzog or Johannes Rau, Germans had (West-German born) Federal Presidents who even occupied formal positions within the Protestant church and—in case of Johannes Rau—came from a family of missionaries and lay preachers. West German voters in the 1980s and 1990s, even if they themselves became more secular, tended to vote for politicians with close ties to their respective churches, whether Protestant or Catholic. It may well be the case that religious affiliation was not the main driver for the decision of voters, but the number of MPs in

[15] Kürschners Volkshandbuch Deutscher Bundestag, 9.-15. Wahlperiode, Darmstadt 1980-2003.

[16] Cf. B. Badura/J. Reese, Jungparlamentarier in Bonn—ihre Sozialisation im Deutschen Bundestag, Stuttgart 1976, 117.

the *Bundestag* with religious affiliations remained stable, while that number became smaller among the general population.

Harding's claim that the political decision makers in Europe are becoming more secular is therefore incorrect, at least in the case of Germany. While the German population may be becoming more secular, the political elite is still made up of members of the churches.

Did this change with German reunification? Does this trend remain prevalent, even when a population of 16 million East Germans, of which only a little over 20% were members of Christian churches, unified with a predominantly Christian West Germany to a nation of 80 million people? An analysis of the religious affiliations in the *Bundestag* of 1998 shows the following numbers:[17] 202 Catholic, 221 Protestant, 1 Muslim, 1 Seven Day Adventist, 3 self-declared Atheists, 259 MPs either not declaring their religious affiliation or without religious confession (Figure 3).[18]

**Figure 3: German *Bundestag* of 1998**

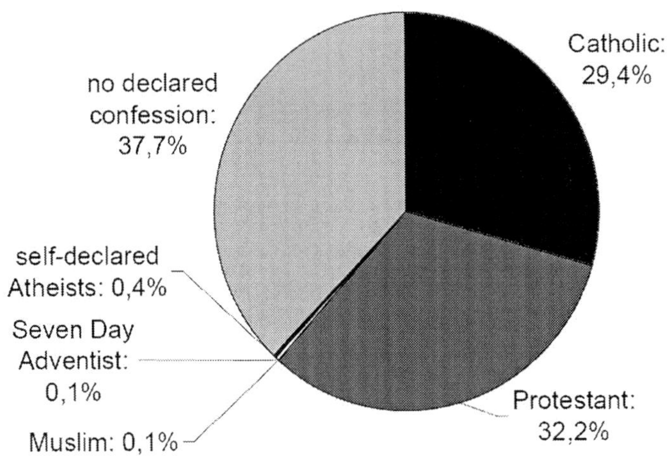


With only 614 members the 16th German *Bundestag* of 2005 became significantly smaller, while one can notice a significant rise in the number of MPs with religious affiliations:[19] 179 Catholic, 209 Protestant, 1 Muslim, 1 self-declared

[17]Based on the CVs of all MPs, published in: Kürschners Volkshandbuch, Deutscher Bundestag, 14. Wahlperiode, Darmstadt 1998.

[18]The increasing number of MPs with no stated religious affiliation mainly stems from the PDS as the former East German Communist Party, where 31 of the 36 MPs do not belong to churches or comment on their religion.

[19]Based on the CVs of all MPs, published in: Kürschners Volkshandbuch, Deutscher Bundestag, 16. Wahlperiode, Darmstadt 2005.

Atheist, 122 MPs either not declaring their religious affiliation or without religious confession (Figure 4).[20]

**Figure 4: German *Bundestag* of 2005**

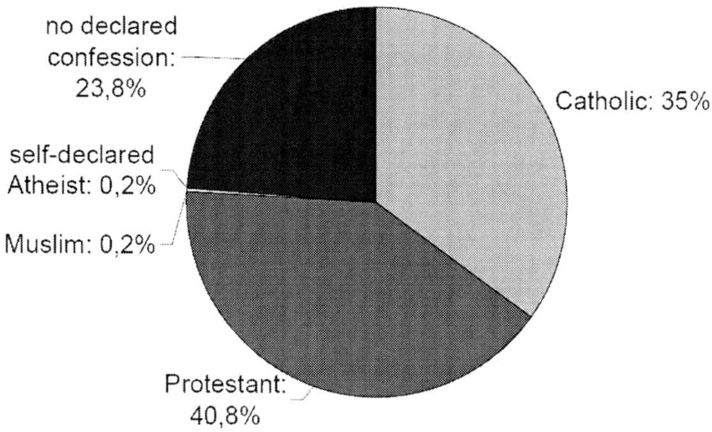


The *Bundestag* in unified Germany tends to be more Protestant as the Protestant church was the largest church in the fromer GDR.

For the West German MPs, not much has changed much since 1980 in terms of their religious affiliation: Contrary to Harding's assessment, the numbers in terms of MP church membership do not mirror the increasing secularization among the general population in Germany. These trends are clear and well documented.[21] In the period after World War II, more than 80% of West Germans were members of one of the two major churches, while in East Germany church membership was reduced to just over 20% by 1989, after 40 years under a self-declared atheist regime. 1989 was expected by many to mark a turning point also for the churches, particularly in East Germany, but it did not turn out this way. The percentage of 20% of East Germans who had remained church members despite political and societal pressure over decades, did not increase with the end of the Cold War, while the numbers of church members in West Germany continued to decline by about 1-2% per year.[22] The West German population is clearly becoming more secular, while East German church membership is now stable, but on an already low level.

[20]The increasing number of MPs with no stated religious affiliation mainly stems from the PDS as the former East German Communist Party, where 31 of the 36 MPs do not belong to churches or comment on their religion.

[21]Cf. D. Pollack, Religiösität in Ostdeutschland, Leipzig 1995.

[22]Survey by the Protestant Churches in Germany, Hannover 2000 (»EKD-Umfrage über Kirchenmitgliedschaft«). Cf. also: World Value Survey Germany, 2000. Cf. as well: Fremde Heimat Kirche. Die dritte EKD-Erhebung über Kirchenmitgliedschaft, hg.v. K. Engelhardt/H. von Loewenich/P. Steinacker, Gütersloh 1997.

*Two types of Christian MPs from East Germany*

The same observation of an increasing secularization does not apply to the politicians in Germany. What has changed is the overall balance between religious affiliations after 1990, which changed because of East German MPs who, compared to their voters, are over-proportionally Christian. Reunification has made Protestants the largest religious group in parliament which may be surprising given that 80% of the East German population does not belong to any church. So why are East German MPs over proportionally Christian?

Firstly, a rapid increase of MPs who were Protestant theologians and pastors from East Germany is noticeable: 6 pastors and one former Professor of Theology were East German MPs in 1998, while there were only 2 West German pastors in the *Bundestag* with an overall population of 60 Million West and 16 Million East Germans. The reason for this over-proportional representation is that the Protestant Church of the GDR provided an important base for the opposition movement within the GDR. Its leaders were widely respected, and several of them became the first generation of East German MPs. In 1998, the number of East German MPs (with exception of the four directly elected, non-religious Communist MPs) identifying themselves as Protestant (41), Catholic (13) and Seven Day Adventist (1) was even much higher than the number of non-religious MPs (23) from the former GDR. This phenomenon is worth analyzing because it is counterintuitive to what Harding states in his *Financial Times* article about increasingly secular European political elites. Two major reasons emerge why there is an over-proportional number of East German Christians among current political elites in the *Bundestag*.

In many cases East German political elites in 1990 were recruited from that group, although their presence in politics has slightly vanished. However, it is no coincidence that the former East German President of the *Bundestag*, Wolfgang Thierse, is Catholic and that the East German SPD was co-founded by Markus Meckel, a pastor, who was part of the former opposition movement in the GDR and became the last foreign minister of the GDR. Richard Schröder started his career as a lecturer of Philosophy of Religion before he became the SPD opposition leader in the last East German parliament, the *Volkskammer*, in 1990 and then member of the 1990 *Bundestag*. In 1991, he was appointed Professor of Theology at Humboldt-University Berlin. And Günter Nooke, a former activist in the GDR opposition movement now serves as the German government's envoy for human rights policy.

Although the GDR made it harder for some of its baptized citizens to attend grammar school, to be Christian implied a choice and often a lifestyle oriented towards family and education. The Theological Faculties and *Kirchliche Hochschulen*, church-run theological seminaries, were amongst the few places where active Christians had the chance to receive their tertiary education. Forming an opposition also required the ability to express one's thoughts effectively, something that was practiced in politically active congregations such as the Zion Church and the Gethsemane Church in East Berlin as well as in the Berlin Theological Seminary, the *Sprachenkonvikt*, from which a number of those new opposition leaders emerged in 1989/90.

The second generation of East German politicians includes somewhat different politicians such as the Catholic Prime Minister of Thuringia, Dieter Althaus, and the current Federal Chancellor, Angela Merkel. Angela Merkel is a pastor's daughter from East Germany, but she was not part of the active GDR opposition claiming the streets in 1989. Instead, she found her niche as a scientist, having gained a Ph. D. in Physics. Merkel, like other scientists, medics or engineers, was able to politically emerge after the reunification without a daunting past in the old Communist system. She was not the only East-German scientist to leave a political mark: the former presidential candidate in 1994, Prof. Jens Reich from East Berlin, is a medical doctor and Professor of Molecular Biology in East Berlin. Another East German and former presidential candidate in 1999 was Prof. Dagmar Schipanski, who served as Dean of a Thuringian Engineering School and was Minister of Science and Research in Thuringia until 2004. Those cvs correlate with the over-proportional number of scientists and engineers amongst the East German MPs since 1990, forming the second major group among East German MPs. Of the 129 East German MPs in the 12th German *Bundestag* (1990),

- 47.3% were scientists/engineers,
- 11.6% were in the medical profession,
- 7.3% were theologians or social workers,
- Only 4.7% were lawyers,
- Only 8.5% were teachers (Figure 5).[23]

[23] J.E. Krieger, Rollenorientierungen, Rollenerwartungen und Rollenverhalten von Ost-Abgeordneten im Deutschen Bundestag. Eine empirische Untersuchung, Frankfurt/M. 1998, 126.

**Figure 5: East German MPs in the *Bundestag* of 1990**

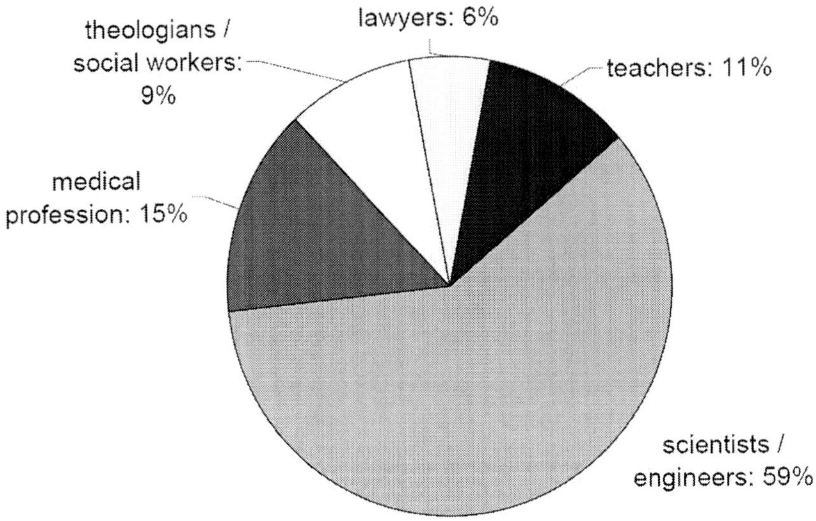


Those numbers differ significantly from West German political elites which show directly opposed professional profile: the majority of West German MPs are lawyers, teacher or trades union officials with only a small number of scientists and engineers in parliament.[24] However, it was almost impossible to be a lawyer or teacher in the GDR without any link to the state administration, since the GDR allocated its college places centrally. Medics or engineers were more likely to work in their societal niche. Secondly, many MPs in the scientist/engineer group are not only educated, but often tend also to be church members, too, even if they end up being less religiously active than members of the first group of opposition leaders with a close church background. Thirdly, there may be a growing group of East and West German MPs who have actually intensified their affiliation with the two main churches. They may perceive that the old West German elites are predominantly Christian and that voters prefer an »honest churchgoer« to a former SED-apparatchik.

The last group of East German MPs is made up of members of the former communist SED/PDS and they are, therefore, more often self-declared atheists.

*Conclusion of the German case study*

In 1990 the former Minister of Defense, Volker Rühe, made the remark that after reunification, Germany would become a more Protestant Germany. This prediction became reality in terms of political elites, while the average population is becoming even more secular. Harding's claim in his *Financial Times*

[24] Kürschners Volkshandbuch, op. cit. (n. 19), 300.

article that »European people« are becoming increasingly secular is certainly correct in Germany's case as well as in Europe in general. However, the East German example as well as the observed stability of religious affiliations of West German MPs between 1953 and 2005 shows that Harding is incorrect in terms of German political elites. Unlike the average citizen, German politicians appear to be increasingly religious in terms of nominal church membership. This may be due to particular historical events like the reunification, or because of an increase of social acceptance of church members. But whatever the reason, the claim that politics in Europe is influenced by increasingly secular political decision makers is clearly wrong, at least in the case of Germany. Looking at the observant Anglican Tony Blair, the Dutch Calvinist Prime Minister Jan Peter Balkenende, or the fact that former Norwegian Prime Minister Kjell Magne Bondevik is an ordained Lutheran pastor, the opposite to what Harding claims seems to be the case in Europe.[25] Europe's political elites seem to become increasingly religious, not in the way of a Christian Coalition like in the US, but certainly in terms of closer ties between politics and churches. In terms of overall national identities this may have little effect, as European citizens are attending fewer services and are less affiliated with churches. However, if the Heads of State increasingly align themselves with churches, one may assume that this leaves at least some mark in the political landscape which in turn shapes national identity. In that respect, is there really a key difference between Europe and the US, as Harding observes? What is the situation in the US?

## 5. Developments in the religious affiliations in the US Congress and Senate between 1965 and 1999

What do the statistics look like in terms of religious affiliations for US politicians and what has changed in the last decades? In the attached table the religious affiliations of Congress and Senate in 1965 and 1999 are listed. »Protestant« includes Episcopalians, Methodists, Baptists, Presbyterians and other Protestant churches. »Other« include Assembly of God, Orthodox, Christian Scientists. For the US Senate, the picture looks like this (Figures 6 and 7 in % of Senators):[26]

[25]For further statistical data on professional politicians in Europe see: J. Borchert (ed.), Politik als Beruf. Die politische Klasse in westlichen Demokratien, Opladen 1999.

[26]N.J. Ornstein/Th.E. Mann/M.J. Malbin, Vital Statistics on Congress 1999-2000, AEI Press, Washington DC 2002, 34-35; A. Ehrenhalt (ed.), Politics in America, CQ Press, Washington DC 1981 [compiled CVs as religious affiliations are not sepeartely listed]; Who is who in Congress, 106th Congress, Congressional Quarterly, Washington DC 2000.

Figure 6: US Senate 1965

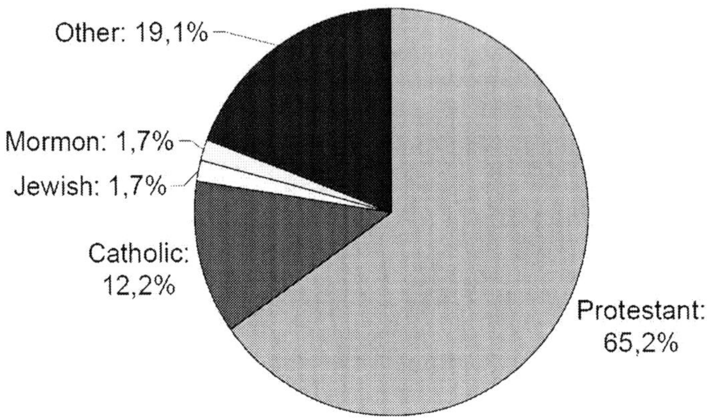


Figure 7: US Senate 1999

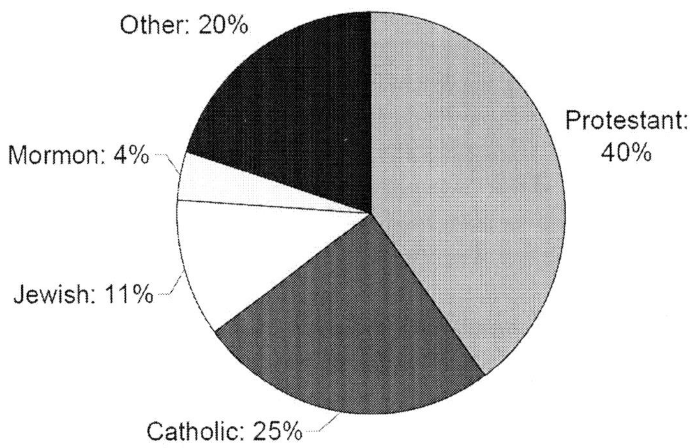


Significantly more Jews, Mormons and Catholics served in the Senate in 1999 than in the 1960s. The changes of religious affiliations among Senators mirror what has been going on in US society in general since the 1960s. Voters are more ready to vote for black or female candidates as well as for religious minorities, while they hardly vote at all for candidates or Senators without religious affiliations. For the current US Governors, a picture similar to the Senate emerges with the exception that there are still no Jewish Governors in 1999/2000[27], while Protestant Christians[28] were in the majority. »Others« include Assembly of God, Christian Scientists and Orthodox (Figure 8).

**Figure 8: US Governors 1999/2000**

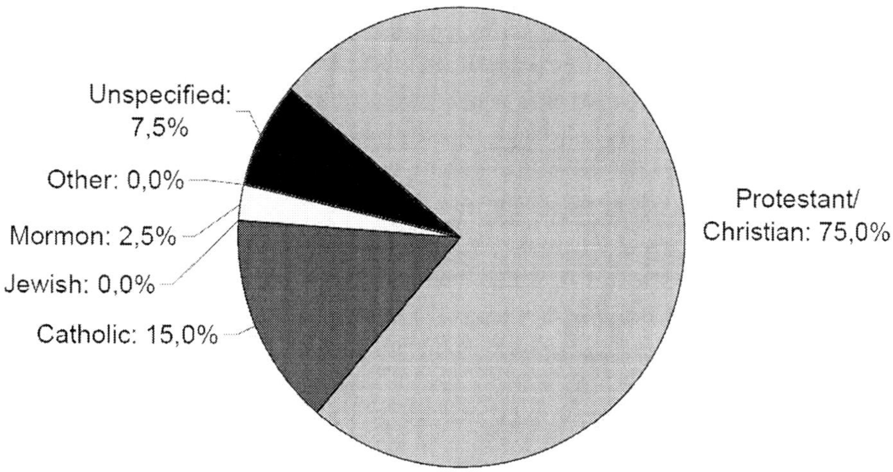


In 1999/2000 many states of the Union were still likely to vote for governors and senators with »Yankee« backgrounds—or, failing that, for those with origins that approach as closely as possible the »Anglo-Saxon ideal«.[29] At least in the 1940-50s that ideal was male and

> was a late-middle-aged or elderly, white, Protestant, native-born man with a rural or small-town and upper-middle class origins, a college-educated lawyer, and a ›joiner‹.[30]

Even if this stereotype may have changed, a Jewish or Mormon candidate will still be struggling to change those thinking patterns in the heads of many local voters in a Governor election in South Carolina or Alabama.

*Religious affiliations in the* US *Congress* 1965-1999

An analysis of the religious affiliations of Congressmen suggests that between 1965 and 1999 there has been a clear trend towards a reduction of the representation of traditional mainstream Protestant denominations (Methodists, Episcopalians, Presbyterian) in the House of Representatives, while the number

[27] Cf. Ehrenhalt (ed.), op. cit. (n. 26); Who is who in Congress, 106th Congress, Congressional Quarterly, Washington DC 2000.

[28] Including Episcopalians, Methodists, Baptists, Lutheran, Congregationalist, UCC and other Protestant churches.

[29] D.R. Matthews, US Senators and Their World, Chapel Hill 1960, 23.

[30] Matthews, op. cit. (n. 34), 44.

of Baptists/Evangelical candidates and Catholics has significantly increased in the past 30 years (Figures 9 and 10):[31]

**Figure 9: US Congress 1965 (89th Congress)**

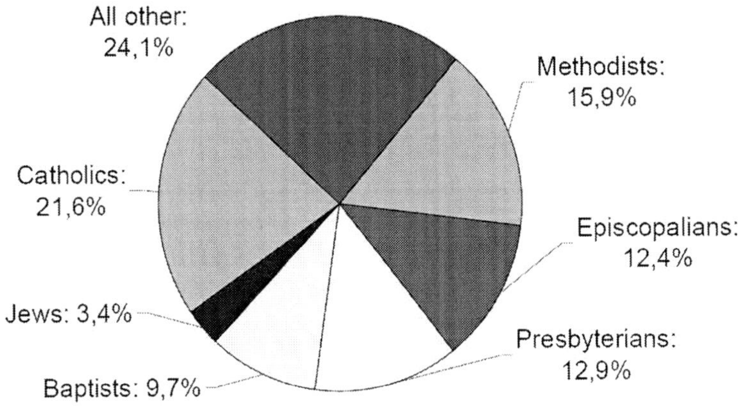


**Figure 10: US Congress 1999 (106th Congress)**

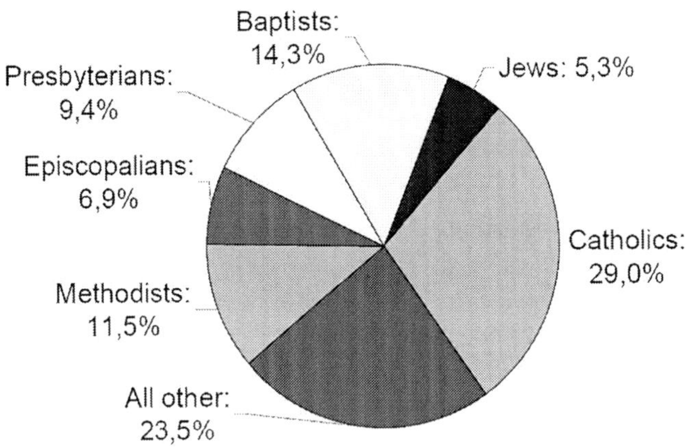


Wald reminds his readers that the same trends exist within US society as a whole, so the question is just whether society mirrors Congress or Congress mirrors society.[32]

[31] N.J. Ornstein et al (ed.), Vital Statistics on Congress, AEI Press, Washington DC 2000, 32-33.

[32] Cf. Wald, op. cit. (n. 13), 341.

An interesting detail is that there were more Catholic Republican Congressmen in 1999 than there were in 1965. The number of Catholic Congressmen between 1965 and 1999 rose about 30%, from 94 to 126. At the same time the numbers of Democrat and Republican Catholic MPs changed from 81: 13 to 76: 50. This confirms one assumption in terms of Catholic religious identity and emancipation: American Catholics are becoming Protestantized and more mainstream because of their Protestant, mainstream environment. While Catholics were distinctly Democrats in the John F. Kennedy era, they have become a reflection of the 50: 50 voting split between Democrats and Republicans in the 2000 elections. In other words: Catholics are no longer politically distinct, either in their voting patterns or in their likelihood to run for political office, and are following the overall trend of declining partisanship during elections.[33] Their increasing presence in Congress is likely to be caused by Hispanic immigrants who vote for their own Congressmen in the South West and Florida. The number of Jewish Congressmen has increased from 15 to 23, but unlike their Catholic counterparts they are overwhelmingly Democrat.

There are several clear trends in the data about religious affiliations of US politicians that confirm Harding's claim for the US that the religious affiliation of political elites in Washington correspond with the religious affiliation of the general US-population: Firstly, Harding is correct when he states that the number of Evangelicals in Congress and Senate has increased. Secondly, Jews and Mormons nearly doubled among Senators, which mirrors their general emancipation in US society. Thirdly, the number of Catholics has also increased among the political elites, which may be due to their increasing emancipation since the election of John F. Kennedy, in addition to the rising numbers of Hispanic immigrants. Catholics have become politically more mainstream, as their preference for the Democratic Party is replaced by the more even numbers of Catholic Democrat and Republican Congressmen. In terms of the US, Harding claims that an evangelical predominance may just mirror trends in the US in general, where moderate Lutheran, Presbyterian, Methodist or Episcopalian churches have experienced a decrease in membership numbers. The decreasing number of moderate Protestants and the rise of Baptists among political elites may just be a reflection of that trend. Harding also points out that G. W. Bush's religious statements are geared towards attracting the increasing numbers of evangelical voters. Although voting patterns are not a key focus of this paper, it is important to see how religious affiliations of voters relate to religious affiliations of politicians in the US and Europe.

[33] Cf. N. Nie/S. Verba/J.R. Petrocik, The changing American voter, Cambridge/MA/London 1976, 72-73.

## 6. Voting patterns and political partisanship in the US and Germany

To conclude the statistical analysis one should briefly look at voting patterns along religious lines in Germany and the US. How do voters react towards politicians of a certain denomination and are there distinct religiously motivated voting patterns emerging? Or is religion less of an issue in Germany and the US when people go to the ballot box? Harding thinks that the religious conviction of the current President is intended to serve an increasingly evangelical electorate, while religion among European voters seems less of an issue in terms of political choice. Is that assumption correct?

Huntington and Wald both point out that American voters through three Great Awakenings have always been influenced by religion in terms of their national identity (Huntington) and in terms of casting their vote (Wald). Are we perhaps just on the brink of a fourth Great Awakening matching the old patterns?

Religion is certainly an important part of US national identity in the sense that liberty implies the liberty to make political and religious choices. Voters identify themselves with politicians because they may approve of the values of the Christian Coalition in general, or because they are specifically against abortion or gay marriage or for school prayers. Religious identity is part of a consciously exercised religious/political liberty which constitutes American national identity. It is no surprise that someone from the Bible belt votes for George W. Bush, not because he is from that geographic region, but because he shares similar religious views held in that particular part of a country which happens to be over-proportionally religious anyway.

In Germany, the picture is somewhat different for historic and geographical reasons: in terms of voting behavior, religious affiliations also play a role, but they follow a structurally different pattern, which has stronger roots in terms of political partisanship and stronger party affiliations than in the US: German Protestants are more likely to vote Social Democrat (SPD), while the majority of Catholics tend vote for the Christian Democrats (CDU) as the main Conservative party. These patterns may have changed, but they have certainly not been eroded. A strong determining factor in German elections is the regional origin of voters and candidates which happen to coincide with their religious affiliation for historic reasons rooted in the Reformation. With the Peace of Augsburg 1555, the leader of a state was able to choose the religion of his subjects to be either Lutheran or Catholic (*cuius regio, eius religio*), which made the different German states both relatively distinct on the outside and at the same time homogenous on the inside, at least in religious terms. To a certain degree the patterns established in the sixteenth century can still be observed today:

In the 2002 elections, the Social Democrats (SPD) achieved a clear majority in the Protestant North and East, while the Catholic South with Bavaria as a Catholic stronghold voted CDU/CSU with an absolute majority. The Northern German, Protestant, Social Democrat teacher, worker or trade union member from a large city is a typical SPD voter while the Southern German, Catholic artisan from a small town is likely to vote for the CDU/CSU. Although one may argue that those voter classifications vanish in a more mixed, secular Germany, the clear religious and geographic voting patterns along those lines in the 2002 elections confirms that the trend is still significant.

Two distinct voting patterns in Germany and the US are emerging in terms of religious affiliation: American voters are concerned that their candidate belongs to a church or shares certain values in terms of a civil religion. In Germany religious convictions of candidates are hardly ever an explicit political topic while candidates from certain regions of the country (which happen to be Catholic or Protestant) are likely to be from a certain party and denomination and are locally supported. Noticeably fewer North and East Germans voted for Edmund Stoiber as the Catholic Chancellor candidate from a small town in Bavaria, while up to 70% of Bavarians, who happen to be mostly Catholic, voted for »their« Bavarian candidate. The religious affiliations of West German politicians often mirror the predominant denomination of the region they are from.

Voting patterns and the development of religious affiliations of elites in West Germany, East Germany and the US are so distinct because of the different historical developments of a Puritan country, a post-Fascist Cold War democracy and a Socialist State. The question becomes whether those distinct patterns make US elites and American national identity in terms of religion »exceptional« in comparison to Germany or Europe in general. Talking about American civil religion,[34] America is certainly distinct, but is it in its national and religious identity (which is interwoven) exceptional as a »beacon on the hill«?[35] To answer this question it is useful to view the data discussed above through a lens which is focused on the *Promise of Disharmony*. Huntington's study characterizes disharmony as a vital necessity in a country with many creeds and ethnicities.

[34]For a definition and in-depth analysis of the term see: R. Richey/D.G. Jones (eds.), American Civil Religion, San Francisco 1974; R. Schieder, Civil Religion. Die religiöse Dimension der politischen Kultur, Gütersloh 1987.

[35]For an analysis of the concept of American exceptionalism see: S.M. Lipset, American Excpetionalism. A Double-Edged Sword, New York 1996.

## 7. Huntington's *Promise of Disharmony* in terms of religious affiliations of political elites

Based on the analyzed data, there are two distinct religious patterns emerging between 1965 and 1999 in the US-Congress and Senate: firstly, more Jewish, Mormon and Catholic members have joined the legislative bodies in the last three decades as an expression of the emancipation of religious minorities. Secondly, Baptists and other Evangelicals as an integral part of the Christian Coalition have gained influence in the 1980s at the expense of decreasing numbers of traditional Protestants (Methodists, Presbyterian, and Episcopalian). Two conclusions emerge: America's rationalism and liberalism is reflected by the fact that religious minorities have managed to integrate themselves among the political elites quickly, while the Christian Coalition is an exceptional and most vivid expression of American Puritanism. Harding only recognizes the latter, while he overlooks the fact that America is also liberal in terms of allowing religious minorities to gain political influence. For other states, like Germany under Bismarck, this would have been unthinkable if the minority happened to be Catholic. In that sense America is »pro-gressive«, although demands that the bare breasts of the goddess *Justitia* be covered may sound disharmoniously »re-gressive« for a majority of Europeans.

What does this imply in terms of American national identity? It is striking to observe how those patterns are an exact match for what Huntington describes as most characteristic for American national identity and what he calls the *Promise of Disharmony.*[36] With that concept, he helps readers to determine what one may do with the conclusion that America has a particular, maybe exceptional identity which manifests itself in a vast range of issues from religion to immigration. The main theme of Huntington's conclusion in *American Politics: The Promise of Disharmony* is to clarify Alexis de Tocqueville's »confusion« of »the values and ideals of American society with social and political reality.«[37] Huntington reminds his readers that this gap, which acutely manifests itself in the development of religious affiliations of elites, is caused by two streams of thought which influenced the American creed in the 17th and 18th century: Protestant moralism and 18th century liberal rationalism which later culminated in developments as diverse as Wilsonianism as one side of the coin and H. Kissinger's *Realpolitik* on the other.[38] American ideals like liberty, equality, individualism and democracy are held up while they were violated at the same time during segregation. Huntington concludes that this »cognitive

[36] S.P. Huntington, American Politics. The Promise of Disharmony, Cambridge 1981, 221-262 (chap. 8 and Conclusion).

[37] Huntington, op. cit. (n. 44), 225.

[38] Cf. Ibid., 229.

dissonance« is not an accident or coincidence, but rather the underlying systemic theme, the »promise of disappointment« which runs through American history and identity.[39] Therefore, one may ask: what are the consequences of this dichotomy in terms of religion and state, in terms of diverse religious affiliations of Congressmen and the policies they support or laws they vote on?

When Huntington states that »power tends to corrupt and absolute power corrupts absolutely, then American power is no exception,«[40] he refers to Lord Acton's classic quotation in regard to the British Empire. According to this analysis, one may ask if America's political elites, »American« religion and identity are exceptional. In terms of motivation, values and religious motives behind political actions they clearly are. Walter McDougall among others also emphasizes this kind of »exceptionalism« in the conclusion of his historically orientated analysis.[41] Huntington explains the dichotomy of American politics convincingly: American politics even in the 20th century has alternated between moralists of the Jimmy Carter-type and realist power politicians like Richard Nixon. What unites both fractions is the American creed and the clear conviction of defending liberty, plurality, civil religion with a puritan flavor and democracy. What makes them different is their understanding of how that creed is to be translated, protected and politically supported. For an outside observer, the dichotomy between questionable American power-politics during the Allende coup and the moralistic human rights approach of Jimmy Carter and others shortly afterwards is nevertheless striking. It is not the success or the failure which are exceptional in American politics, but the dissonances with which Americans attempt to come to terms with »through some combination of moralism, cynicism, complacency, and hypocrisy.«[42]

In some of his conclusions, Huntington clearly goes too far in asserting American uniqueness, such as his statement that »American political institutions are more liberal and democratic than those of any other human society past or present.«[43] Surely, citizens of the Weimar Republic would have made the same argument, probably with even greater validity. However, the general explanation of this gap between the declared goal of American institutions to protect liberal, democratic ideals at home and abroad as well as their failure oftentimes to achieve those goals is convincing: liberty and democracy are part

[39]Ibid., 259.
[40]Ibid., 255.
[41]Cf. W.A. McDougall, Promised Land or Crusader State. The American Encounter with the World Since 1776, Houghton Mifflin 1997, 172-222. St.A. Renshon, One America? Political Leadership, National Identity, and the Dilemma of Diversity, Washington 2000, 28-66.
[42]Huntington, op. cit. (n. 44), 261.
[43]Ibid., 261.

of the American creed and a major value. A religiously diverse Congress is an expression of that liberty.

America is at least unique, if not exceptional through its creed, its specific form of civil religion and because of the apparent gap between its religious missionary spirit and its political reality. Renshon's specific analysis of dual citizenship in *One America* illustrates this gap between idealism and reality: there is at least a dissonance when one swears allegiance to one country and denounces all allegiances to other countries in an oath, while one holds two passports declaring allegiance to both countries. For Europeans it may also seem dissonant when a US-President in the 21st century talks about crusades, or when Eisenhower suggested that in terms of having values it only matters that one goes to church somewhere, whichever church or faith does not matter. This gap and promise of disharmony lead back to the development of religious affiliations of political elites.

On the one hand, the election of a Jewish or Mormon MP represents the American dream that anyone can join the American political elite irrespective of religion or ethnicity. In terms of US-*Realpolitik*, Jews and Catholics have a greater chance of having political impact in America today than they had in 1950. At the same time America remains extremely diverse: the ideal of the religious liberty of Jesse Ventura, the only Governor not to declare his religious affiliation, clashes with the moralistic ideals of the American President. Those opposing values have the potential to divide a society where the liberal values clash with the evangelical voices from the Bible belt or George Bush's views of Jesus of Nazareth as the political philosopher of his choice. What makes America exceptional and able to endure disharmony, can also become its greatest threat to itself. Fortunately, political elites with firm roots in their various beliefs seemed to have often managed in US history to prevent this domestic clash of cultures. Huntington concludes:

> Critics say that America is a lie because its reality falls so far short of its ideals. They are wrong. America is not a lie; it is a disappointment. But it can be a disappointment only because there is also a hope.[44]

Harding in his article in the *Financial Times* addresses a potential danger—that of an evangelical church/state coalition among the legislative bodies—but he fails to recognize that the religious diversity of those bodies within themselves is a dominant and constituent part of American national and political identity. For Germans and the political elites they vote for, the conclusions in terms of national identity are seemingly the other way round: homogeneity becomes a virtue guaranteeing societal stability. However, not everyone is accepted as a full-part of this society: even after three generations there

[44] Ibid., 262.

are hardly any Turks in parliament. Diversity in terms of ethnicity and religion does not make it into parliamentary ranks or societal elites in Germany. Looking at the religious affiliations of their political elites, Germans and their politicians seem to opt for the main-stream: the middle-aged, Christian MP from their region as the promise of homogeneity who comes with the promise of harmony.

## 8. Conclusion

*What would Jesus drive?*[45]

The analysis has shown that the underlying assumptions in Harding's article prove to be if not false, at least too simplistic. In the case of the United States, his assumptions hold true to a certain point: it comes as no surprise that there are more Mormons, Jews and Catholics in Congress and Senate in 2000 than there were in 1965. Some of those groups are overrepresented within US society in terms of their total numbers, but the same could be said about an over-proportional representation of Mormons at Harvard Business School. The overall increase of Evangelicals in Congress and Senate correlates with the increasing political strength of those groups in American society. In that respect the political elites mirror what is going on in American society in general. M. Fox in an analysis of religion featured in TIME magazine, correctly concluded in terms of the United States:

> That the answer to the question Where is living religion in America? is simply: Everywhere. (...) The most fundamental far-reaching conclusion we can make regarding the spiritual in American culture today is simply that people very often are leading lives of living religion (...) without knowing it.[46]

While Joseph Lieberman, Orin Hatch or John F. Kennedy did not run for office to make America more Orthodox Jewish, Mormon or Catholic, the Christian Coalition has the explicit political goal to promote Christian family values, school prayers in order to »re«-shape American national identity in terms of their values. The Puritan roots of America are explicitly evoked by the Christian Coalition as part of their campaign and voters increasingly voted for those politicians in the 1980s and 1990s.

[45] Article in the German newspaper DIE WELT on 11 January 2003 about how Americans believe in two basic truths: that it is no one's business what religion they follow and what car they drive. The link of the two rather disharmonious truths is described by a journalist reporting from a group called Detroit Project at the Detroit Car Fair. This group argues that it would be ethically irresponsible and only supportive of oil-producing dictatorships to drive SUVs. See also: www.whatwouldjesusdrive.org.

[46] M. Fox, Religion USA. An Inquiry into Religion and Culture by Way of TIME Magazine, Dubuque/Iowa 1971, 430.

Therefore, two apparently contradictory observations appear to be correct: on the one hand, the political elites are simply a mirror of what is going on in society in terms of religion, a society where Catholics, Jews and Mormons are fully emancipating themselves. On the other hand, the increasing importance of the Christian Coalition and the Evangelical movement show that one particular religious group, i.e. born-again/evangelical Christians who make their religious affiliation a part of their political program, have managed to gain support based on religious affiliations and shape national identity that way. Moralism and rationalism mirror themselves in religious affiliations of American politicians at the same time who are religiously diverse, but hardly ever agnostic. They shape national identity as much as they are shaped by it. Developments as diverse as the emancipation of religious minorities as well as the puritan roots of the 17th century are reflected among political elites.

In the case of Germany, however, Harding's initial assumption that religious affiliations of political elites are a mirror of what is going on in an increasingly secular European society does not hold true, mainly because of the effect of Germany's division in 1949 and German reunification in 1990 on the relationship between religious and political life in East and West Germany. While nominal church membership stagnates, German voters tend to opt for politicians who are active or at least nominal Christians.

What does this trend say in terms of German national identity? Germany is certainly not becoming more religious, but German voters seem to elect culturally homogenous, Christian political elite. Churches were always highly respected as being involved in building what Putnam calls a »civil« society in post-war Germany as a well-functioning democratic society.[47] Key institutions of that civil society such as hospitals, kindergartens, youth and social clubs, music societies were and are still run by church members or churches themselves. German civil society embraced the churches as an integral part of it, independent from nominal membership. Therefore, there is hardly any hostility, at least on the basis of religious affiliation between non-Christian voters and politicians who are active Christians.

In comparison to the United States, German society may be less religious, but it is striking that secularism is not gaining momentum among political elites, which are still predominantly religious. What differentiates the two societies is Puritanism: Germany has no strong moral, Puritan/Calvinist stream constituting its national identity and the same applies to most Northern and Central European countries. Christianity in the form of a US-Christian Coalition is not present in Germany's political landscape, but national identity is

[47]Cf. R. Putnam, Bowling Alone, New York 2000. See also: R. Inglehart, Culture and Democracy, in: L.E. Harrison/S.P. Huntington (eds.), Culture Matters. How Values Shape Human Progress, New York City 2000, 81.

shaped by Christian values and so are German elites to an even larger extent. Most of all: Germany may have become secular, but in terms of religion it is still rather homogenous and nominally Christian in its majority. Its political elites do not follow trends of secularism, but belong to the two mainstream churches for religious, moral or nominal reasons.

While many German citizens may feel alienated by a religious vocabulary in American politics, as Harding correctly points out, they themselves, for very different and diverse reasons, vote for politicians who are over proportionally religious in comparison to the rest of their respective societies. The difference may be just the tone in politics, and not a massive »faith gap« which Harding has identified. While political elites in the US mirror what is going on in their society in general, German elites tend to be at least nominally and maybe even in substance more religious than their voters, while the latter still seem to connect church membership to certain values such as honesty, trust, fairness and charity in the midst of an outwardly more secular continent.

# Fundamentalist Elites and the Politics of Identity

KARSTEN FISCHER

A decisive part of the lasting horror spread by the terrorist attacks of 11 September 2001 is due to the fear that at its roots we might find a worldwide social movement articulating its protest against a world economy felt to be deeply unjust. The fear that poor people take what they claim theirs regularly serves as an argument for the increase of Western development aid.

For example, during Germany's 2002 federal electoral campaign religious charitable trusts issued an appeal that 0.7% of Germany's gross national product should be spent for development aid, implying a trade-off between the latter and potential threats to the West. US-President George W. Bush has argued in exactly the same way—as have Bishop Desmond Tutu, Elie Wiesel and the Dalai Lama. Tutu believes that poverty is the primary reason for terror, while Bush explains that »We fight poverty because hope is the answer to terror«, and both Wiesel and the Dalai Lama assert that education is the means to eliminate terrorism. However, these well-meaning considerations may rest on a serious fallacy. Fundamentalist elites might feel even more provoked and motivated to terrorist attacks by a higher commitment to aid on the part of Western welfare-states: if, that is, these elites regard Western involvement as both authoritarian capitalistic imperialism and a hegemony of decadent consumerism. After all, fundamentalist terrorists demand widespread economic prosperity in their native regions only rhetorically, while in reality they defend their so-called cultural identity at all costs, including especially socio-economic disadvantages for large sections of the population. Thus there is a danger that intensified development aid, justified as a means of combating terrorism, may only lead to even greater disappointment and a subsequent slackening of aid efforts in the face of imminent terrorist attacks.

The assumption that fundamentalist activities correlate significantly to the existence of social elites is supported by empirical data. With regard to al-Qaeda it is well-known that Ayman al-Zawahiri, the influential Egyptian chief-ideologue behind bin Laden, was born into a prosperous and well-educated family of physicians residing in the wealthy Cairo suburb Maadi. Al-Zawahiri finished his studies in Cairo in 1974 and worked as a surgeon in the Egyptian armed forces before moving to Afghanistan in 1980, where he worked for the Red Crescent in Peshawar. In 1985 he met bin Laden in Djeddah, and the two became accomplices.[1] A study carried out by the Pakistani, Nasra Hassan, between 1996 and 1999 examined nearly 250 instructors and relatives of suicide bombers as well as those suicide bombers who failed in their attempts. It shows that by and large the suicide bombers are men between the ages of 18 and 38, socially well integrated and neither poor nor uneducated.[2] In addition, a survey by the Palestinian Center for Policy and Survey Research (PCPSR) conducted in the West Bank and the Gaza Strip found that the approval of violence against Israeli targets including suicide bombings is greater the higher the standard of living and the level of education.[3] A UN report covering 40 countries published in December 2002 established that the general approval of al-Qaeda amongst function elites is significantly higher than the societal average, and a full 2002 Gallup survey within almost every relevant Muslim country showed that the approval of the sentence: »Tolerance is one of the three most important values that are to be imparted to children in the course of their upbringing,« decreases as the level of education increases.[4] Hence *Jihadists* [5] by no means act out of despair or hopelessness, on the contrary.

Contrary to the assumptions quoted above, it is, then, rather, a *Dialectic of Enlightenment* that is to be expected, *cum grano salis*: educational and poverty relief programmes may not reduce the threat of terrorism, indeed they could be counterproductive with regard to its prevention. This suggests an understanding of fundamentalism in terms of particular patterns of cultural critique and of the politics of identity pursued by social elites. These patterns have, as will be outlined below, comparable nature in both Orient and Occident.

## Occidentalism—a career between self-definition and outside description

The terrorist attacks of 11 September 2001 were greeted with approval in only a few of the so-called underdeveloped countries, and such approval as came forward was conditioned not by social but by political and socio-cultural factors. This is indicated by its absence from the non-Arab parts of Africa, the ›poor

[1] L. Wright, Der Mann hinter Bin Laden. Dr. Ayman al-Zawahiri aus Ägypten—eine islamistische Karriere, in: Lettre International 59 (IV/2002), 28-44.

[2] S. Atran, Genesis of Suicide Terrorism, in: Science 299 (07. March 2003), 1534-1539. 1537.

[3] A.B. Krueger/J. Maleckova, Education, Poverty, Political Violence and Terrorism. Is There a Causal Connection?, National Bureau of Economic Research, Cambridge/MA: Working Paper 9074, July 2002, `http://www.nber.org/papers/w9074` [accessed: 26.03.2003].

[4] The Gallup Organization. Gallup Poll of the Islamic World 2002. Subscriber Report, 21: Iran: 73:55, Lebanon: 77:61, Jordan: 78:65, Morocco: 80:69, Turkey: 88:82, Saudi-Arabia: 68:63; the only exception is Kuwait (72:70), the ratio is equal in Pakistan (60:60).

[5] For the term cf. N.N. Ayubi, Political Islam. Religion and Politics in the Arab World, London/New York 1991, 142.

man« of the globe. Moreover, as we now know, the attacks were planned and carried out by individuals who were anything but underprivileged people who had previously been excluded from the merits of modernisation and recently rapidly acquired the technical knowledge and practical skills needed for their crimes in the West. On the contrary, they came from polyglot elites, whose socialisation, as in the case of those hijackers based in Hamburg, bore all the marks of modernity. As beneficiaries of Western educational systems or indeed, in the case of Osama bin Laden himself, of the Western economy and its international financial markets, these elites pursue a *selective modernisation*, that is, they put modern achievements to work for anti-modernist goals.

This elitist project of an anti-modernist fundamentalism which rejects such values of civilization as freedom, tolerance, rationalism, pluralism, and the individual pursuit of happiness and castigates the Western lifestyle as decadent moral decline refers to a retrograde notion of Islam and defines itself according to it.[6] If modernity is understood as the *legitimation of continual change* and as the specific character of occidental developments compared with other forms of social change,[7] the interpretative problem of fundamentalist elites becomes apparent: as a reaction to the experience of such cultural and social change, they find themselves recommending even more cultural change. That is, under conditions of permanent socio-cultural change and unconstrained cultural overlap induced by a globalized Western modernity, the fundamentalist strategy of isolationist regression implies not a stopping of transformation processes altogether but, at best, a renewed orientation of them. The paradoxical project of fundamentalism—opposition to secularisation while being caused by secularisation[8]—means that it is only suited to such societies as have already been seized by modernization, even if that modernization is limited to imported military machinery and an imposed form of regime as was the case in Afghanistan. If to this extent fundamentalism is »not a rudimentary traditionalism of the pre-modern era but a novel reaction accompanying modernity itself«[9], then its essence cannot be explained as primarily a religious phenomenon, but rather as a *political strategy*.

[6]It is well known that the name of bin Laden's terror network al-Qaeda means foundation or base. As in the case of the term totalitarianism that goes back to Mussolini, the term fundamentalist can be used both as affirmative self-description and pejorative outside perspective. US-American Protestants published a periodical entitled The Fundamentals. A Testimony to the Truth form 1909 to 1912, before they founded the World's Christian Fundamentals Association in 1919 and thereby had coined the term. The similarity to the al-Qaeda-semantics is obvious.

[7]F.-X. Kaufmann, Religion und Modernität. Sozialwissenschaftliche Perspektiven, Tübingen 1989, 35.

[8]N. Luhmann, Die Religion der Gesellschaft, Frankfurt/M. 2000, 295.

[9]M.Th. Greven, Die politische Gesellschaft. Kontingenz und Dezision als Probleme des Regierens und der Demokratie, Opladen 1999, 132.

Alluding to the *Orientalism* diagnosed by Edward W. Said, this phenomenon has been described as *Occidentalism*: opposing urbanity, a bourgeois way of life, rationality, and feminism,[10] a phenomenon not at all limited to Islamist movements but in fact wide spread throughout the West. Ideological formulas, such as the rejection of urbanity, contrast sharply with the urban provenance of fundamentalist elites and serve power-strategic purposes, especially the attraction of large sections of the population.[11] Typically, this occurs in the context of opposition movements: as a rule fundamentalist elites are revolutionary counter-elites, or to be precise *niche-elites*,[12] whose seizure of political power is motivated above all by their desire to maintain a moral order beneficial to their own, often economic, interests. Elitist fundamentalism of any religious character also remains a »typical intellectual's attitude«.[13]

The Occidentalism hypothesis is particularly important because it is not only an analytic perspective from the outside but also an affirmative self-description. Hassan Hanafi (born 1935), the inventor of the ›Islamic left‹ who earned his doctoral degree in France and today holds a professorship at Cairo University, uses the term *Occidentalism* as an affirmative self-descriptive concept intended to counterbalance the tendency of westernization in the Third World.[14] Although Hanafi's version of this concept is little elaborated and not militant, it is clear, at the same time, that the bias of such a decolonialization concept is culturist, rather than economic or political. The concept includes both diagnosis and remedy: it can be observed that that cultural critique can clearly serve as ferment for fundamentalist ideologies in the sense of an Occidentalist politics of identity which is at home both in Orient and Occident.[15]

---

[10] I. Buruma/A. Margalit, Occidentalism, in: The New York Review of Books, Vol. XLIX, No. 1, 17 January 2002, 4-7. For the term »Occidentalisme« cf. already Abdallah Laroui, Islam et modernité, Paris 1987, 162 ff. For the debate on Orientalism cf. Georg Stauth, Islam und westlicher Rationalismus. Der Beitrag des Orientalismus zur Entstehung der Soziologie, Frankfurt/M. 1993.

[11] Cf. Buruma/Margalit, op. cit. (n. 10), 4.

[12] Cf. E. Sivan, The Enclave Culture, in: M.E. Marty/R.S. Appleby (eds.): Fundamentalisms Comprehended, (The Fundamentalism Project, Vol. 5), Chicago/London 1995, 11-68, 17.

[13] N. Luhmann, Die Gesellschaft der Gesellschaft, Frankfurt/M. 1997, 807. Ayubi, op. cit. (n. 5), 158f. shows empirically that the middle classes and intellectuals, not traders, peasants, and the industrial proletariat form the socio-economic basis of militant, political Islam in all of the Arab countries apart from Syria.

[14] H. Hanafi, Islam in the Modern World, Vol. I, Religion, Ideology and Development, Vol. II, Tradition, Revolution and Culture, Cairo 1995.

[15] Cf. G. Stauth, Religiöser Fundamentalismus zwischen Orient und Okzident. Religiöse Identitätspolitik und ihr Verhältnis zur Demokratie, in: D. Loch/W. Heitmeyer (Hg.), Schattenseiten der Globalisierung. Rechtsradikalismus, Rechtspopulismus und separatistischer Regionalismus in westlichen Demokratien, Frankfurt/M. 2001, 140-166.

## The Road to Mecca—Leopold Weiss alias Muhammed Asad

Muhammed Asad is a telling example.[16] Asad was born in Vienna in 1900 under the name of Leopold Weiss. As son of a Jewish lawyer and a banker's daughter, according to his own statement, he enjoyed a happy youth. After the First World War, he dropped out of university where he had been studying art history and philosophy, and increasingly found himself confronted with the then widespread cultural pessimism. In his autobiography he confesses: »I wanted to find by myself an approach to the spiritual order of things which, I knew, must exist but which I could not yet discern.«[17] He does not attribute these difficulties to himself but rather views his own »vagueness« as »the vagueness of an entire generation«.[18] Clearly influenced by Spengler and Nietzsche, he laments that »the opening decades of the twentieth century stood in the sign of a spiritual vacuum.«[19] »All the ethical valuations to which Europe has been accustomed for so many centuries had become amorphous under the terrible impact of what had happened between 1914 and 1918«.[20] Their place, he said, was taken by materialistic wellbeing:

> The average European—whether democrat or communist, manual worker or intellectual—seemed to know only one positive faith: the worship of material progress, the belief that there could be no other goal in life than to make that very life continually easier or, as the current expression went, ›independent of nature‹. The temples of that faith were the gigantic factories, cinemas, chemical laboratories, dance halls, hydroelectric works; and its priests were the bankers, engineers, politicians, film stars, statisticians, captains of industry, record airmen, and commissars. Ethical frustration was evident in the all-round lack of agreement about the meaning of Good and Evil and in the submission of all social and economic issues to the rule of ›expediency‹—that painted lady of the streets, willing to give herself to anybody, at any time, whenever she is invoked (...).[21]

With regard to their origin, and also their powerfully eloquent and polemical consistency, these thoughts could easily have derived from the so-called Conservative Revolution, one of the hallmarks of which was the fear of uncertainty.[22] Asad, however, turned not to the political right but to Islam, where he found

[16] I am indebted to Sidonia Blättler for drawing my attention to Asad. For Asad cf. M. Kramer, The Road from Mecca. Muhammad Asad (born Leopold Weiss), in: M. Kramer (ed.), The Jewish Discovery of Islam. Studies in Honor of Bernard Lewis, Tel Aviv 1999, 225-247; G. Windhager, Leopold Weiss alias Muhammad Asad. Von Galizien nach Arabien 1900-1927, Wien u.a. ²2003.

[17] M. Asad, The Road To Mecca, Lahore ²1982, 57.

[18] Loc. cit.

[19] Loc. cit.

[20] Loc. cit.

[21] Op. cit., 70.

[22] St. Breuer, Anatomie der Konservativen Revolution, Darmstadt 1993, 44 f.

»an emotional lightness of approach to all questions of life—a supreme common sense of feeling, if one might call it so«.[23] For Asad this led »not only to the spiritual perfection of the individual but also to the creation of such social conditions as might be conducive to the spiritual development of all, so that all might live in fullness«.[24]

A liberal and secular understanding of religion rooted in the Enlightenment tradition was thereby precluded, and Asad consistently felt himself called to join the »Jihad«, as he confesses in the chapter of his memoirs which bears that title. Portraying his battle against the Italian occupation of the Cyrenaica in the north-east of Libya in 1931, he engages with the question of why he had voluntarily put his life at risk, stressing that his conversion to Islam generated in him

> a desire to pursue it among like-minded people—and not only to pursue it in a personal sense but also to work for its social fruition within the community of my choice. To me, Islam was a way and not an end—and the desperate guerillas of Umar al-Mukhtar were fighting with their lifeblood for the freedom to tread that way, just as the Companions of the Prophet had done thirteen centuries ago. To be of help to them in their hard and bitter struggle, however uncertain the outcome, was as personally necessary to me as to pray (...).[25]

Asad's journey from the profoundly European cultural *fin de siècle* pessimism of the interwar period to political Islam seems to be symptomatic of the elitist project of a religiously fundamentalist cultural critique and politics of identity, which draws on Occidentalist concepts of the enemy.

## The occidental ethic and the spirit of crusade: Sayyid Qutb

A far more influential exponent of such way of thinking, however, is the Egyptian fundamentalist Sayyid Qutb. Qutb was born into an Egyptian middle class family in 1906. After completing his university studies he joined the Ministry of Education and initially worked as teacher and literary critic. As a critical opposition columnist he displayed western, liberal, skeptical, existentialist attitudes and discovered the now famous Nagib Mahfus. After a stay in the USA between 1948 and 1950 Qutb became an Islamist ideologue and joined the Muslim Brotherhood, a militant underground movement founded in 1928 by Hassan al-Banna, which was mainly made up of members of the urban lower middle class.[26] On account of his increasingly radical works, Qutb was impris-

[23] Asad, op.cit. (n. 17), 100.

[24] Op. cit., 128.

[25] Op. cit., 327.

[26] Cf. Ayubi, op. cit. (n. 5), 81; 218; A. Al-Azmeh, Die Islamisierung des Islam. Imaginäre Welten einer politischen Theologie, Frankfurt/M./New York 1996, 132; R.P. Mitchell, The Society of the Muslim Brothers, New York/Oxford 1993.

oned for many years by the Nasser-regime and severely tortured before, in 1966, he was sentenced to death, executed and became an Islamist martyr. Qutb's influence on the whole breadth of the militant Islamist movement, including al-Qaeda, can hardly be overestimated. Both bin Laden's chief ideologue al-Zawahiri (mentioned above) and bin Laden himself are strongly influenced by Qutb. Bin Laden studied at Djeddah University, where he came into contact with the Muslim Brotherhood and particularly fell under the spell of Abdullah Azzam and Sayyid Qutb's brother Muhammad.[27]

The decadence motif only too familiar from European cultural critique is—now recontextualized in fundamentalist terms—of central importance for Qutb's Occidentalist ideology. A key notion is the shifting concept of *jahiliyyah*, used to denote *barbarism*, *ignorance*, *decay*, and *moral degeneracy*. Related to it is the differentiation between *external imperialism* and *internal imperialism*: Whereas *external imperialism* refers to violent and armed occupation, *internal imperialism* denotes a conscious or unconscious collaboration caused by indifference or betrayal as a result of despondency, passivity, and moral degeneracy, a *jahiliyyah* of the colonialized themselves. If the decadence of the Muslim society is partly held responsible for colonialism, in the sense that its moral weakness has made heteronomy possible in the first place, then this is a stereotype of cultural critique well known since the time of Machiavelli. Qutb simply adds the differentiation between active and passive decadence, according to which Oriental civilizations have suffered passive decadence over the last couple of centuries whereas the apparently successful Occident was subject to active decadence, i.e. an especially lasting decline of values. Qutb goes back to antiquity and presents the Roman Empire as sowing the seeds of Western decadence and arrogance which have persisted since:

> The idea upon which the Roman Empire was based was suppression by force and the exploitation of other nations for the sole benefit of the motherland, and to provide a good life for the elite. (...) The famous ›Roman justice‹ was justice for the Romans alone. (...) The Romans in reality knew no religion. Their traditional gods were but pale copies of the Greek myths, indistinct figures whose existence was unimportant and whose worship was a matter only of social custom. They were never permitted to interfere in the affairs of real life. (...) Such was the soil in which modern Western civilization grew.[28]

[27] P.L. Bergen, Holy War, Inc. Inside the Secret World of Osama bin Laden, London 2001, 56.

[28] W.E. Shepard, Sayyid Qutb and Islamic Activism. A Translation and Critical Analysis of Social Justice in Islam, Leiden etc. 1996, 292f. Hassan Hanafi, a critical, but intensive reader Qutb's, also still sees the Pax Romana at the heart of the European consciousness, cf. H. Hanafi, Development from without—Development from within, `http://www.dse.de/ef/cultures/hanafi.htm` [accessed 05.06.2003], 2.

Qutb subsequently quotes another well known theme from the Western conservative cultural critique, the castigation of materialistic greed in occidental industrial societies:

> The ordinary European, whether democrat or fascist or bolshevik, worker or intellectual, knows only one positive religion and that is the worship of material progress (...). The temples of this religion are the large factories, the cinemas, the chemical laboratories, the dance halls and the electrical power plants, while its priests are the bankers, the engineers, the movie stars, the leaders of industry and the heroes of aviation.[29]

The dependence of this passage on the quotation from Asad cited above is striking. Qutb was familiar with Asad's pamphlet *Islam at the Crossroads*, which he had read in its Arabic translation.[30] However, whereas Asad regards materialism as the consequence of moral erosion, Qutb expounds the problem of moral degeneracy as the result of excessive materialistic individualism, which he blames for licentiousness and discord, moral irresponsibility, degeneration, social chaos, the humiliation of women, and the weakening and destruction of the family. Symptomatic of this view is a passage from Qutb's influential *Milestones* which led to his accusation and subsequent conviction of high treason:

> If (...) ›free sexual promiscuity‹ and illegitimate generation become the foundation stone of the society with mutual relations of man and woman erected on carnal desires, sexual hunger and animal provocation, shunning the family responsibilities according to natural attitudes and the principle of division of work, woman preoccupying hereself [sic!] with adornment, embellishment, attractiveness and enchantment, forsaking and relinquishing the basic charge of upbringing and protecting the new generation and preferring to serve as hostess in a hotel, passenger-vessel or an aeroplane of her own accord or under the call of society, thus directing her creative energies and capabilities towards material benefits and amassing material comforts instead of producing human beings (...)—when things come to such a pass then it should be deemed a harbinger of civilizational decay and decline. This state of affairs is termed Jahili in the Islamic terminology.[31]

Even though prudery and anti-feminism are distinctive in those maxims and the specifically Islamist notion of *jahiliyya* is enforced, the similarity to stereotypes of Western cultural critique is striking. When Qutb denies that the industrially, economically, and scientifically advanced societies are truly civilized, then his view corresponds to the confrontation of supposedly ›true‹ (German) culture with ›mere‹ (Western) civilization. From here the road leads to the extremism of the European 20th century, such as social Darwinism (which Qutb adapted

[29]Shepard, op. cit. (n. 28), 294.

[30]M. Asad, Islam at the Crossroads, Lahore 1955. Kramer, op. cit. (n. 16), 235.

[31]S. Qutb Shaheed [Qutb, Sayyid], Milestones, Karachi 1981, 180. Cf. also S. Qutb, The Ideological Bankruptcy of Europe and the Future Prospects of Islam, in: The Voice of Islam. A Monthly Magazine Devoted to the Promotion of True Human Progress, Vol. XII, Karachi 1963, 5-16.65-77.85.

from the French fascist Alexis Carrel[32]), an open rejection of democracy as one form of polytheism, and aggressive anti-Zionism, which was conveyed to Qutb by Werner Sombart's polemic *Die Juden und das Wirtschaftsleben* and the *Protokolle der Weisen von Zion.*[33]

Moreover there are immediate parallels between Qutb's Islamic fundamentalism and Protestant fundamentalist movements in the USA. Qutb might well be thought to be quoting the leading New York fundamentalist John Roach Straton, so similar are his remarks to those of Straton in 1920:

> The most sinister and menacing figure of our modern life is the cigarette smoking, cocktail drinking, pug dog nursing, half-dressed, painted woman, who frequents the theaters, giggles at the cabarets, gambles in our drawing-rooms or sits around our hotels, with her dress cut ›C‹ in front and ›V‹ behind! She is a living invitation to lust, and a walking advertisement of the fact that many of our modern women have lowered their standards of life![34]

For Qutb this state of affairs not only justifies the declaration of Jihad, but is its original motive and legitimation. Against decadence it is essential »to establish the Sovereignty and Authority of God an earth, to establish the true system revealed by God for addressing the human life; to exterminate all the Satanic forces and their ways of life, to abolish the lordship of man over other human beings«, which he believed »reasons and factors (...) enough to declare Jihad«.[35]

Qutb consistently advocates an uncompromising Manichaeism, not only evoking the *clash of civilization* (Huntington) *avant la lettre* but, so to speak, existentializing it:

> European and American Crusaderist imperialism cannot leave out of its account the fact that the Islamic spirit is a bulwark resisting the spread of imperialism (...). Those who reckon that Jewish financial influence in the United States and elsewhere is what leads Westerners in this direction (...) and those who reckon that the struggle between the Eastern and Western blocs is the effective factor—all of these neglect a real element in the matter which must be added to all these others. This is the Crusader spirit that all Westerners carry in their blood and that lies hidden deep in their minds, to which is added imperialism's fear of the Islamic spirit (...).[36]

---

[32]Vgl. Al-Azmeh, op. cit. (n. 26), 136 ff.; Youssef M. Choueiri, Islamic Fundamentalism, London 1990, 142ff.

[33]Vgl. Choueiri, op. cit. (n. 32), 112.119.

[34]Rev. J.R. Straton (Pastor of Calvary Baptist Church, NY City), The Menace of Immorality in Church and State. Messages of Wrath and Judgment. New York 1920, 49.

[35]Qutb, Milestones, op. cit. (n. 31), 133f.

[36]Shepard, op. cit. (n. 28), 286f.

His main concern is thus *intellectual* and *spiritual colonialism* since, according to his *jahiliyya* theory, *internal imperialism* is a decisive factor for Islamic inferiority. He consistently propagates a cultural battle against any *westoxication*,[37] and along with that also, explicitly and particularly, against Western development aid and the UNESCO:

> The ›free world‹ fights us, apart from time to time, not with tanks and rifles. Rather it fights us with tongues and pens, with charitable organizations in important educational centers, in form of the UNESCO (...). It fights us with those societies and organizations that are brought into being, founded and supported and which dominate the sensitive centers of our country.[38]

In as much as Qutb ascribes central importance to this cultural battle, he declares any co-operation and any cultural exchange that aims at promoting understanding to be categorically unwelcome. Not only is the West denied any good intentions at all and accused of acting with purely imperialistic deliberation, but Qutb also rejects any intercultural contact in principle, regardless of the West's intentions, since he considers it to be the cause of the *passive decadence* of the Orient.

## The political challenge of the transcendental idealist

This completes the picture with regard to the scepticism towards the usefulness of poverty relief programmes and campaigns against illiteracy as means of combating fundamentalism and terrorism which has been expressed at the beginning of this article. It also explains why fundamentalism as the project of an elite politicizes and agitates at all costs, even and especially the cost of socio-economic disadvantages for large sections of society.[39]

This raises a number of questions which are both current and practical questions. How great is the real ›risk of infection‹ by an elitist fundamentalism opposed to decadence for the bulk of the population in underdeveloped countries? What are the prospects of such elites of initiating a *social movement* as has occurred in Algeria and Iran? Under what conditions will a culturalist construction of identity that accepts a stagnation of prosperity be able to

---

[37] For the term cf. Ayubi, op. cit. (n. 5), 150.

[38] Sayyid Quṭb, Dirāsāt Islāmiyah, Beirut/Kairo [5]1982 [1402], 161. Mitchell, op. cit. (n. 26), 50 connects this with the burning of English-language books in Egypt in November 1946.

[39] For example, in Algeria the Armée Islamique du Salut (AIS), known as Movement Islamique Armé (MIA) before 1994 and the armed wing of the Front Islamique du Salut (FIS), wages its war against ›westernization‹ and also against women not wearing veils, girls eager to be educated, teachers, journalists, development aid workers, tourists, and the average Algerian citizen by signaling through the bombing of public spaces that visits to coffee houses, reading newspapers, watching television etc. are anti-Islamic transgressions deserving death. By comparison, the improvement of the conditions of life, e.g. fighting the high percentage of illiteracy, has to take second place.

exercise such fascination that the project of an intellectual elite moves out of socially marginalization and becomes »the sharpest weapon to be used in any mass movement«?[40] How can an elitist cultural critique, which is hostile towards Western consumption, be socially and politically marginalized so that its anti-Western polemic is prevented from having a mass impact? After all, even the majority of Muslims would prefer »Disneyworld to paradise if in doubt«.[41] And finally, how can the destructive ways of reception of Occidentalist thought that still await careful study be changed constructively?

One possibility of interpretation could lie in the connection of de-modernization and social mobility described by Peter L. Berger. When members of the upper middle class break free from their careers, positions become available for successors, which is the reason why elitist anti-modernism accelerates the social mobility of members of the lower classes who are typically less prone to act on impulses of de-modernization.[42]

At the same time, one should not entertain any illusions about the nature of fundamentalist terrorism, i.e. *Jihadism*, regarding which a quote by Heinrich Heine sounds almost prophetic:

> There will come upon the scene armed Fichteans whose fanaticism of will is to be restrained neither by fear nor by self-interest; for they live in the spirit; they defy matter like those early Christians who could be subdued neither by bodily torments nor by bodily delights. Yea, in a time of social revolution these transcendental idealists will prove even more pertinacious than the early Christians; for the latter endured earthly martyrdom in the hope of attaining celestial blessedness, whilst the transcendental idealist looks on martyrdom itself as a vain show, and is invulnerable within the entrenchment of his own thought.[43]

Heine's allusion to Fichte refers to his *Addresses to the German Nation*, in which he propagates the idea, well known since Machiavelli, that moral revival is a pre-condition for state-based national self-assertion against foreign domination. This is a notion that is very attractive to the Islamic fundamentalists of today, as can be seen from the lasting effect of Qutb's work.[44] Qutb thinks the political challenge of the ›transcendental idealist‹ is to stop the *entrenchment of his own thought*, so that the *fanaticism of the will* can override

[40] Hanafi, Islam in the Modern World, op. cit. (n. 14), Vol. II, 19.

[41] M. Lüders, »Wir hungern nach dem Tod«. Woher kommt die Gewalt im Dschihad-Islam? Zürich 2001, 43.

[42] P.L. Berger/B. Berger/H. Kellner, The Homeless Mind. Modernization and Consciousness, New York 1973, 219f.

[43] H. Heine, Religion and Philosophy in Germany. A Fragment, transl. by J. Snodgrass, Albany 1986, 159.

[44] It is no coincidence that Hassan Hanafi too considers Fichte an important mentor of the Islamic liberation movement. Consistently he even presented a paper entitled The Structure and Development of Fichte's Philosophy: 1810-1814 as a Model at the conference of the International J.-G. Fichte-Association that took place from October 14-18, 2003 in Munich.

the survival instinct and the striving for prosperity. This cannot be achieved by socio-economic means or by taking military action, but must instead begin with the different ways of reception of occidentalist critique of culture and decadence. It is therefore clear that the notorious speech by President Bush given aboard the aircraft carrier USS Abraham Lincoln on 1 May 2003, in which he declared that the Americans stand for freedom anywhere in the world, could achieve nothing. To start with, the very meaning of the term freedom as used by Bush categorically ignores the counterpart of that freedom, freedom from the sometimes dire consequences of globalization. Additionally, and perhaps more importantly, outside the West an understanding of freedom is gaining general acceptance which takes its maxim from, of all things, the chorus of the Kris Kristofferson song *Me and Bobby McGee* made famous by Janis Joplin: »Freedom is just another word for ›nothing left to lose‹«.

# Churches as ›Value Mediators‹ Religion and Collective Identity in Germany

JOHANNES ZACHHUBER

## 1. Religion and politics—the transatlantic divide

It is a truism to speak of the stark contrast between attitudes to religion in Western Europe and the USA. Europeans coming to North America, from Alexis de Tocqueville and Max Weber to Peter Berger and José Casanova, have been struck by this particular divergence between the Old and the New World. Nevertheless, given the present feelings of increasing alienation on both sides of the Atlantic, it may be not without significance that this particular aspect of social life seems to be, once again, an area specifically prone to mutual misunderstandings and, at least occasionally, suspicions. It would appear useful in this situation to reflect on the precise differences between these two religious cultures specifically on the political aspect of those differences.

Such an endeavour would seem to me beneficial not only for the hermeneutics of mutual understanding. On both sides of the Atlantic, societies are currently undergoing rather profound changes, which clearly interact with, and may in some cases even be caused by, developments in their religious cultures. In such a situation the comparative look at another model is often helpful to understand one's own range of options as well as future perspectives. Others may consider whether this is at all applicable to the present American situation; I confine myself here to the observation that the benefit of such a cross-bench view for the German discussion appears rather obvious.

What are these differences? I suggest offering here only a fairly general and sweeping characterisation that lands me at the point where I wish to start off with my proper argument. What I find important is that we are duly aware that this difference is not one-dimensional. Certainly, what springs to mind initially are the huge, apparently increasing numbers of believers in the USA, as opposed to shrinking attendance of religious services in Germany and in Western Europe generally. In a frequently cited opinion poll 60% of Americans said religion played a crucial part in their lives, while in Germany only 21% would concur with such a statement.[1] While it is true that these, as any

[1] Pew Global Attitudes Project, »US Stands Alone in its Embrace of Religion,« 19 December 2002.

statistical figures, are open to various interpretations, I nevertheless take it that there are strong indicators for a ›religious divide‹ across the Atlantic.[2] The American society as a whole seems to be permeated by religion in a way that many people in Germany find difficult even to comprehend. It suffers no doubt that certain aspects of this religiosity appear to substantial parts of the German public only either ridiculous or menacing.

There is, however, another side to this story. If, on account of the shrinking number of churchgoers, a country such as Germany is seen as becoming increasingly less religious, one must not ignore some surprisingly stable bonds which continue to hold religion and society together. Interestingly, a number of those are decidedly unthinkable in the USA with its strong tradition of separation between state and church. Just consider Religious Education. This is still an official subject at state schools in most parts of Germany.[3] As a matter of fact, it is often pointed out that it is the only school subject whose existence is guaranteed by the constitution.[4] Legally it would be more complicated to scrap Religious Education than mathematics, even though, admittedly, the latter is unlikely to happen any time soon. This subject, it must be understood, is not simply the teaching of basic knowledge in Christianity and other world religions (even though this ought to be covered by the curriculum); it is decidedly religious instruction »given in accordance with the tenets of the religious community concerned« (Basic Law, Article 7, Paragraph 3). What precisely this amounts to is a matter of debate, and among German Protestants it is acknowledged that it does not mean preaching to school children, but rather the cultivation of a critical discourse about what religion is and could be.[5] Be this, however, as it may, the fact remains that the German political and legal system allows for this kind of co-operation between the state and religious

[2]E.g. J. Casanova, Public Religions in the Modern World, Chicago 1994, 27f. Cf. also various contributions to the issue 4/2005 of Internationale Politik.

[3]Exceptions are, currently, the states of Brandenburg, Bremen and Berlin. They all invoke the so called ›Bremen Clause‹ (Article 141) of the German Constitution (Basic Law), which defines an exception from the stipulation of Article 7, Paragraph 3. Cf. for the following: N.O. Oermann/J. Zachhuber, Einigkeit und Recht und Werte. Der Verfassungsstreit um das Schulfach LER in der öffentlichen und wissenschaftlichen Diskussion, Münster 2001.

[4]Article 7, Paragraph 3: »Religious instruction shall form part of the regular curriculum in state schools, with the exception of non-denominational schools. Without prejudice to the state's right of supervision, religious instruction shall be given in accordance with the tenets of the religious community concerned. Teachers may not be obliged against their will to give religious instruction.« (Official translation; source: `http://www.bundesregierung.de` as on 25 September 2006). Cf. Oermann/Zachhuber, op. cit. (n. 3), 55-62.

[5]Oermann/Zachhuber, op. cit. (n. 3), 154-165. The Roman Catholic Church has been reluctant to subscribe to this agenda officially (cf. the 1996 official paper: Sekretariat der Deutschen Bischofskonferenz (ed.), Die bildende Kraft des Religionsunterrichts. Zur Konfessionalität des Religionsunterrichts, Fulda 1996). Arguably, it still characterises much of Catholic Religious Education in practice.

communities, which would be excluded by a complete separation of state and church.[6]

It is quite interesting, then, that today, in spite of the occasional squabble, overall acceptance of this kind of institution is still high.[7] Many parents let their children attend Religious Education classes, even though they do not go to church and do not consider themselves particularly religious either. Why, then, do they find it at all worth the while? Certainly, the idea that their children obtain some factual knowledge of the world of religion and, in particular, their own, Christian tradition is cherished by some. One might think, however, that this objective could be achieved through a different kind of subject. Religious Education clearly plays a particular role at state schools, and parents are mindful of that. Their option in favour of Religious Education as a school subject in part reflects their willingness to accept that religious communities have a specific contribution to make to society. This contribution is often expressed by the words that they are ›value-mediators‹ (*Wertevermittler*). Teaching religion, then, is more or less tantamount to imparting values to our children, and many people in Germany, including a considerable number of decision makers, are happy for the Churches to be trusted with such a job.

## 2. The German perception: Churches as ›value mediators‹

This way of putting the matter seems to me quite characteristic for the way the social relevance of religion is commonly seen in Germany, and I therefore propose to explore this particular concept in the remainder of this paper. It is not my intention here to speak about Religious Education as such; others are more qualified than I am to do this. I took this as one example illustrating the very particular way in which religion and society have been, and in many ways still are, related in Germany.

Various questions seem to arise at once. For a start, it is not at all obvious what people mean when they express this expectation. What are values and why should we attach importance to them? Secondly, why do we need churches to make young people accept them? Put differently, is there any relation between values and religion and, if so, what is it? Yet, thirdly, if it is thus unclear whether societies ought to rely on religion for such a task, it is equally questionable whether religious communities should see this as part of their mission.

---

[6] As far as the German state is concerned, a more ›confessional‹ approach would be acceptable. Cf. the ruling of the Constitutional Court of 1987 (BVerfGE 74, 274).

[7] Cf. (e.g.), Religionsunterricht. Welchen Stellenwert sollte er an unseren Schulen haben?, in: Chrismon 8/2003 where c. $\frac{3}{4}$ of those polled agreed that Religious Education ought to be a regular subject at state schools.

In what follows I shall try to address these questions in turn. It will become apparent, or so I hope, that the underlying concept is deeply ambiguous and goes to the heart of the quite severe problem of how modern, pluralistic societies can develop some form of shared identity and which role, if any, religion is to play in this endeavour.

*a) What are values?*

Let me start with a brief terminological and conceptual clarification.[8] It is probably easy to demonstrate that people who yearn for the transmission of values in education are not at all in agreement about the exact meaning of such an expression. With only a trifle of exaggeration one might say that it is convenient to agree on our society's need for values precisely insofar as nobody knows what exactly it is that we need. ›Value‹ seems very much the kind of vague term that comes in handy to articulate a somewhat blurred feeling of uneasiness with the way our affairs are going. Quite often what people have in mind would seem something earlier generations might have termed virtues: truthfulness, respect, fairness, courage. Quite understandably, people are anxious that the young generation is brought up properly, including the implantation in them of a good measure of good behaviour. On top of this there is the inevitable pinch of conservatism, the yearning for the ideals of some bygone age when things were supposedly better than they are now because values were still what they ought to be.

Yet, in spite of all that vagueness and resentment, the value discourse does express something substantial, and it is therefore not appropriate to dismiss it out of hand. What is this? A brief historical detour may be helpful.[9] It is generally accepted that the term value has been introduced into moral theory from economics only in the 19th century, a fact which later caused Martin Heidegger to complain that this was merely another expression of the fatal developments of that age.[10] Whatever the concept's background in economics may signify—and I propose to leave this to one side here[11]—it is fairly obvious that the

[8]The following draws on Oermann/Zachhuber, op. cit. (n. 3), 113-124. One of the best accounts to date is: H. Joas, Die Entstehung der Werte, Frankfurt/M. 1997 (= The Genesis of Values, Chicago 2001).

[9]Cf. H. Schnädelbach, Philosophie in Deutschland 1831-1933, Frankfurt/M. 1983, 197-231 (= Philosophy in Germany. 1831-1933, Cambridge 1984, 161-191).

[10]M. Heidegger, Einführung in die Metaphysik, Tübingen 1966, 151 (cited by Schnädelbach, op. cit. (n. 9), 230 (= 190 ET). Interestingly, in the same passage Heidegger blames »the muddy waters« of »values« and »totalities« for the distortion wrought by a so called »philosophy of National Socialism« on »the inner truth and greatness of this [sc. the NS] movement« (op. cit. 152). The lectures reproduced in this book were delivered in 1935, but Heidegger republished them virtually unchanged in 1953 and thereafter.

[11]Cf. Th. Adorno, Einleitung zum »Positivismusstreit in den Geisteswissenschaften«, in: id., Gesammelte Schriften, vol. 8, Frankfurt/M. 1972, 280-370, here: 346-348.

development of the value discourse in the 19th century is intimately connected with the rise of scientific reductionism on the one hand, historical and cultural relativism on the other. Traditionally, ethics had simply made the metaphysical assumption that there were goods, a class of beings whose desirability was universally acknowledged. They would culminate in one supreme good (*summum bonum*), such as happiness. For two reasons, throughout the 19th century this notion became ever more elusive. Scientists increasingly claimed to hold the key for a full understanding of human nature. Desire then would be merely a psychological reality; there was no need to posit any particular, intelligible object of desire. Emerging historicism, on the other hand, suggested that human beings at different times and in different cultures had desired wildly different things. Ironically, both these developments converged in their rejection of a moral theory on the basis of an objective *summum bonum*. Without undue oversimplification it may be said that the concept of value was introduced to stem this dual challenge to traditional ethics. Values would be functionally equivalent to the goods of traditional ethics, but rest on the individuals' subjectivity. They were needed as a concept, it was argued, because our valuations imply ›validity‹ which cannot be reduced to a psychological phenomenon. And while values may not be the same always and everywhere, the acceptance of their validity was not purely the individual's choice either. Rather, individuals would always find themselves as part of a given historical and social order within which values *for them* had their validity fixed.

Admittedly, the major advocates of philosophical value theory in the 19th and early 20th century believed that, in order for this theory to work properly, one needed to establish absolute values on top of those cultural ones. To this end they employed neoKantian transcendentalism[12] or phenomenology,[13] but it is now widely recognised that those attempts failed spectacularly and were, probably, the main reason for the scorn poured on those attempts by later thinkers.[14] This failure may also have initiated the emergence of a concept of value that, contrariwise, accentuated their complete contingency, their total subjection to the arbitrary will of the individual. Such a concept we find in Friedrich Nietzsche and, with some modifications, in Max Weber.[15] Yet, while they were right to protest the excesses of philosophers in search for absolute and eternal values, one might wonder whether they were equally correct in

[12] E.g. W. Windelband, Einleitung in die Philosophie, Tübingen 1914, Part II, esp. §13, 244ff. (= An Introduction to Philosophy, tr. by J. McCabe, London 1921, 208ff.).

[13] M. Scheler, Der Formalismus in der Ethik und die materiale Wertethik. Neuer Versuch der Grundlegung eines ethischen Personalismus, Bern $^{4}$1954 (= Formalism in Ethics and Non-Formal Ethics of Values. A New Attempt Toward the Foundation of an Ethical Personalism, Evanston $^{5}$1973. Cf. Joas, op. cit. (n. 8), ch. 6.

[14] Cf. Schnädelbach, op. cit. (n. 9), 230 (= 190f. ET).

[15] Cf. Joas, op. cit. (n. 8), ch. 2.

reducing values to a matter of purely individual choice. Once a clean dichotomy is accepted between universally and eternally valid truths on the one hand, and merely subjective ones on the other, that consequence is inevitable.[16] The legitimacy of the value discourse, which I claimed above, might be said to reside precisely in the space created in between those two categories which are not dichotomous in social and cultural life. It could be easily demonstrated that none of our ›values‹ neither democracy nor individual freedom nor justice or fairness, would stand the test of historical or cultural invariance. Yet this does not lessen their importance for today's world. Individuals and communities stake their lives on their validity, and rightly so. Even were one to deny the ›value‹ of any of the goods mentioned, this would not alter the principal point. No one could conceivably avoid drawing on ›values‹ in their lives even though they are necessarily to some extent contingent.

Values, then, are what people value, and thus they are what we want to attain in and through our actions. They are what traditional ethical theory has called goods, objectives of our actions which, as such, determine what we do and how we do it. If we make decisions we use such ›values‹ as criteria. Those decisions are often insignificant, but some are fundamental for our lives and the lives of others; thus the values governing those decisions determine to a considerable extent the overall picture we have of ourselves and others have of us.

It is not difficult to see, then, that values are important not only for what we do, but also for who we are. They play a crucial role in the formation of our identities insofar as those identities are the products of our actions. Thus values are at the very core of our personal being; they make up our character, the particular stamp that marks out the beings we are.

This, I think, is all the more true as they are not freely at our disposition, a point which is often lost in public debates. We do not *decide* from one day to another whether or not to accept one particular value; they are acquired over a long period of time. They are all the more powerful as it is, precisely, not in our hands to change them out of a moment's consideration. If we truly value another person's integrity, this forbids us to choose certain actions involving this person. If we do not, then we are in a different position. I am not saying, though, that we cannot at all alter our values or that they could not be altered. It is, I suppose, as with favourite dishes. We choose them from the menu because we like them (we value them!), and it does not normally occur to us in a restaurant to question the preferences which we have acquired over a lengthy period of time. It may happen, though, that we realise we should change our habits, for example because our favourite dish happens to be terribly unhealthy.

---

[16]This is I think the rationale underlying Alasdair MacIntyre's radically anti-modern polemic in his famous After Virtue. A Study in Moral Theory, London [2]1985.

As all those who have been in this situation know, this is difficult enough, even though it is possible. In a similar way we are not necessarily and invariably bound to the values we have at one time obtained, but nor do we relate to them as to objects of our choice. Rather, they are normally the basis for the choices we make.

This being so it is immediately clear that values as such cannot disappear; we must have values in order to act. They can certainly, and do, change. There can be no doubt that major shifts in societies are always to some extent shifts in values. It has, for example, been pointed out that Western societies, which have reached unprecedented wealth in their transition from industrial to post-industrial societies over the last decades, have tended to move from values linked directly with survival (such as economic security) towards so-called ›self-expression‹ values many of which are ›post-materialist‹ such as environmental protection and tolerance of diversity.[17] Where poorer societies put the well being of their families on top or near the top of their value systems, wealthier societies become usually more individualistic.

People who complain about the ›loss‹ of values would thus more properly be said to observe that they change; and this is what they do not like. This is what I have called, at the outset of this paper, the inherent conservatism of the value discourse, which is, I think, not necessarily identical with the political affiliation of individuals engaged in this kind of debate. More generally, it says that people are concerned about values if they worry that the loss of what used to be is more problematic than anything society might gain in its turn by undergoing those changes.

Let me adduce a further observation here. Values are never purely individual. They are always shared. Their emergence is thus always linked to the social structures of a particular community. This community could be a nation, but it could also be a family—to name perhaps the two extreme places in which the generation of values takes place. Due to their character as shared values they contribute to ›collective‹ identities. People are not only identifiable as individuals of a particular character, but also as members of a family, as inhabitants of a particular region, members of a social class and, not least, nationals of this or that state. Any such identity rests on a variety of shared features, such as language, including dialect, external appearance, economic situation, education, but not least on shared values. Values, then, are both the product of the interaction within communities and the very properties by which members

[17] This shift from materialist to post-materialist values was first predicted by R. Inglehart in a seminal 1971 paper: The silent revolution in Europe. Intergenerational change in post-industrial societies, in: American Political Science Review 65 (1971), 991-1017. Cf. now the major study based on large-scale empirical research in the early 90s: P.R. Abramson/R. Inglehart, Value Change in Global Perspective, Ann Arbor 1995.

of such a community are recognised; they are thus to a considerable extent the cement holding communities together. As such, they are the more important the more elusive the community's character otherwise is.

This, we can now easily see, is particularly and often painfully obvious in modern societies, and this seems to me to be the major reason why these societies debate about values with such delight, such zeal and, often enough, such resentment. We generally do not speak about things that we take for granted. A community which is quite sure of its own identity and its internal cohesion, a community, that is, in which everyone knows why he belongs to it and, actually, wishes it to be so, such a community might not even know the words for ›values‹ and ›identity‹.

*b) Values and religion—an ambiguous relation*

We can see, then, why people are interested in ›values‹. They guarantee their identities on both an individual and a collective level. Interest in this kind of identity naturally increases the more elusive it appears in practice. But, to proceed to my second question, why would this search for identifying values be associated with religion, specifically with organised religion? I think two answers must be given.

The first is this. Religion generally holds a strong emotive sway over a person's deepest convictions (thus giving proper weight to them) and determines many of their actions in a way that both deeply informs their values and also causes them to persevere in them. The close relation between religion and values is generally accepted, which does not mean that all values are religious in the traditional sense of the word. For religious individuals it is, nevertheless, true that many of their central preferences, the goods they value above others, are intimately connected with their religious faith.

This specific perseverance, the strong emotive attachment to values once accepted seems to me, incidentally, an aspect of some relevance in more recent debates, in Germany and beyond. It is certainly and generally the case that values can be stronger or weaker; there are preferences about which we feel more passionate than about others. In recent years, however, the further possibility has been much debated that our value systems as such become weaker. In an age of postmodernism, it has been suggested, nobody will take any value too serious any longer.[18] Our identities will, accordingly, become more fractured, made up of small bits collected here and there into a consciously incoherent whole.

[18] G. Vattimo, Belief, Stanford 1999 and R. Rorty, Contingency, Irony, and Solidarity, Cambridge 1989. Cf. also G. Vattimo/R. Rorty/S. Zabala, The Future of Religion, New York 2005.

If I am not much mistaken, the renewed interest in the values which traditional religion might entail is at least partly due to some disillusionment with postmodernist ideologies.[19] It certainly seemed to me that the utter respect and even admiration which the most unexpected parts of the German public showed towards the late pope in the weeks and months surrounding his death were to some extent due to the recognition that he represented a kind of personality which has become rare, but may still be needed. Not so much because his views had become more palatable to them than they used to be, but because he held fast to them in the face not only of criticism, but of a time which seemed to have progressed beyond them altogether.[20]

***

However important this notion of stable value orientation may be in the present situation, for the German tradition of assigning the task of ›value mediation‹ to the churches another factor certainly carries more weight. The churches have been credited for a long time with the task of providing collective identity to society at large.[21]

I have mentioned how crucial this aspect of values is; they are always shared values thus providing not only individual, but also collective identities. As things are, the latter has been a political problem for modern Western societies for quite a while, for the German society arguably in particular. Social and economic developments, in combination with the absence of a nation state, have meant that, in the 19th century, identities were much more obvious on sub-national levels. On the national level they were, however, considered politically necessary as the foundation of the nation state. In this situation, which emerged in Germany in the latter half of the 19th century, the Christian churches stepped in and, in a move which could appear to be of mutual advantage, offered religious identity as a backup for the elusive national unity. The advantage was mutual because Christianity had, in fact, lost its sway over much of the educated public at that time or was in the process of losing it. It is for this reason that, in the words of a leading scholar, »the success of nationalism [i.e. in the Wilhelmian era] could also be read as the success of ›rechristianisation‹«.[22] Christianity, and in Germany this was decidedly

[19]Cf. the insightful criticism of Rorty in: Joas, op. cit. (n. 8), ch. 9.

[20]Cf. K.O. Hondrich, Die Divisionen des Papstes, in: FRANKFURTER ALLGEMEINE ZEITUNG, 16 April 2005, 8.

[21]Cf. now for this interrelation: M. Geyer/H. Lehmann (eds.), Religion und Nation. Nation und Religion. Beiträge zu einer unbewältigten Geschichte, Göttingen 2004.

[22]F.W. Graf, Dechristianisierung. Zur Problemgeschichte eines kulturpolitischen Topos, in: H. Lehmann (ed.), Säkularisierung, Dechristianisierung, Rechristianisierung im neuzeitlichen Europa. Bilanzen und Perspektiven der Forschung, Göttingen 1997, 32-66, here: 64.

Protestant, Lutheran Christianity, provided the German nation state of the late 19th and the early 20th century with much needed values and gained in turn a reinvigoration of its public acceptance as the guardian of a concept which at that time was cherished by large parts of the population.

In a way, the same happened again in the years after World War II, albeit in a slightly varied setting. This time, national identity had been tarnished by the violent nationalism of the Nazis and the atrocities committed in its name. This time, the values reintroduced to sustain collective identity were of a clearly Catholic brand in line with the generally strong political and social influence of the Roman Catholic Church on Western German institutions in the 1950s and 60s.[23]

I am not saying, of course, that all those who today expect the Churches to mediate values to our society are harking back to Wilhelmian times or, indeed, long for a return of the Adenauer years. Nor would I suggest that religion has only in the last 150 years begun to function as the glue for society. Quite clearly the opposite is the case. What has been new since then, however, is that this function has been presented to religious institutions agonising about their loss of influence over the population and thus tempted to adopt this value-providing scheme quite consciously as a means to regain a position in society which they had all but lost or, at least, which they feared they would lose soon.

We can see, then, that the still widely-held assumption in Germany that Churches are good for the society as ›value mediators‹ has its roots mainly in a worry about shared values, about collective identity on the level of the society at large, and it has its background in a historical situation in which religious institutions would come forward with this kind of support for a nation desperate to discover what actually constituted its unity. That this is so would seem evident not least on account of the fact that the issue of ›values‹ is frequently brought up on the backdrop of criticisms of multiculturalism and in the context of debates about the need for a common national ›lead culture‹ (*Leitkultur*).[24]

[23] A. Langner (ed.), Katholizismus im politischen System der Bundesrepublik. 1949-1963, Paderborn et al. 1978. Particularly interesting is the contribution by R. Morsey, Katholizismus und Unionsparteien in der Ära Adenauer, op. cit., 33-59 which concludes that »der deutsche Katholizismus hat die Unionsparteien in der Aufbau- und Konsolidierungsphase der Bundesrepublik direkt wie indirekt in entscheidendem Ausmaß unterstützt. Er gewann dadurch (...) politische Mitgestaltungsmöglichkeiten wie nie zuvor und hat sie, aufs Ganze gesehen, positiv genutzt« (58). The author continues to argue, however, that for this achievement Roman Catholicism paid the price of reduced internal cohesion both as a social group and within the Catholic Church proper (loc. cit.). Cf. on this problem at n. 29 below.

[24] The phrase was coined by the oriental scholar Bassam Tibi, but then utilised partly against his intuitions in a major public debate in Germany in 2000. As a result the term was widely denounced. Cf. B. Tibi, Europa ohne Identität. Die Krise der multikulturellen Gesellschaft, Göttingen 1998; id., Leitkultur als Wertekonsens—Bilanz einer missglückten deutschen Debatte, in: Aus Politik und Zeitgeschehen (Das Parlament), B 1–2/2001, 23-

I summarise, again briefly. The connection between values and religion is generally accepted. One recent debate has focussed on the importance of traditional religion for stable value orientation on the backdrop of the postmodernist endorsement of generally weak values. More specific and more traditional for the German situation is the interest to muster the support of the churches to underpin the notoriously elusive national identity in the late 19th century and again in the years after World War II.

*c) Churches as ›value mediators‹–a critical assessment*

I proceed to my third question. Is this interest in the churches as guardians of collective identity at all tenable? As it stands, this idea seems to be confronted with two main sets of problems. One is political, the other theological in nature.

The need for a community to have a common identity by means of shared values seems to me evident. The question is what kind of values should they be? It would seem clear that they must fulfil three main criteria:

1. They must be specific enough to mark an entity off from other similar entities.

2. They must, at the same time, be wide enough to extend to all those they are meant to represent.

3. They must have a certain emotive element which makes them truly cherished, valued by all.

I will not offer an exhaustive discussion of these three criteria, but only remark briefly that the third of them makes it difficult to confine those identifying values to those which make up the democratic creed. Even though people will agree that our political systems are built on a constitutional order, that we need due process of law and the separation of powers, freedom of speech and so forth, this may not be enough, as it works mainly on the rational level and fails to give people the feeling of belonging which they need to cherish truly their national identity.

Of immediate relevance for my paper, however, is the second of these points, and there can be but little doubt that it has been the major stumbling block for all more recent attempts to draw on religious institutions for the founding of national identities. The reason, of course, is that this idea depends crucially on the assumption that one particular religion or, specifically, one particular church is able to offer the bond of unity which the nation covets. While one might speculate about the extent to which this has ever been the case, it is

26. The political debate was started by the CDU politician Friedrich Merz, cf. his article: Einwanderung und Identität, in: DIE WELT, 25 October 2000.

indubitable that it has not been the case at any point in German history over the past 150 years. And thus, what helped arguably a majority of Germans to develop their feelings of national identity in Wilhelmian times produced considerable difficulties for those who were effectively excluded by the decidedly Protestant brand of this political religion. The largest group affected was that of Catholics, who felt consistently the strain between their religious and their national identities. Most notorious, and rightly so, became the pressure on the Jewish population which faced an increasing confrontation with an aggressive nationalism which was constructed in a way that would by definition exclude them from its notion of community.[25]

It would, of course, be grossly unfair and indeed wrong to see the identity politics of post war Western Germany simply as a continuation of this problematic tradition. What was attempted, rather, was a much more inclusive model which trusted religious communities more generally with the generation of the foundations which the modern, secular state required without being able to bring them about.[26] In other words, starting from the conviction that a modern society needs values for its internal cohesion, but that the state is banned from promoting any particular set of them, a system was developed in which this task was entrusted to the major religious communities. Few would doubt, perhaps, that this system has been quite successful as it helped reform German society from the shambles of the Nazi era into a modern democracy.[27]

At the same time, it has become increasingly clear that the growing religious diversification and, indeed, the increase in the number of people who consciously reject membership in any religious community have strained this system to breaking point. The debates about the integration of Islam into the legal and political framework of Germany have displayed traces of willingness to abandon the traditional system in favour of a more rigid version of the separa-

[25] K. Pickus, Native Born Strangers. Jews, Catholics and the German Nation, in: Geyer/Lehmann (eds.), op. cit. (n. 21), 141-156.

[26] This conviction has been classically expressed by E.-W. Böckenförde in his seminal paper: Die Entstehung des Staates als Vorgang der Säkularisation, in: Säkularisation und Utopie. Ebracher Studien. Ernst Forsthoff zum 65. Geburtstag, Stuttgart 1967, 75-94: »Der freiheitliche, säkularisierte Staat lebt von Voraussetzungen, die er selbst nicht garantieren kann. (...) So wäre noch einmal—mit Hegel—zu fragen, ob nicht auch der säkularisierte weltliche Staat letztlich aus jenen inneren Antrieben und Bindungskräften leben muß, die der religiöse Glaube seiner Bürger vermittelt. Freilich nicht in der Weise, daß er zum ›christlichen‹ Staat rückgebildet wird, sondern in der Weise, daß die Christen diesen Staat in seiner Weltlichkeit nicht länger als etwas Fremdes, ihrem Glauben Feindliches erkennen, sondern als die Chance der Freiheit, die zu erhalten und zu realisieren auch ihre Aufgabe ist« (93f.).

[27] Not least, its nationalism became ›sublimated‹ into Europeanism as R.J. Granieri has argued: Thou shalt consider thyself a European. Catholic Supranationalism and the Sublimation of German Nationalism after 1945, in: Geyer/Lehmann (eds.), op. cit. (n. 21), 336-363.

tion between church and state, with obvious repercussions for the mainstream churches.

I shall return to the question of what might be a future perspective for Germany. Meanwhile there are also theological objections against the ›value-mediating‹ that has so often been assigned to religious communities.[28] They too must be taken seriously. Does not such a function transform religions into ideologies supporting whatever is the political order of the day? Could not one say that religious communities contribute to their societies at least partly by calling into question certain ›values‹ these societies cherish—on account of the religious message to which they are bound in the first place? I think that it is no coincidence that in all the major religious traditions we have strands of a close alliance with the political and social order, but also strands of a very conscious rejection of such an alliance. It is not at all obvious that only the former had a bearing on political and social life; one could certainly argue a strong case for the specific influence of groups that have quite consciously kept aloof from direct involvement with the political realm, such as the Quakers.

On a more pragmatic note, the present situation of European churches might provide some illustrations also of the dangers to the religious institutions themselves of too close an alignment with the value systems of a particular political or social order. What increases their relevance at the heyday of such an order brings them down whenever the latter tumbles. This seems to me important to note, not least in order to assess whether an integration of Islam within the traditional framework of state-church relations in Germany is at all attractive from the Muslim point of view. It seems to me quite possible that the example of the major churches in Western Europe functions precisely as a deterrent against such a move.[29]

## 3. Perspectives

So what is the future for the relation of religion and society in Germany? I am not claiming prophetic powers, so these are merely a few alternatives which seem to me to exist at the moment. The future of the traditional West German

[28] Cf. the passionate attack against the use of values in Lutheran theology by Eberhard Jüngel: Wertlose Wahrheit. Christliche Wahrheitserfahrung im Streit gegen die »Tyrannei der Werte« in: Id./C. Schmitt/S. Schelz, Die Tyrannei der Werte, Hamburg 1979, 45-75. Following the political thought of Carl Schmitt, Jüngel draws on a sharp contradistinction between »truth« and »value«. For him, theology is responding to the truth of the God, not to idolatrous »values«. A more moderate argument is advanced by T. Hüttenberger, Was leistet der Wertbegriff für die Aufgaben von Theologie und Kirche, in: A.-K. Finke/J. Zehner (Hgg.), Zutrauen zur Theologie, Berlin 2000, 316-332. While essentially accepting the problems posed by Jüngel, he points out the inevitability of human ›valuation‹ and thus argues that the Church has a responsibility to assist people with this existential challenge.

[29] See n. 23 above.

system of semi-engagement and the lingering of a strong influence of religious institutions in the public sphere will depend crucially on two factors. One is the success of the integration of Islam into the existing framework. I cannot see at the moment that this is going to happen in the near future, but I am certainly not saying that it is likely to fail altogether.

The second interesting development over the coming years will be the role of those who are consciously not members of any religious group—whatever this may say about their ›religion‹. This group is growing in quantity, but has not, so far, voiced its disagreement with the existing framework effectively. Up to now a considerable number out of this group seemed, on the contrary, content to accept the importance of the churches for ›values‹ if not for anything else. Once again, it is not clear what is to happen in the future.

While it is arguably ever more difficult for any religious institution to support collective identity on the national level in the way churches in Europe have done for a long time, a case could be made for a lasting (and perhaps actually increasing) relevance of their contribution to the formation of identities on the level of smaller communities. It seems clear that in an age of growing individualism on the one hand and ever more complex national and supranational structures on the other, the relevance of small communities grows—for individuals themselves, but also for civil society which remains strongly dependent on their contributions to social tasks. It might be helpful, vis-à-vis ›values‹, if religious communities developed their responsibility more on that level where they indubitably have an important rôle to play in an increasingly pluralistic society.

This leaves open, I admit, the issue of collective identity on the national level. If religion is to play a role there, this could only be in a form which is consciously transcending the boundaries of denominations and religions.[30] Europeans are only beginning to turn into this direction,[31] and it seems to me that much theological and political work needs to be done before we know whether this kind of concept will be feasible in our own context in the future.

[30]The most well known of such cases is the so called ›civil religion‹ in the US. Cf. R. Bellah, Civil Religion in America, in: Id., Beyond Belief. Essays on Religion in a Post-Traditionalist World, Berkeley 1970, 168-189.

[31]R. Schieder, Wieviel Religion verträgt Deutschland? Frankfurt/M. 2001.

# Growing Religious Pluralism
# A Contrarian View

PATRICK J. DENEEN

It is often pointed out that a major challenge facing today's democracies and democratic institutions is whether they can adequately address the phenomenon of ›growing religious pluralism.‹ I find it difficult to answer this question, in part because I do not in the first place automatically assume the existence of ›growing religious pluralism.‹. It is, therefore, perhaps appropriate first to address the unstated assumption in the question: in what way, if at all, can it be said that religious pluralism actually is ›growing‹? Part of the difficulty in recognizing the validity of this question lies not in the existence of religious pluralism *per se*, but rather in the long history of the problem itself—the prevalence of religious pluralism in democracies is far older than modernity, dating back at least to the execution of Socrates by the Athenian democracy after being convicted of, among other things, introducing new gods to the city. If history suggests that religious pluralism has always been with us and was perhaps even more problematic in the past—after all, modern democracies do not regularly execute individuals who introduce new gods to the city—then why is there a widespread assumption that religious pluralism is ›growing‹? Why is the growth of religious pluralism taken to be a simple observable fact?

Perhaps what underlies the perception that ›religious pluralism‹ is increasing is the implicit acknowledgement that, in reality, what is increasing are the numbers of people following religious traditions that have not previously had a significant presence in Western societies, particularly Islam, but also Hinduism, Sikhism, Confucianism, and Buddhism. This reformulation of the question suggests that what modern Western democracies are labeling an increase in religious pluralism is, rather, an increase in the numbers of people of non-Western religious traditions, not those traditions *per se*. Many of these traditions have however, been acknowledged by Western societies for a long time—for example, John Locke argued for the need to tolerate the Jewish, Hindu, and ›Mohammandan‹ traditions in his 1689 treatise, *Letter Concerning Toleration*.[1] So, again, are modern democracies actually experiencing more religious diversity than before?

Religious pluralism has been part of Western societies to one extent or another for its entire existence. It can therefore be suggested that the perception that religious pluralism is a ›growing‹ phenomenon is not necessarily based on

[1] J. Locke, A Letter Concerning Toleration, ed. J.H. Tully, Indianapolis 1983.

increasing numbers of religious sects, but is instead inspired by an underlying assumption that religion, as a phenomenon, would decrease in salience and significance with the advance of modernity.[2] Underlying observations about increasing religious pluralism is the subtle realization that the ›secularization thesis‹ has not come to pass.[3]

Put another way, the sense that religious pluralism is a ›growing‹ phenomenon may not be the result of any actual increase in pluralism but is rather the consequence of unconscious disappointment borne of the realization that long-standing Enlightenment assumptions about the results of certain historical processes—particularly, that ›modernization‹ would result in ›secularization‹—have not come to pass. What is perceived as ›growing religious pluralism‹ in Germany and the United States may not be an increase in religious pluralism as such, but rather the awareness a) that religion does not seem to be withering away as expected, either its Christian variety in America, nor its Muslim variety in Europe, and b) that the kind of religion that seems in particular to be maintaining its hold and remaining visible in the public sphere is that with a ›traditional‹ or ›conservative‹ bent that is, to a greater or lesser extent, against ›modernization‹ in general and liberalism in particular.[4] Perhaps, then, what is growing are religious voices that stand directly against certain longstanding assumptions by modern intellectual elites about the undergirdings of modern liberalism, including the privatization of religion, the preeminence of conscience, individual autonomy, and formal legal equality.[5]

A rather striking potential implication of the above scenario, if it is in any way correct, is that it may very well be the case that religious pluralism, in every significant sense, is actually shrinking. This suggestion requires justification. Historically, religious pluralism has created problems by inspiring clashes *within* religious traditions, a situation often referred to as ›sectarianism.‹ Indeed, the most ferocious forms of sectarianism have often occurred not between different religious traditions, but within the *same* tradition. The Thirty Year War between Christian sects in the Middle Ages and the current conflagration in Iraq between Shiite and Sunni Muslims are powerful examples of this phenomenon. The word ›sectarianism,‹ which is not commonly employed in contemporary

[2]A classic argument on behalf of secularization can be found in: P.L. Berger, The Sacred Canopy. Elements of a Sociological Theory of Religion, New York 1967.

[3]P.L. Berger repudiated his earlier belief in the ›secularization thesis‹ in: The Desecularization of the World. A Global View, in: P.L. Berger (ed.), The Desecularization of the World. Resurgent Religion and World Politics, Grand Rapids 1999.

[4]Cf. R.S. Appleby, The Ambivalence of the Sacred. Religion, Violence, and Reconciliation Lanham/MD 2000.

[5]The elite fostering of the ›secularization thesis‹ is chronicled in Christian Smith, Introduction. Rethinking the Secularization of American Public Life, in: The Secular Revolution. Power, Interests and Conflict in the Secularization of American Life, Berkeley 2003.

discourse, might be understood as a less benign form of religious pluralism. The term denotes far more religious intensity than ›pluralism‹ can convey. Traditionally, the problem with pluralism is that it results in sectarianism—that is, divisions both between and within religious traditions.[6]

Relatively recent instances of religious sectarianism in America provide a way to draw contrasts between earlier forms of sectarianism and the contemporary belief that the world is in the throes of ›growing pluralism.‹ Consider the title of an essay written in 1967 and published in a well-known book by American sociologist and religious historian Sidney Mead—»The Fact of Pluralism and the Persistence of Sectarianism.«[7] Only forty years ago, Mead could write about ›pluralism‹ and ›sectarianism‹ as essentially the same phenomena. The challenge for liberal societies at that time was to negotiate the differences between religious traditions. For much of recent American history, this amounted to negotiating some of the differences between Protestant sects, but from the mid-nineteenth until the mid-twentieth century, it meant, above all, addressing the differences between Protestants and Catholics. Catholics were long regarded as traitorous and downright evil by many American Protestants. Suspicions of Catholics date back to colonial times, when the state of Virginia banned »popish priests,« Georgia forbade the inheritance of land by Catholics, and a relatively tolerant Maryland circumscribed the public celebration of Mass; forbade Catholics the ownership of firearms, and placed a special tax on new Catholic residents in order to discourage growth in their numbers.[8] Hostility towards Catholics can be traced back into English history as well as to theological contests in the times of Martin Luther in Germany and John Calvin in the Netherlands.[9] The height of Protestant-driven anti-Catholicism in the United States occurred in the 1840-50s, following a large influx of Catholic immigrants into Northeast urban areas. This circumstance led to the rise of the nativist »Know-Nothing« Party, which sought to prevent Catholics, who were viewed as pawns of the Vatican, from undermining American values and democracy; for a time, this party enjoyed considerable electoral success. For their part, Catholics tended to separate from the dominant Protestant society, building an extensive network of ›alternative‹ institutions, a Catholic sub-culture that

[6] While John Locke notes the need for toleration of non-Christian religious sects, his main emphasis is upon the need to tolerate the variety of Christian religious sects, including »Lutherans, Calvinists, Remonstrants, Anabatists, and other sects...,« op. cit. (n. 1), 57.

[7] S.E. Mead, The Fact of Pluralism and the Persistence of Sectarianism, in: Id., Nation With the Soul of a Church, New York 1967, 29-47.

[8] Th.H. O'Connor, Religion and American Society, Reading/MA 1975, 25-26.

[9] In his Letter Concerning Toleration, Locke disallows toleration toward two distinct groups: atheists and religionists who acknowledge a foreign Prince, and thus, presumably, Catholics. Locke, op. cit. (n. 1), 50.

is still discernible in some large Northeastern cities. Indeed, Catholic identification with their faith was so intense that many American Catholics fought with their Catholic ›compatriots‹ on the Mexican side during the Mexican-American war.[10] Occasionally, violence broke out between Protestants and Catholics. Anti-Catholic violence was frequently perpetrated by the Ku Klux Klan, which was started as a primarily anti-Catholic organization. Violence also came in the form of a pitched battle fought in 1844 in Kensington, Pennsylvania, over which translation of the Bible should be assigned to students. The use of battlefield artillery in this battle resulted in fifteen deaths and over thirty wounded.[11]

Sectarianism of this sort has persisted until relatively recent times. The continued separation of Catholics from wider society was decried in a 1951 article entitled »Pluralism: The National Menace.«[12] In 1955, religion scholar Will Herberg wrote in his classic study *Protestant-Catholic-Jew* that, »American Catholics still labor under the heavy weight of the bitter memory of non-acceptance in a society overwhelmingly and self-consciously Protestant. Hardly a century has passed since Catholics in America were brutally attacked by mobs, excluded from more desirable employment, and made to feel in every way that they were unwanted aliens.«[13]

Nevertheless, in less than forty years, American Catholics have left behind the days when they were suspected as minions of the Pope and tradition-bound ritualists dubiously loyal to America. Today, Catholics are at the center of mainstream American society. Certainly, much of this has to do with the ›mainstreaming‹ of Catholicism, a process undertaken by design, through elements such as Horace Mann's ›common schools,‹ the rise of an identifiably non-sectarian but vaguely Christian—later, Judeo-Christian—›civil religion,‹ and, perhaps most importantly, through the historical contingency of anti-communist sentiments among Protestants and Catholics alike.[14] Remarkably, in the 2004 American presidential election campaign, Democratic candidate John Kerry's Catholicism was almost a non-issue, except to the extent that traditional Catholics pointed out what they considered his doctrinal shortcomings.

A noteworthy new phenomenon is perceptible in this opposition against a nominally Catholic candidate *by* Catholics. In the contemporary American

[10]R.R. Ruether, When the Irish Were Mexicans, in: National Catholic Reporter, 1 September 2006.

[11]O'Connor, op. cit. (n. 8), 79.

[12]Pluralism—The National Menace, in: Christian Century 68, 13 June 1951, 701-11

[13]W. Herberg, Protestant, Catholic, Jew. An Essay in American Religious Sociology, New York 1960, 232.

[14]Herberg, op. cit. (n. 13), 86-7.96-7.137-53; cf. also St. Macedo, Diversity and Distrust. Civic Education in a Multicultural Democracy, Cambridge/MA 2000, 41-148.

landscape, the greatest allies of self-professed traditional or orthodox Catholics who opposed Kerry—Catholics who seek to adhere to traditional teachings predating Vatican II, who prefer the Latin Mass, and for whom recent sexual scandals within the clergy reveal the dangers of liberal influences in seminaries—are ›traditionalist‹ evangelical Protestants. That is, conservative Catholics are most firmly aligned with many whose forbears would have belonged to the Know-Nothing Party, if not to the Ku Klux Klan. Traditional Catholics, along with conservative evangelical Protestants, are now more inclined to oppose a Catholic candidate for political office if the candidate is liberal than they are to identify, above all else, with a co-religionist, as they did in 1960, when John F. Kennedy successfully ran for President. As further evidence of this striking shift, consider that five of the nine current Supreme Court Justices are Catholic; the nominations of four of these Justices—Antonin Scalia, Clarence Thomas, Chief Justice John Roberts, and, most recently, Samuel Alito—were successfully vetted largely through the efforts of conservative Protestant evangelicals.

Doctrinal and sectarian differences between Protestants and Catholics have not disappeared, but, in the context of contemporary America, these sects are united through shared views on key political issues such as abortion, stem cell research, euthanasia, and the strict separation of religion and politics. Opposition to certain aspects of liberalism, particularly those that emphasize lifestyle choice, individual autonomy, and moral relativism, has also united conservative Protestants, Catholics, and Jews. The journal *First Things* serves as the sounding board for the continued political alliance between conservative Catholics and evangelical Protestants.[15] The journal's editor is Father Richard Neuhaus, a former Lutheran minister who converted to Catholicism and is now a priest.

All in all, there is little evidence of ›growing religious pluralism,‹ at least not in the most important classic historical sense, where religious pluralism manifests as outright sectarianism between and among various religious faith traditions. Rather, in the United States in particular and to a growing extent Europe, one sees two great ›parties‹ forming: on one side, an increasingly unified ›traditional‹ party of religion, and on the other, a secular-minded party of ›progressives.‹ In the United States, the division between these two parties is captured by the colors of maps shown on television during election coverage, where the country is divided between ›red states,‹ most of which are located in the interior of the country and whose populations are comprised mainly of religiously-minded individuals, and ›blue states,‹ located primarily on the East and West Coasts and whose populations are comprised mainly of more secular-

[15]Cf.: Evangelicals and Catholics Together. Christian Mission in the Third Century, in: First Things 43, May 1994, 15-22.

minded ›progressives‹. In contrast, Europe is decidedly more ›blue‹ than ›red‹, a fact regarded with jealousy by denizens of blue states and with dismay, if not outright disdain, by citizens of red states. Nevertheless, the demographic shifts taking place in Europe as a result of high rates of immigration and high fertility rates among immigrant populations, the majority of whom are Muslim, it may well be expected that Europe too will eventually be divided between conservative ›red‹ and progressive ›blue‹.

The issue at the core of the division between ›red‹ and ›blue‹ is reflected in the question, »Can democratic norms, institutions, and practices be reconciled with growing religious pluralism?« In this question too lurks a set of assumptions, in that what is at issue is the very definition of »democratic norms, institutions, and practices.« Should the definition be based on traditional religious principles or on the secular values that have been assumed to be the bedrock for democracy for so long? Basic assumptions about how human beings are to conceive of themselves in relation to other human beings are being called into question. Are human societies conceived of primarily as autonomous individuals coming together by choice and agreement, under the philosophic aegis of ›voluntarism,‹ or are they constituted primarily through relations with others as defined by specific duties and obligations that stress family and community, nation and generation? The first model is captured in the Social Contract theory inaugurated by Thomas Hobbes and John Locke in the 17th century; the second is, at its core, Aristotelian, and was described by Edmund Burke in the 18th century and has been defended by more contemporary thinkers such as Gilbert Keith Chesterton, Alasdair MacIntyre, Christopher Lasch, Wendell Berry, and Jean Bethke Elshtain.

The question, as posed above, suggests that, at the very least, there is a tension, if not an outright contradiction, between ›growing religious pluralism‹—which might more accurately be described as growing religious traditionalism—and the ›practice, norms, and institutions‹ of democracy. However, it also begs the question that lies at the heart of the difference between the two dominant ›parties‹ on the scene today—whether secularists can assume, as they so often do, that their position comprises the fundamental definition of democracy.[16] Indeed, the hostility between adherents of ›red‹ and ›blue‹ positions may be stoked by the unconsciously dismissive nature of the question whether democracy can be reconciled with religious pluralism, which just adds fuel to the anger

[16]While examples that conclude that religious belief is incompatible with democracy, take this recent instance drawn from a scholarly article: »Christian fundamentalism also makes a virtue of submission to this truth and to the authority that speaks or wields it. It is anti-democratic and anti-intellectual insofar as it devalues not merely facts but also deliberative autonomy and deliberation themselves.« W. Brown, American Nightmare. Neoliberalism, Neoconservatism, and De-Democratization, in: Political Theory 34 (December 2006), 708.

of religious adherents whose views secularists often automatically regarded as thoroughly anti-democratic, if not entirely unreasonable.[17]

Whether questions about democracy and religious pluralism can be addressed in a more productive and peaceful manner in coming years in the United States is an open question. There are some grounds for hope that secularists will move away from their most condescending and dismissive positions and that religiously based voices will move beyond defensive reactions and playing the victim. These positions are being moderated by religious and secular voices alike. The Democratic Party, which once claimed the great preacher, William Jennings Bryan, as a standard-bearer, is seeking to reclaim its that historically-based religious voice.[18] Conservative evangelicals and Catholics alike no longer view their affiliation with the Republican Party as having been ordained by God, a fact demonstrated in the recent 2006 mid-term Congressional elections.

It may very well be that the ›norms, practices, and institutions‹ of democracy lie somewhere between the secular and the religious positions, in an area of creative tension that accords respect to individual autonomy while also acknowledging its limits, and that views tradition with a healthy suspicion while simultaneously acknowledging it as a rich source for a sense of community and mutual obligation, not only between members of families, communities, and nations, but also between generations, including those generations as-yet unborn.

Issues of democracy and religion are no less relevant to contemporary Europe. It may well be that the relative triumph of the secular worldview in European countries such as Germany will have unique implications for these issues in Europe. The United States provides an example of one possible implication, which centers on demographic issues. It is interesting to note that birthrates in America's ›blue‹ states are similar to those in Germany and Europe, that is, below replacement rate. However, birth rates in ›red‹ states are regularly above replacement rates, which suggests that there may be a connection between a worldview that rejects the idea of complete individual autonomy, one that embraces traditionalism—including religious traditionalism—and the willingness to compromise one's ›freedom‹ for the joys and burdens of bringing up children. Those holding a religious worldview, it might be concluded, are more willing to accept values of duty and self-sacrifice, and might be thereby less susceptible to appeals to more individualistic forms of self-satisfaction. Thus,

[17]The classic statement that would bar religious claims public legitimacy based upon their lack of universal »reasonableness« is J. Rawls, Political Liberalism, New York 1993. Richard John Neuhaus critiques this general view in: The Naked Public Square, Grand Rapids/MA 1986.

[18]For a reminder of Bryan's importance in the Democratic Party, and in American politics, see M. Kazin, A Godly Hero. The Life of William Jennings Bryan, New York 2006.

those people less wed to a ›progressive‹ worldview are more likely to produce families in larger numbers. Ironically, one might conclude on this basis that conservatives have a greater belief in the future than progressives![19]

Although the United States faces its own demographic challenges, they are slight in comparison to the inability of most European nations to repopulate their cities and towns through reproduction. Financial incentives for starting families have proven largely ineffective, suggesting that devotion to bringing a new generation into the world ultimately has little to do with monetary compensations, and therefore has a difficult time registering in the liberal mindset so dominated by market considerations. Europe faces a profound challenge arguably arising not from religious pluralism, but from its absence—divided, as it is, between two great parties, the party of secularism and a growing party of Islam—an absence that may contribute to the ›Islamization‹ of Europe in approximately half a century given current demographic trends and that may have the ironic result of a religiously *singular* Europe in several decade's time. It may very well be that the ›norms, practices, and institutions‹ of democracy, rather than being hindered by ›growing religious pluralism,‹ in fact depend upon the creation of *actual* religious pluralism for their continued existence. Ironically, what Europe may need in order to remain Europe is a genuinely growing religious pluralism.

[19]Ralph Waldo Emerson contrasted the worldviews of conservativism and »innovation« thus: »it is the opposition of the Past and Future, of Memory and Hope (...).« (Emerson, The Conservative). By contrast, see Christopher Lasch's argument that associates middle-class religious conservatives with the virtue of »hope« in: The True and Only Heaven. Progress and its Critics, New York 1995. Cf. also P.A. Lawler, Aliens in America. The Strange Truth About Our Souls, Wilmington/DE 2002, and: Id., Stuck with Virtue. The American Individual and Our Biotechnological Future, Wilmington/DE 2005.

# About the Authors

PATRICK J. DENEEN

Patrick J. Deneen is associate Professor at the Department of Government at Georgetown University, Washington DC where he holds the Markos and Eleni Tsakopoulos-Kounalakis Chair in Hellenic Studies. His interests include ancient political thought, American political thought, democratic theory, religion and politics, and literature and politics. He is the author of »The Odyssey of Political Theory« (2000) and »Democratic Faith« (2005). His current research is centered on the »Division of Labor« as a recurring theme in the history of political thought. He has presented work and lectured widely, including at Berry College, University of Chicago, Harvard University, Indiana University, Rutgers University, University of Tulsa, Valparaiso University, and Yale University.

KARSTEN FISCHER
*Born* 1967

Karsten Fischer holds a research and teaching position at the Department of Social Science at Humboldt-University, Berlin. He studied Politics, Philosophy and Public Law/International Law at the Universities of Bonn (M. A. 1994), Frankfurt/M. and Berlin (Dr. rer. soc. 1998, *habilitation* 2006). He co-ordinated the interdisciplinary research group »Common Good and Civic Spirit« at the Berlin-Brandenburg Academy of Sciences and Humanities. His research interests comprise theory and methods of politics, politics and religion, governance/theory of state/theory of democracy, and the future of state and democracy.

He is a founding member of the Program on Religion and Politics at Humboldt-University as well as a member of the German Society for Politics and of the Social Science Research Center, Berlin.

CATHLEEN S. FISHER

Cathleen S. Fisher is Vice President for Institutional Relations at the Center for Strategic and International Studies and International Studies (CSIS) in Washington, DC. Previously, she was Deputy Director at AICGS where her responsibilities included projects on Religion and Politics in the United States and Germany, and on German-American Relations after the Iraq War. Earlier, she had served for ten years as Senior Associate at The Henry L. Stimson Center, Washington DC, focusing on international and national security issues.

She has been an Adjunct Associate Professor in the National Security Studies Program at Georgetown University. She holds a Ph.D. in government and politics from the University of Maryland and an M.A. in international relations from the Johns Hopkins University School of Advanced International Studies.

BRUCE GRELLE
*Born* 1956

Bruce Grelle is Professor at the Department of Religious Studies at California State University, Chico. He is director of the Religion and Public Education Resource Centre (RPERC) and a member of the Center for Applied and Professional Ethics. He studied at Indiana University, Indianapolis, and at the University of Chicago Divinity School (M.A. Div. 1981, Ph.D. 1993).

He is co-editor of »Explorations in Global Ethics. Comparative Religious Ethics and Interreligious Dialogue« (1998). Recent research has focused on religion and public education, and on religion, globalization, and global ethics.

NILS OLE OERMANN
*Born* 1973

Nils Ole Oermann is personal advisor to the Minister of the Interior of the Federal Repulic of Germany. From 2004-07, he worked for the Federal President of the Federal Republic of Germany. He studied Protestant Theology, Law, Philosophy and History at Leipzig, Münster and Oxford/UK, and holds doctoral degrees from Oxford (DPhil) and Leipzig (Dr. theol.). In 2006 he submitted his *habilitation thesis* to the Theological Faculty of Leipzig University. In 2002-03 he was McCloy scholar at Harvard University focussing on Business Ethics, Economics and International Relations. His research interests lie in religion and politics, education on values, economics and ethics.

He is a founding member of the Program on Religion and Politics at Humboldt University, Berlin.

MARCIA PALLY

Marcia Pally is Associate Professor (Ajt.) in Multilingual Multicultural Studies at New York University, where she received her doctorate in 1995. She is a permanent Fellow of the New York Institute for the Humanities, and a guest at the Wissenschaftskolleg zu Berlin in 2007. She is the author of *The Religion, Values and Foreign Policy of the Country with the Biggest Guns: A user's manual* (forthcoming, 2008) and *Lob der Kritik. Warum die Demokratie nicht auf ihren*

*Kern verzichten darf* (2003). She has lectured widely at universities and professional associations including Harvard, Columbia, The University of Chicago and Humboldt University, Berlin. For the past 20 years, Prof. Pally has also been a columnist for major US and European publications including THE NEW YORK TIMES, THE NATION, DIE ZEIT, SÜDDEUTSCHE ZEITUNG, MERKUR, and INTERNATIONALE POLITIK (German Council on Foreign Relations), and she served on The Media and Communications Committee of the American Civil Liberties Union. Her research interests include the intersection among culture, religion, and US politics, and the influences of culture on language use and learning.

Jeffrey M. Peck

Jeffrey M. Peck is a Professor in the »Communication, Culture and Technology« Program at Georgetown University and has been a Senior Fellow in Residence at AICGS since 2002. After receiving his M.A. (University of Chicago, 1974) and his Ph.D. in Comparative Literature (University of California, 1979), he was faculty member at the University of Washington, Seattle, in the Departments of German, Comparative Literature and in the Program in Jewish Studies. From 1992-1999 he directed the Jewish Studies Initiative at Georgetown University, from 1999-2002 he was the first Director of the Canadian Centre for German and European Studies at York University, Toronto, and the University of Montréal. His research focuses on questions of national and minority identities, particularly German-Jewish life since unification and contemporary responses to the Holocaust in a transatlantic context.

Dagmar Pruin
*Born* 1970

Dagmar Pruin holds a research and teaching position in Old Testament Studies at Humboldt-University, Berlin, after studying Theology at the Universities of Hamburg, Göttingen (M. Div. 1997) and Berlin (Dr. theol. 2003), and Jewish Studies at the Hebrew University in Jerusalem. Her research interests include the Old Testament and the history of the ancient Near East, interreligious, especially Jewish-Christian dialogue, and religion and politics in Germany, Israel, and the US.

From 2002-05 Dagmar Pruin sat on the Commission for Gender Studies at Humboldt-University. She is a founding member of the Program on Religion and Politics at Humboldt University, and co-chairs the program's exchange project Religion and Politics in Germany and the US. In 2006 she was DAAD-Fellow at AICGS, the Johns Hopkins University.

Rolf Schieder
*Born* 1953

Rolf Schieder is Full Professor at the Department for Practical Theology / Religious Education at Humboldt-University, Berlin. He studied Protestant Theology at the Universities of Neuendettelsau, Göttingen and München (1986 Dr. theol., 1994 habil.) and became Professor for Religious Education at the University of Koblenz-Landau in 1994. He is the author of »Civil Religion. Die religiöse Dimension politischer Kultur« (1987) and »Wieviel Religion verträgt Deutschland?« (2001). His research is focused on religion and politics, civil religion, interreligious education and standards and competences for Religious Education at public schools.

He is the spokesman of the Program on Religion and Politics and organises the Berlin Lectures on Religion and Politics.

Karsten D. Voigt
*Born* 1941

Karsten D. Voigt has been the German Federal Government's Coordinator of German-American Cooperation since 1999 after serving for many years as foreign policy spokesman of the SPD. He studied History, German Language, and Skandinavian Studies at the Universities of Hamburg, Kopenhagen and Frankfurt and joined the SPD in 1962. From 1976-1998 he was a member of the German Bundestag. He has held various positions within the Bundestag and the SPD, notably as member of its executive committee from 1984-95. He has been Member, Vice-President and President of NATO's Parliamentary Assembly, as well as Chairman of NATO's Defence and Security Committee. He is a member of numerous boards and organizations, among them the German Council on Foreign Relations, the Aspen Institute, Berlin, and Atlantik-Brücke. He is one of the initiators of the Program on Religion and Politics at Humboldt University.

Johannes Zachhuber
*Born* 1967

Johannes Zachhuber is Fellow and Tutor in Theology at Trinity College and Lecturer in Modern Theology at the Theology Faculty of Oxford University. He studied Theology in Rostock, Berlin and Oxford (M.St. 1995; DPhil. 1997). He held a research and teaching position in Systematic Theology and Philosophy from 1997-2002 and was Junior Professor of Philosophical Theology from 2002-2005, both at Humboldt University, Berlin. His research interests lie in the area of late ancient theology and its reception, history of theology in the 19th century, philosophical theology, and religion and politics.

He is a founding member of the Program on Religion and Politics at Humboldt-University.